CALGARY'S ELECTRIC TRANSIT

An illustrated history of electrified public transportation in Canada's oil capital

Streetcars, Trolley Buses, and Light Rail Vehicles

Railfare DC Books

ABOUT THE AUTHORS

Colin Hatcher spent his early years in Montreal, when streetcars and commuter trains were the principal means of local transportation. His family moved to Sudbury, Ontario while the streetcars were still operating and there were lots of trains nearby. He returned to Montreal, securing his BA degree at Sir George Williams (now Concordia) University, and became involved with the Canadian Railroad Historical Association. Colin subsequently took up a position with the Regina YMCA, and his CRHA friends encouraged him to research the Regina streetcar system, resulting in the book *Saskatchewan's Pioneer Streetcars – the Story of the Regina Municipal Railway* (Railfare: 1971).

Calgary Transit expressed an interest in a similar publication as their contribution to the City of Calgary's 75th Anniversary celebration, resulting in the 1975 release of *Stampede City Streetcars – the Story of the Calgary Municipal Railway* (Railfare). Following a move further north, Colin tackled the Edmonton streetcar story, meeting up with Tom Schwarzkopf who had an interest in trolley coaches. Railfare published their joint work *Edmonton's Electric Transit* in 1983.

Colin continues to be actively involved in railway preservation and operation efforts (Edmonton Radial Railway Society), is a volunteer archivist and often operates streetcars on both the High Level Bridge and at Fort Edmonton Park. He writes for Edmonton Radial Railway Society's *Trip Sheet*, CRHA's *Canadian Rail*, and helped Geoff Lester prepare an on-line *Atlas of Alberta Railways*. He has written two volumes on the Northern Alberta Railways (BRMNA, Calgary), booklets on the Edmonton Transit LRT system's first 25 years, and also the Edmonton YMCA's first century.

Tom Schwarzkopf's introduction to urban transit was at age five with a move to Toronto where, when riding on the Peter Witt streetcars, he competed with the conductor in calling out car-stop names.

Whether getting up at 6 AM to see the Barnum & Bailey Circus train unload, or riding the new PCC streetcars, railways and transit have always been an integral part of Tom's life. In his Cornwall, Ontario high school years, Tom enjoyed riding the new electric trolley buses, thus starting a life-long interest in this urban "track-less trolley" transportation mode.

A move to Edmonton in 1973 renewed his contact with trolley coaches. A mutual interest in electric transit led to a friendship with Colin Hatcher, culminating in their co-authorship of *Edmonton's Electric Transit*. In that book, Tom added to Colin's work on the streetcars and light rail vehicles with an extensive history of that city's longest-operating trolley bus system in Canada. (The book won the 1983 Alberta Culture Regional History Award). With *Calgary's Electric Transit*, Tom's collaboration with Colin continues, despite a relocation to Ottawa, where Tom is now preparing a history of all Canada's trolley coach systems for future publication by Railfare*DC Books.

In addition to Tom's historical writings, he is the author of the popular children's series "The Angela and Emmie Adventures" – now into the fourth book. The second of those adventures, *Danger at Mason's Island*, was short listed for the Hackmatack Children's choice and the Silver Birch Awards in 2008. In between writing, Tom is also an English professor at Ottawa's Algonquin College, and is a proud new grandfather.

See photo of authors opposite page.

Book designed and typeset in Adobe Garamond Pro, ITC Garamond, and Myriad MM by Eric Clegg, with overall guidance from David Henderson. Graphic grid designed by Primeau & Barey, Montreal. Printed and bound in Canada by Transcontinental Printing. Distributed by Lit DistCo.

Copyright © Railfare*DC Books, 2009.

Legal Deposit, *Bibliothèque et Archives nationales du Québec* and the National Library of Canada, 4th trimester, 2009.

Library and Archives Canada Cataloguing in Publication
Hatcher, Colin K., 1939-
Calgary's electric transit : streetcars, trolley buses, and light rail vehicles / Colin K. Hatcher & Tom Schwarzkopf.
Includes bibliographical references.
ISBN 978-1-897190-55-5 (pbk.).--ISBN 978-1-897190-56-2 (bound)
1. Street-railroads--Alberta--Calgary--History. 2. Trolley buses--Alberta--Calgary--History. I. Schwarzkopf, Tom, 1943- II. Title.
HE4509.C3H38   2009 388.4'609712338   C2009-903997-4

For our publishing activities, Railfare*DC Books gratefully acknowledges the financial support of the Canada Council for the Arts, of SODEC, and of the Government of Canada through the Book Publishing Industry Development Program (BPIDP).

Railfare ❈ DC Books
Ontario office:
1880 Valley Farm Road, Unit TP-27
Pickering, Ontario L1V 6B3

Business office and mailing address:
Box 666, St. Laurent Station
Montreal, Quebec H4L 4V9
railfare@videotron.ca
www.railfare.net

Cover: In this signature Calgary setting, a C-Train travelling west on the 7th Avenue SE transit mall passes the stately City Hall located on the Macleod Trail, formerly known in this downtown setting as 2nd Street SE. This May 21st 1985 view captures an emerging new transit mode beside the sandstone heritage City Hall building. With a large architecturally-modern addition built behind, the 1911 building continues to preside over a changing, modern, bustling downtown core. (Ted Wickson)

Canada Council for the Arts   Conseil des Arts du Canada

Société de développement des entreprises culturelles
Québec ❈❈

CONTENTS

DEDICATION

This book is dedicated to each of the thoughtful people who pursued, documented, recollected and shared information about Calgary's streetcars, trolley buses and its light rail transit system. The art of many photographers – some of whom took perfectly-positioned documentary "roster" shots, and others who took carefully composed photos of equipment in service – is clearly evident. Some folks created diagrams and drawings. Still others shared their ephemera and stories. Their invaluable foresight, inquisitiveness, tireless commitment, and kind co-operation is what made this book possible.

July 2009

Above: Authors Colin K. Hatcher and Tom Schwarzkopf

ACKNOWLEDGEMENTS

THE streetcar text and roster for *Calgary's Electric Transit* is based on information found in *Stampede City Streetcars* published by Railfare in 1975. At that time, author Colin K. Hatcher had access to the City of Calgary official records through the offices of Calgary Transit. Of significant value were the interviews with retired and former Calgary Municipal Railway streetcar motormen and conductors and sometimes members of their families. Several people who held a strong interest in Calgary streetcars, but had no formal street railway staff ties, shared their stories, recollections and photographs. Hobby photographers who visited Calgary to document the last few years of streetcar operation willingly shared the results of their work, which is individually identified with each photograph. Many of these resource people were very elderly in 1975, indeed a few were World War I Veterans. Over the past 34 years, many of these people have passed on. The names of those individuals and organizations who assisted with *Stampede City Streetcars* are as follows:

L.A. Armour, Tim Humphries, D.C. McDermid, Harry Sales, R.H. Wray, all staff from Calgary Transit and the City of Calgary; Georgeen Barrass and Esther Kreisel, archivists from Glenbow and the Provincial Archives of Alberta respectively; George Adie, J. K. Gush, James Hughes, Les Longpre, Homer McBride, Doreen McBride (daughter of Mr. Hughes, daughter-in-law of Mr. McBride), T.W. Ridley, T.C. Scatcherd, retired motor-conductors and family; Ken Liddell, *Calgary Herald* columnist; J.A. Beatty; Richard M. Binns; James J. Buckley; Canadian National and Canadian Pacific railways; E.A. Toohey collection courtesy S.S. Worthen; Anthony Clegg; William Coo; Raymond F. Corley; Peter Cox; Janet Cumming (daughter of motorman-conductor Robert Cumming who was killed at Vimy Ridge during World War I); Lucien Dauphinais; John Ewing; Glenbow Archives; Robert W. Gibson; W.H. Grant; David Henderson; Heritage Park; Omer Lavallée; Stephen D. Maguire; H.W. McCauley (son of Calgary Municipal superintendent T.H. McCauley); John M. Meikle; Foster M. Palmer; Douglas V. Parker; C. Dwight Powell; Provincial Archives of Alberta; Robert Sandusky; Jim Scott; Bill Simpkins, *Calgary Herald* photographer; W. C. Whittaker; A. Wright, Regina Transit System; Wally Young.

Following publication of *Stampede City Streetcars*, readers wrote to share further experiences and photographs. A significant contributor in this respect was Percy W. Browning. Like John M. Meikle, C. Dwight Powell and John Ewing, Percy Browning grew up in Calgary and was fascinated with all aspects of its streetcar operations. Excerpts from the late Mr. Browning notes and many of his photographs appear throughout the streetcar section of this book.

In April 1981, with the impending opening of Calgary's new light rail transit system and with the encouragement of David Henderson of Railfare, the author and Paul McGee journeyed to Calgary to meet with Sandra Bell, then Calgary Transit's Communications Coordinator, who took us to CT's Anderson Shops where LRVs were being assembled, even while work to complete the building was still underway. Sandra introduced us to Calgary Transit people who were keen to share their interest, information and enthusiasm about the new LRT technology surrounding us. In October 1985, a completed manuscript was presented to John Hubbell, Calgary Transit's Superintendent of Service Development and Marketing, and Cheryl Mocan-Brazell, Communication Coordinator, Marketing and System Resources. They encouraged an expanded version be prepared to include not only the northeast line that had by then begun operating, but also the northwest leg on which construction was then under way. We were learning that we were writing about a dynamic growing technology and means of transportation that required a different approach from dealing with an historical analysis of a past technology. In 1987, another tour and series of interviews was arranged to help provide a wider view of an expanded system. Calgary Transit staff in the persons of Diane Rennie, A.H. (Andy) Bleackley, Project Coordinator Engineering Services, Harry Bumstead, Control Centre Victoria Park Garage, and Don Hurley, Enforcement Supervisor, all assisted with information and explained the various aspects of their work related to LRT operations.

In the meantime, Tom Schwarzkopf completed a trolley coach history of the Calgary system. A condensed History of Calgary Transit sent many years ago to author Schwarzkopf by Leslie D. Knaus, Public Relations, City of Calgary Transportation Department, provided supportive information for the trolley bus manuscript. In addition, the extensive CTS clipping collection of the Glenbow Archives and its *Calgary Herald* file provided much of the data for the trolley bus portion. With the further assistance of Brenda Kitaguchi, Communications Coordinator, Service Development and Marketing, a third draft manuscript was presented to Calgary Transit in July 1988. Shortly afterwards, City of Calgary budget problems required the project to be placed in abeyance.

In the fall of 2008, Railfare and the authors concluded it would be appropriate to proceed with the project. We quickly learned that Calgary Transit had already engaged Harry Sanders, a local Calgary historical writer, to produce a story of Calgary Transit to celebrate its 100th Anniversary on July 5th 2009. Despite that, Railfare felt that its wide circle of readers all across the world would welcome its usual high quality electric transit treatment – this time including Calgary's trolley coaches and its renowned LRT system – so we pressed on with the project. Harry Sanders and the author did engage in helpful consultations. Having been given copious information support by Calgary Transit in

Above: From the crowds and decorations in the above view, taken from the corner of 8th Avenue sw and 1st Street sw, it would appear that Calgarians were celebrating an important event. It is believed that the event was the opening of the new Hudson's Bay store, one block to the north of this busy intersection, on August 18th 1913. On this occasion, The Bay chartered the CMR's 65 trams for a four-hour period and all passengers were carried free of charge. The imposing sandstone was built on the corner housed the Bank of Montreal and the Bank of British North America. It was later replaced by a substantial-looking flat stone structure fronting on 8th Avenue sw with four columns housing the Bank of Montreal.
(Glenbow Archives NA-644-11)

the past, and given that Calgary Transit was already engaged in its own historical project, the manuscript was researched prmarily outside of the offices of Calgary Transit. When Calgary Transit's assistance was needed at key points, Ron Collins, Communications Coordinator, responded quickly and very effectively.

A call for photographs to known transit historians, collectors and photographers resulted in many very significant contributions. These include the work of a new generation of photographers and collectors who have documented the operation of Calgary's trolley coach and LRT system. Ted Wickson of Toronto and Robert "Bob" Sandusky, also resident of the Toronto area but a knowledgeable resident of Calgary for a number of years, have both made significant contributions to the LRT section. Ted also provided several trolley coach slides, and Bob provided some excellent streetcar illustrations. Steve Scalzo of Park Forest, Illinois generously shared trolley bus wire maps he sketched during his visits to Calgary and many of the trolley coach colour slides he has posted on Tom's Trolley Bus web site. Art Peterson of Chicago provided many beautiful streetcar and trolley bus slides from several photographers featured in the Krambles-Peterson archives. John M. Day of Vancouver, former editor of *Canadian Coach* magazine, scanned many of his excellent black and white photos, without which

the trolley bus section would be much poorer. Peter Cox of Edmonton furnished a rare slide taken by Robert Loat of the Toronto Transportation Commission demonstrator trolley coach in Calgary. Author Schwarzkopf is grateful to Hal Wright at Sandon, British Columbia for information on the fleet of preserved coaches, including the two Calgary ones, in his collection. Wally Young, in Victoria, British Columbia, former editor of *Canadian Coach* magazine willingly answered many requests. Whenever we needed a contact or help, Wally provided it, and he also put us in touch with several excellent photo collections.

Robert J. Halperin, an author of two pictorial volumes about Canadian streetcars, shared his collection of Calgary streetcar photographs. Many of those coloured images that Mr. Halperin shared with us were taken by Robert W. Gibson on colour slide film. Mr. Halperin obtained copies of those images from the Electric Railway Historical Society in Chicago, where the Gibson collection now resides. John Thompson of Toronto assisted by sharing his network of contacts. Managing the response from the call for photographs and the large inventory of photographs already on hand from the original streetcar book has been ably carried out by Paul McGee of St. Albert, Alberta. About 1000 images have been sent to and digitized by Paul. His work at getting the clearest possible images for this publication is evident. Sometimes images come to us unexpectedly. Jim Scott of Calgary got up early on the morning of June 15th 2009 to document some of the first CTrain operation at the new Crowfoot station. He shared that work with us and it appears in the colour section. Rich Krisak of Atlanta, Georgia forwarded streetcar photos which illustrated some scenes new to us. Peter Murphy and Archivist Josée Vallerand of the Canadian Railroad Historical Association's Exporail at Montreal searched the Raymond F. Corley fonds and the William Bailey fonds for Calgary streetcar images. We had the privilege of having Foster M. Palmer's photographs available to us for use in *Stampede City Streetcars*. We have kept those photographs on file and they appear again in this work. Mr. Palmer travelled from his home in Boston to many Canadian cites to record streetcar operations in the closing years of streetcar service. The late Mr. Palmer's photographic collection is now deposited in the archives of the New England Electric Railway Historical Society of Kennebunkport, Maine. A very prolific photographer of Calgary streetcars was W.C. Whittaker. The late Mr. Whittaker used to visit Calgary annually between about 1946 and 1949 from his home in Mill Valley, California. We were fortunate to collect a number of Mr. Whittaker's pho-

tographs for use in *Stampede City Streetcars* and are pleased to present them again in this work. Mr. Whittaker's collection is now held by a private collector, Dave Shaw of Mississauga, Ontario in his Railway Memories Collection. Calgarian A.H. Coverdale, a railway photographer of considerable note whose collection is also part of the Railway Memories Collection, did take at least one Calgary streetcar photo. The author found a clean 1945 post-card size print with A.H. Coverdale's stamp on it recently and it appears in this publication. Ernie Plant of the Vancouver area took a number of streetcar photos and one of his photos now in the Andrew Merrilees collection at the National Archives of Canada appears in this publication as well.

The text from the original LRT manuscripts and from *Stampede City Streetcars* was copied with the assistance of Heather Green. The design of this book was by Eric Clegg, under the able guidance of publisher Dave Henderson. Thanks to all folks above, and also to any whose names were inadvertently omitted above.

Colin K. Hatcher, Edmonton, Alberta
Tom Schwarzkopf, Ottawa, Ontario
July 2009

Below: "Main Street" in Calgary during the electric railway era was 8th Avenue SE/SW between 2nd Street SE and 4th Street SW. This 1929 view of 8th Avenue SW looking eastward from 1st Street SW shows Calgary Municipal Railway car 29 loading passengers destined for the Elbow Park district. (Canadian National 31836)

CHAPTER ONE

Early Calgary

THE growth of the City of Calgary can be likened to the flooding of the Bow and Elbow River Valleys if a huge dam were to be built across the valley downstream from their confluence. The city spreads itself over the wide river valleys, climbs up the steep valley hills, and spills out over the top onto the undulating grassy plains above. These grassy plains stretch north, east and south as far as the eye can see, but to the west, the sky line is broken by the distant crags of the Rocky Mountains. The circumstances leading to the development of a thriving city at this point go back many years before the 1875 arrival of the North West Mounted Police under Inspector Brisebois.

The plains from the Red Deer River south to the Missouri River in Montana were inhabited by the Indians of the Blackfoot Confederacy, comprising the Sarcee, Blackfoot, Blood and Piegan tribes, approximately in that order from north to south. Further east on the plains between the same river boundaries lived the Gros Ventres, also part of the Blackfoot Confederacy. All of the Great Plains tribes appeared to have wandered south from the wooded area of the North Saskatchewan River, along a trail closely followed today by the old highway and the Canadian Pacific Railway line between Edmonton, Calgary and Fort Macleod. The Old North Trail, as it came to be known, became a well-travelled Indian route across the plains through Blackfoot country between the North Saskatchewan and the Missouri, crossing the Bow River about mid-way between the two major valleys.

Strangely enough, the country around the Bow and Elbow was left to the Blackfoot almost until the final quarter of the 19th century. The Hudson's Bay Company traders – and before them the North West Company traders – found little interest displayed by the Blackfoot in trapping furs and trading them for guns and knives, as they seemed content to retain their old customs. Consequently the very few early trading posts set up in the Bow and Elbow area quickly fell into disuse.

The American Fur Company experienced outright hostility from the Blackfoot tribe and was delayed in establishing Fort Benton on the Missouri at the edge of Blackfoot country until the 1840s.

In 1864, the American Fur Company folded, leaving the southern Alberta plains open to independent trading. The demise of the well-established firm marked the end of fair trading practices. On the Canadian plains, no law enforcement agency existed, and some of the independent traders from the US got into a brisk whiskey trade with the Blackfoot. Sometime after 1869, Fort Whoop-Up was established just south of present-day Lethbridge on the Old North Trail, which quickly became known, for this reason, as the "Whoop-Up Trail", while the Blackfoot country itself became known as "Whoop-Up country". Bad whiskey which the Blackfoot received in trade rapidly deteriorated their way of living and resulted in considerable needless loss of life. The whiskey trade spread east to the Cypress Hills and north to the Bow River with "whiskey" forts being established across the area. In 1871, Fred Kanouse, a trader formerly employed with the American Fur Company, established a small post on the banks of the Elbow River about three miles upstream from its confluence with the Bow. This un-named post is regarded as Calgary's first permanent building.

Below: The overland trail from south to north is called the Old North Trail. It became a trade route following the arrival of the Canadian Pacific Railway in Calgary in 1883 and is now the route of the main south to north highway in Alberta. (Map by Anthony Clegg)

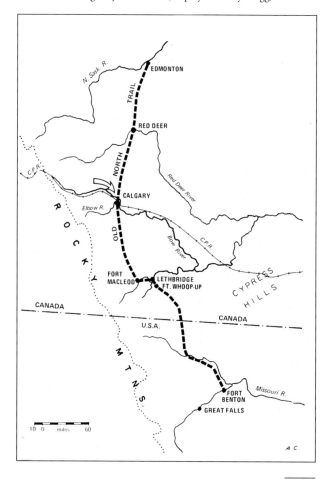

Above: Looking west from the corner of Centre Street and 8th Avenue in 1918, the former Hudson's Bay store is now occupied by the Royal Bank of Canada.
(Glenbow Archives ND-8-208)

Below: A summer morning panorama of the City of Calgary from the hill northeast of the Centre Street Bridge.
(Canadian National 31839)

The whiskey trade continued to spread until in 1873, three years after the Hudson's Bay Company transferred its territory of Rupert's Land to the new Dominion of Canada, the federal government decided to establish a police force for the west. In the summer of 1874, a trained, well-equipped force under Colonel Macleod arrived without incident at Fort Whoop-Up, hoping to purchase it for their own use. Unsuccessful in this bid, the force continued along the Whoop-Up Trail to the Oldman River crossing, where they established a fort and named it after their Colonel. The following summer, 1875, Colonel Macleod chose F Troop under the command of Inspector Brisebois, to go north to establish another fort. Brisebois chose a site at the confluence of the Bow and Elbow rivers, adjacent to the Whoop-Up Trail. Emulating the precedent set by his Colonel, the Inspector named the new fort after himself. A few months later, however, Colonel Macleod overruled the choice of name and called it Fort Calgary. (sometimes spelled Fort Calgarry.)

Years later, the site of the fort along 9th Avenue SE was taken over by the Grand Trunk Pacific Railway as the location for its Calgary terminals. Canadian National Railways subsequently developed its city freight handling facilities on the site. These were closed and removed in the early 1970s. A reconstructed Fort Calgary and interpretive centre now occupies the site.

Calgary's beginnings were small. The new fort attracted a handful of merchants, serving the police and others having a growing interest in large scale ranching. Fort Calgary grew slowly until its big boost came in 1883 when the CPR, building westward to the Pacific, finally reached the Bow River. Calgary never looked back. The ranching trade grew rapidly; the railway brought a constant flow of settlers; agriculture became feasible, spurred on by irrigation; mineral deposits in the eastern Rockies, coal at the edge of the mountain ranges and later, the discovery of oil all contributed to the rapid growth of the Bow River community as a supply centre.

Calgary grew to a community of almost 30,000 people by 1909, where only 34 years earlier two rivers joined in a quiet glade frequented occasionally by the Blackfoot and the buffalo. The community has continued to thrive. Some 134 years after Fort Calgary was first established, the City of Calgary boasts a population of over one million.

In the early years of the Twentieth Century, one of the accepted marks of municipal maturity was the possession of a street railway system. Calgary was the owner of just such a transit enterprise, which was publicly owned from its inception in 1909 to its demise in the closing days of 1950. This system had a profound influence on the growth and prosperity of Calgary.

This is its story.[1]

Below: The Canadian Pacific Railway played an important role in Calgary's formative years. This photograph shows a special train carrying Lord Stanley of Preston, the Governor-General of Canada, from Calgary to Gleichen in October 1889.
(Canadian Pacific)

Above: Calgary's first public transit was provided by the Calgary Car Company, which operated three such British-built buses during 1907 and 1908. Poor roads and high fares soon forced the vehicles off the streets, although the company was not formally disbanded until October 1915.
(Glenbow Archives (NA-647-1)

Below: Calgary's first streetcar, photographed at the Stampede Gate to the Exhibition Grounds. The inaugural run of the street railway, known as the Calgary Electric during its formative years, took place on July 5th 1909. Shown from left to right: Commissioners A.G. Graves and S.J. Clarke, an unidentified crewman, Superintendent T.H. McCauley and Mayor R.R. Jamieson. (Glenbow Archives NA-644-22)

CHAPTER TWO

Introduction of Urban Transportation

THE STREETCAR did not represent the first attempt at public transportation in Calgary. The Calgary Car Company Limited commenced service with chain-driven buses in 1905 but, because of bad roads and high fares, the business was not very successful and did not last for long. The city was becoming serious about operating a street railway system as early as 1906.

In March 1907, Bylaw 740, providing $250,000 for the building and equipping of a street railway system, was passed by the citizens and received third reading in Council on May 6th 1907.[1] A plan drawn up by the City Engineer and dated September 13th 1907[2] described a system which appears to have been designed as a series of belt lines, with 8th Avenue SE-SW as a double track trunk line from 6th Street SE to Mewata Park on 11th Street SW. A parallel east-west line was planned on 4th Avenue SE-SW from the Langevin Bridge at 4th Street SE to the Louise Bridge at 9th Street SW where it angled south west to connect with a proposed line on 11th Street SW. Another pair of east-west lines was planned for 12th Avenue SE-SW and 17th Avenue SE-SW between 11th Street SW and 5th Street SE. North-south trackage was planned as follows: 11th Street SW and 1st Street SW to connect all of the avenue lines; 2nd Street SE between 8th Avenue SE and 17th Avenue SE; 4th Street SE between 4th Avenue SE and 8th Avenue SE; 5th Street SE between 12th Avenue SE and 17th Avenue SE. A single track was planned to run east from the 8th Avenue SE line via 6th Street SE and 9th Avenue SE across the Elbow River to the Cushing Brothers' factory at 15th Street SE.

Council passed a motion on May 6th 1907 concurrent with the final reading of Bylaw 740, that the electric street railway system be built, equipped and administered by a special body to be known as the Street Railway Commission which was to be appointed by the City Council. It was also ordered that no steps be taken toward the carrying out of the street railway bylaw until such a commission had been established.[3] In effect, however, the July 15th 1907 council meeting countermanded this resolution by authorizing the Public Works Committee to call for tenders pending the appointment of the Street Railway Commission. The Public Works Committee handled street railway construction matters for some time, as Council wrestled with the alternatives of operating the railway under municipal auspices, or letting a franchise to outside parties for its operations. Eventually, tenders were sought for the proposed thirteen miles of street railway track, overhead and six semi-convertible cars with electrical equipment. However, the only complete tender received came in at $357,756[4] – nearly 50% more than the amount authorized the previous year.

On March 13th 1908, the City Clerk issued a second call stating that City Council was open to receiving offers for the installation, construction, equipping and operation of a street railway in the city for a limited period of franchise.[5] One interesting response to the franchise tender came from R.T.D. Aitken representing the Montreal Engineering Company of Montreal. He pointed out that a temporary tramway in a city with a population smaller than 40,000 which was spread out over a wide area was unprofitable, but that his firm would consider a forty-year franchise on reasonable terms and conditions. He also requested permission to generate and sell power in the city subject to such reasonable and proper considerations and restrictions as may be agreed upon.[6]

Apparently, while working through an agreement with Mr. Aitken, who appeared to be the only serious contender for a franchise, the City Engineering Department called for tenders to lay a double track line on 8th Avenue SW-SE between 4th Street SW and 3rd Street SE, as well as through the 1st Street SW subway (under CPR tracks), in conjunction with plans to pave these roads.[7] The rails arrived in October 1908[8] and were subsequently laid as planned. Indeed, the first rail vehicle to operate on Calgary streets was an 8 HP gasoline car, which ran along 8th Avenue SE-SW between 2nd Street SE and 4th Street SW for a test run of the steel at 3 PM on Thursday December 24th 1908. It was manned by Superintendent Giles, accompanied by Commissioner S.J. Clarke, F.W. Alexander, H. Haskings, A. Nichols and A. Wagner.[9]

In the meantime, Council and Mr. Aitken were attempting to reach an agreement. It seems that the City was holding out for a franchise maximum of twenty years while Mr. Aitken could not see his way clear to go less than a 25-year franchise. Mr. Aitken also wanted the right to haul freight cars over the proposed system, while the City wanted to maintain the right to restrict freight car haulage over city streets.[10] No agreement was ever reached, and Council decided to construct and operate the street railway under municipal auspices with a July 1st 1909 target date for its inauguration.

A Municipal Enterprise

On January 6th 1909, the City Commissioners issued a contract to Charles Taylor, an electrical engineer and the superintendent of the Edmonton Radial Railway – also a municipal operation – to act as a consultant. The recommendations presented in Mr. Taylor's ensuing report were most significant in that they triggered the actual construction and equipping of the Calgary Electric Railway.

The report recommended a track layout essentially as subsequently built, amounting to 10.2 miles of street trackage and 12.5 miles of lineal track. The estimated cost of the total proposal was broken down as follows:[11]

Construction and material:	$234,770
Additional cost on account of heavier concrete base, filler and drainage to accommodate double track street railway on paved streets	97,591
Car barn	15,000
Twelve cars	84,000
One sweeper	3,000
One sprinkler	5,000
Engineering and contingent account	4,388
Street grading	6,000
Total	$449,749
Provided in By-Law 740	$250,000
Required to be raised	$199,749

In addition, a petition by property owners on 1st Street sw between 4th Avenue sw and 8th Avenue sw for a car line was considered favourably by Council. A double track line plus the cost of removing the already installed special work and replacing it with a double wye crossover in pavement was estimated to be $25,988, making a new total of $225,737 to be raised.[12]

The purchase of six additional cars, a sweeper and a sprinkler was also proposed over and above the equipment authorized by the original bylaw. It was estimated that the routes scheduled for completion before the end of 1909 would require twelve cars in order to provide a ten-minute service on each line. The report recommended pay-as-you-enter, double-truck, forty-passenger cars about forty-two feet in length. This report favoured the belt system of routing. The commissioners noted as well that the $97,591 item for additional concrete base for paving was the estimated cost of constructing the street beyond that normally required to pave the street without streetcar tracks. This was not originally budgeted in Bylaw 740 and would leave the property owners to pay only normal costs associated with paving their street, the same as if the street railway were not built on their street. All phases of the report were adopted at the January 18th 1909 council meeting.[13] The only feature which was not followed through was the purchase of a sweeper.

On April 2nd 1909, a second bylaw for street railway funds was passed by the ratepayers with 378 favouring and 60 against the borrowing of a further $226,000 for the electric street railway.[14] This Bylaw 921 was given third reading and passed in Council on April 13th 1909.[15] The final total approved for the initial building and equipping of the Calgary Electric Railway was $476,000.

In the meantime, the commissioners had been authorized by Council to call for tenders for street railway material, cars and equipment, as well as engines and boilers for the power house. These contracts were subsequently awarded by the Commissioners under authority of a motion passed in Council on March 1st 1909.[16]

Contract	Firm	Amount
3 boilers	Babcock & Wilcox	$28,560
1 induced draft dystem	Babcock & Wilcox	5,500
1 engine 500 KW	Robb Engineering Co.	14,300
1 generator 500 KW	Allis-Chalmers-Bullock	15,950
1 motor generator set		
1 switchboard		
12 car bodies	Ottawa Car Co. (8) and Preston Car & Coach Co. (4)	34,240
12 car motors	Canadian Westinghouse	24,945
1100 tons rail	Gorman, Clancey & Grindley, Calgary	67,500
Rail bonds	Canadian General Electric Co.	3,040
Overhead material	Northwest Electric	2,900
Trolley wire	Northwest Electric	4,340
Feed wire aluminum	Federal Electric Co.	4,550
Wooden poles	Stuart Lumber Co.	3,440
Ties	East Kootenay Lumber Co.	14,600

Other contracts let for the supply and construction of the system included car barn special and intersection special trackage, the building of the car barn, trucks for the streetcars and a 5000 gallon water sprinkler from Preston Car & Coach Company Limited of Preston, Ontario.

Commissioners were given the authority to apply to the Governor-in-Council for permission to extend the Calgary Electric Railway beyond the city limits if deemed necessary in the interests of the City.[17]

With most of the contracts let, the commissioners set about the task of seeking a superintendent for the railway. The commissioners recommended the hiring of Thomas H.

McCauley − formerly superintendent of the Port Arthur Electric Light Plant − as the superintendent of the Calgary Electric Railway at a salary of $175 per month effective April 1st 1909. Mr. McCauley was described as a man with fourteen years' experience in this field and a qualified electrical engineer with both construction and operating experience in electric light and railway work. Mr. McCauley accepted the position, and reported for duty on April 1st, beginning immediately to superintend the construction of the system.[18] After establishing himself, he received permission to call an associate from the Port Arthur-Fort William system in the person of Charles Comba, who was assigned the duties of general foreman of the system.[19] Mr. McCauley also successfully enticed James Holmes from the same system to become the barn foreman in charge of motor repairs for the electric cars.[20]

Tenders continued to be called and awarded while Council deliberated on various aspects of the routing. The previously-agreed-upon extension north of 8th Avenue sw on 1st Street sw was changed to Centre Street as a result of objections by churches on the former thoroughfare, who feared that streetcar noise would disturb religious services. The commissioners also felt that the Centre Street trackage would be more economical, as it would eliminate the expense of taking up the special work already installed at 8th Avenue sw and 1st Street sw in 1908. Centre Street,

moreover, provided a direct line between a proposed bridge over the Bow River and the CPR station, making it a logical alternative to 1st Street sw.[21]

Construction of the track-work was held up for several weeks in late April, May and early June 1909, as delivery of rail and fixtures was delayed by a shipping strike on the Great Lakes.[22] This retarded construction long enough for a number of 4th Avenue sw residents west of Centre Street to petition against building that line. Instead, the 9th Avenue SE line was double tracked to 12th Street SE, thus enabling the cars to offer better service to St. George's Island Park.[23]

Below: In June 1910 the same group as that illustrated on page 10 inspects CMR 18, one of the new Preston-built cars. From left to right are Commissioner S.J. Clarke, Commissioner A.G. Graves, Mayor R.R. Jamieson, and T.H. McCauley, Street Railway Superintendent. Those behind the official party of four have not been identified. (Glenbow Archives NA-644-23)

The Stage was Set … The Drama About to Begin

As the July 1st target for operation approached and passed, work was being rushed day and night on the essential portion of the line from downtown to the Fair Grounds. Correspondence with respect to the finer details of the cars grew more abundant until July 3rd 1909, when a letter went from the Mayor of Calgary to the Ottawa Car Company advising that the first two cars had arrived in the city.[24] Last-minute installation of the power plant was progressing favourably and, as all of these activities were co-ordinated toward final completion by Mr. McCauley, a strong sense of expectation developed among Calgarians. This anticipation was over-shadowed somewhat by the great provincial fair which opened on Monday July 5th, the same day that cars 1 and 2 made their first run over incomplete track under newly-erected overhead wiring.

Though there were only two "props" and a small cast of players, the stage had been set and the curtain was about to go up on the first act of the ongoing dramatization depicting the growth and development of Calgary and its transit system.

Above: Billy Cairns (conductor) and George Adie (motorman on step) pose with Belt Line tram 46 some time during early 1900s. Note the prominent air whistle and route destination board with moveable destination arrow. Lettering on these larger trams spelled out the new *Calgary Municipal* name.
(Glenbow Archives NA-2891-13)

Opposite top: Centre Street between 7th Avenue and 8th Avenue about 1912. Offices of the Canadian Estates Company, owners of Tuxedo Park, were in the first building on the left side. The CPR station is at the end of the street on 8th Avenue and the observation car is parked just south of 8th Avenue. (Glenbow Archives NA-644-12)

Opposite bottom: Calgary's No. 1 shown entering the carbarns, as Mayor Jamieson and Commissioners Clarke and Graves pose with Superintendent McCauley and an unidentified conductor, July 1909. (Glenbow Archives NA-2891-1)

Tickets courtesy of Edmonton Radial Railway Society
Fonds Leslie Corness

CHAPTER THREE

Enter the Streetcars

"At 3:10 this morning, under the direction of Supt. McCauley, the first streetcar ever run in Calgary got under way. Car No. 2, which made the run was lined up at the entrance to the Exhibition grounds on 2nd Street East. The staff in charge was composed of Supt. Thomas H. McCauley, Charles Comba at the motor, Clifton Williams, conductor, George Williams and J. Giles.

The passengers were Sergt. Mackie, W.M. Davidson and A.W. DeGraves of the Albertan.

The electricity was turned on at 2:30 and everything was in readiness.

Everything went as smoothly as could be. The car journeyed slowly along 2nd Street East, through the subway, and to the Queen's Hotel and returned.

Later this morning another trial run will be made to the Alberta hotel and the official start from the Alberta at 8 o'clock this morning."[1]

The day was Monday July 5th 1909, and *The Morning Albertan* was on the streets a few hours later with the almost secretive trial run story. Later the same day, unobtrusively tucked away at the bottom of page one, *The Calgary Herald* described the official run under the heading "Street Cars Are Running to the Fair."

"Promptly at 8 o'clock cars No. 1 and 2, which were occupied by Mayor Jamieson, Aldermen Mitchell, Green, Erb, King, Speers, Commissioner Graves, Supt. McCauley, and other citizens, and two press representatives left the corner of 8th Avenue and 1st Street west and ran to the car barns at Victoria Park and returned. There was no formal opening remarks or address of any kind..."

"As the cars passed down 8th Avenue and 2nd Street west (sic), they were heartily cheered by many business men and others who cast grateful eyes on the long looked-for trolleys."[2]

At the conclusion of the inaugural run, Mayor Jamieson made the following statement to the press, "This is an epoch in the history of the remarkable progress in the growth of the city of Calgary."[3] The two cars then began operating a reliable five-minute service which continued throughout the week of the fair between the Alberta Hotel at 8th Avenue sw and 1st Street sw, via 8th Avenue sw-se and 2nd Street se to the Fair Grounds at Victoria Park.

When service concluded a the close of "Day One" for the Calgary Municipal Railway, a total of $450 had been dropped into the two fare boxes, representing the carriage of about 9000 passengers.[4] These two trams had embarked upon a

lifetime in Calgary which would span 41 years. Considering the millions upon millions of people they would carry, the extremes of climate they would experience, the number of times they would squeal and lurch around the many sharp curves in the city's narrow streets and the absolutely countless occasions on which they would stop and start, it is an understatement to say that they were a tribute to the designers and craftsmen who built them.

These two streetcars were part of the original fleet of twelve similar cars: numbers 1 to 8 ordered from the Ottawa Car Company Ltd. of Ottawa, and numbers 9 to 12 purchased from the Preston Car & Coach Company Limited of Preston, Ontario. The five pairs of arched body windows on each side of the cars displayed a graceful and popular design of the day. A very distinctive characteristic of all Ottawa-built passenger cars delivered to Calgary over the following few years was the semi-elliptical sash on the front and rear platforms and on the end windows of the cars. The words CALGARY ELECTRIC on the Ottawa-built cars and CALGARY ELECTRIC RY on those from the Preston Company were centered on the body sheathing below the windows on each side. The Ottawa-built cars carried the road number on the same plane as the lettering at each end of the car body under the first and ninth window posts. The road number also appeared on either side of the front dash and in the centre of the rear dash. The Preston-built cars carried road umbers on each side of the front and rear dashes, but not on the car sides. Six brass guard rods, three inches apart, were fitted to the windows on the left (*blind* or *devil-strip* side) of the car body as safety features.

Interior paneling and moulding was of first quality red cherry, smoothly finished and highly polished. Ceilings or headlinings were three-ply wood veneer with bird's eye maple face. Joints in the headlinings were covered with band moulding and the side mouldings were arranged for advertising cards.

All of the units in this series were designed for two-man, pay-as-you-enter single-end operation. The car design reflected these features, with a short front platform for the motorman who was responsible for operating the car, and a long rear platform where passengers boarded and deposited their fares with the conductor who was actually in charge. Passengers could exit at either platform. Polished bronze hand railings on the rear platform separated the paths of the embarking and disembarking passengers. There were no doors on the rear platform but a bulkhead with sliding doors on each side separated the platform from the main body of the car. There was also a bulkhead at the front of the car body with a sliding door in the centre. Conductors and

Above: Robert Cumming, motorman of CMR "dinky" 29, poses with his children,
Robert Gordon and Cissy, for a photographer at the Killarney Loop, circa November 1912.
(Miss Janet Cumming collection)

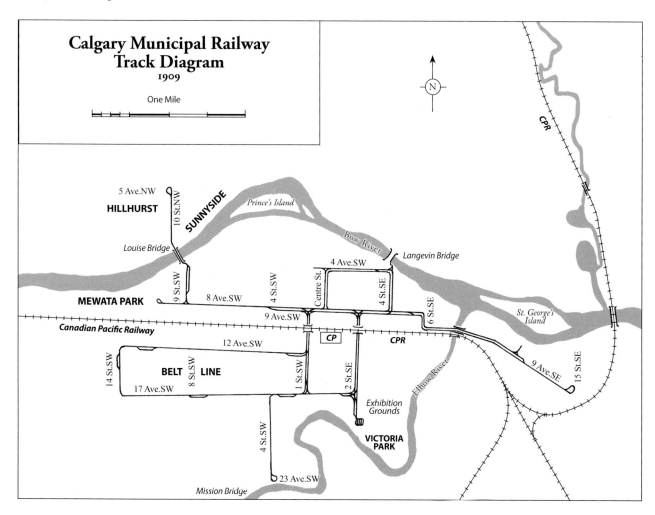

motormen could signal *stop*, *start* or *back up* to one another by means of a pull cord on the ceiling which activated small bronze bells mounted on each platform.

In the Ottawa-built cars, seating for thirty-six passengers was provided by ten double transverse seats and longitudinal benches at the rear.[5] Seats were stationary, sprung, and finished in rattan weave topped with brass grab handles. The Preston-built cars had fourteen double transverse walk-over seats and two stationary seats, with the same finishing and upholstering as their Ottawa-built counterparts.[6] Other passenger comforts included clerestory window vents operated by brass handles extending down to outstretched arm level, known commercially as standard ventilator sash openers, as well as the semi-convertible feature permitting side sashes to be dropped into side pockets. These combined features provided plenty of ventilation in warm weather. The first sign of winter temperatures was the cue to bring out the storm sashes and draw heat from the electric heaters below the seats.

Throughout the week of the Fair, the two new trams plied with dispatch over the short route between the city centre and the Fair Grounds, carrying capacity crowds over the open trackwork on 2nd Street SE. On Monday July 12th, immediately following the close of the Fair, streetcar service was restricted to a few blocks on 8th Avenue SW-SE to allow paving operations on 2nd Street SE to continue unhampered by car traffic.[7] By Wednesday of the same week, the cars were running every ten minutes along 8th Avenue SW-SE to 9th

Street SW and then north to 4th Avenue SW at the Louise Bridge. They returned via the same route to terminate at 8th Avenue SE and 2nd Street SE.[8] On Tuesday July 20th, the 9th Avenue SE line to Cushing's factory (15th Street SE) was in service, as was the Louise Bridge-Hillhurst section.[9]

The Question of Sunday Operation

As track construction was being hurried along and more of Calgary Electric's streetcars continued to arrive from the builders, the whole question of Sunday operation was thoroughly discussed at great length. Editorials appeared in the press, and sermons were given from the pulpits by the Calgary clergy. On the very eve of the first run, the Reverend Mr. Kerby of Central Methodist church prefaced his evening sermon with these remarks:

" There is no necessity for Sunday street cars in Calgary until the city has a population of 50,000, and then the question should be submitted to the people.

That is the way they do it in Ontario and we can still learn something from the people of old Ontario.

There is no reason why we should have Sunday cars now. The city is not congested, and everybody with two legs can walk out to the parks or the hills if they want fresh air, and the exercize (sic) will do them good.

I hope the time will be long delayed when the majority of the people of Calgary will vote for Sunday Cars."[10]

Above: A view of the 8th Avenue sw – 1st Street sw corner looking eastward. The photo, taken in July 1914, shows CMR 55, a Red Line "West Calgary" car making transfer connection with the Grand Trunk loop car, followed by a single-truck tram carrying "City – Fair" route sign. Incandescent street lighting had replaced the arc-lamps pictured in the view on page 15.
(Provincial Museum and Archives of Alberta, Pollard T.N. 1476)

Opposite: A new Preston-built streetcar No. 12 stands at the south end of the White Line known as the "North-South" route in 1910. The Blue Rock Hotel was on 4th Street sw between 25th and 26th avenues sw.
(Colin K. Hatcher collection)

The Morning Albertan's positive editorial stance supporting the operation of Sunday cars was at odds with the Reverend Mr. Kerby's views. The editorial construed his statement to mean that the Sunday streetcar question was to be decided upon population entirely, and that the Commandments were to be left out of the argument. The editorial concluded: "The *Albertan* believes that a city with a population of 29,265, with suburbs of at least 1,000 more, is populous enough for Sunday cars."[11] *The Calgary Herald* also editorialized in favour of Sunday streetcar operation on the basis of convenience, and observed that no apparent injurious effects could be foreseen.[12] Dean Paget of St. John's Church was reported to be in favour of Sunday cars, as he felt that they were an inexpensive means of transit to church,

parks and homes. He cautioned, however, that the street railway employees must still get their day of rest.[13]

Calgarians, by means of a plebiscite on Wednesday August 4th 1909, decided strongly in favour of the Sunday car issue, the count showing 654 in favour and 80 against.[14]

Hot on the heels of the decision, Superintendent McCauley announced that streetcars would be running Sunday August 8th 1909, every twenty minutes beginning at 9 AM on 8th and 9th avenues sw-se and every ten minutes during the afternoon and evening throughout the whole system.[15]

The System Expanded

On Friday August 13th 1909, the 17th Avenue sw-se line was opened for traffic; in spite of somewhat awkward operating conditions, it reportedly attracted several riders. The service was slow because the special track intersection at 2nd Street se was incomplete. Cars coming from 17th Avenue se to turn northbound onto 2nd Street se could only turn onto the southbound track on 2nd Street se. At 8th Avenue se they could only turn into opposing traffic, so they turned into the eastbound track. Then they backed east along 8th Avenue se to 6th Street se where they were able to cross over onto the westbound track and proceed forward to 2nd Street se and into the southbound

Above: Preston-built car 18 pauses for the photographer in front of the Stampede Grounds gate at 2nd Street SE and 17th Avenue SE along with a number of civic officers shortly after its delivery in 1910. According to the square route indicator over the rear entrance, the car was assigned to the "East-West" route or the Red Line.
(Glenbow Archives NA-2891-2)

Opposite: CMR 6 – one of the original Ottawa-built cars on the Burns Avenue line, circa 1912. R.G. Salloway is conductor and Henry Howard the motorman.
(Glenbow Archives NA-1299-1, copy of PA 855-8)

track which in turn led into the 17th Avenue SE-SW line. This complicated turning arrangement terminated about Wednesday August 18th[16] when the special track work at 17th Avenue SE and 2nd Street SE was completed. Eastbound 17th Avenue cars could then turn into the northbound track on 2nd Street SE and "wye" or turn back at 8th Avenue SE and 2nd Street SE to begin the return trip to 17th Avenue.

By the end of August it was expected that track would be completed on 4th Street SW between 17th Avenue SW and the Mission Bridge, and that all paving and track would be completed on 2nd Street SE.[17] Meanwhile, construction was pressing forward on 17th Avenue SE-SW, 14th Street SW, 12th Avenue SW and 1st Street SW; people in this southwest area were becoming anxious to know how Superintendent McCauley planned to get them to the city centre without a roundabout trip via 14th Street SW, 12th Avenue SW-SE and 2nd Street SE, when the 1st Street SW track directly connected 8th Avenue SW and 17th Avenue SW.[18] On September 15th, the issue was pressed when a passenger boarded an eastbound Belt Line car on 17th Avenue and was refused a transfer to the 1st Street West line. His destination was the corner of 8th Avenue and Centre Street and the transfer would have saved him a needless trip of four blocks at a very busy time of the day. The conductor stated that the Belt Line car was going downtown and that he was acting under instructions.[19] The final outcome of this incident is unknown, but the Belt Line route never changed (except

for one brief span in the 1930s) during the whole period that streetcars operated in this section of Calgary.

Amid the pressure to provide reasonable service while completing construction, Superintendent McCauley found himself faced with several unexpected difficulties. One was a financial matter that the commissioners were able to correct with dispatch. It was discovered that the original street railway construction bylaw of $476,000 was overspent by $40,000 because the cost of paving the 19'6" strip between and beside the tracks on 8th Avenue SW-SE from 4th Street SW to 6th Street SE had been charged against the street railway, when in fact only the cost of heavier concrete base, filling and drainage to accommodate double track on paved streets was properly chargeable.[20] The actual cost of paving was never intended as a charge against the railway, so the commissioners recommended to Council that a bylaw be prepared providing for a refund of the $40,000 unlawfully taken from the street railway for the 8th Avenue paving. Council concurred, and on October 26th 1909, Bylaw 998 for $40,000 was presented to the citizens. It was carried, 106 in favour and 47 against,[21] indicating that only a scant number of voters turned out to cast a ballot on the issue.

Some Early Labour Troubles

The first hint of labour difficulties arose early in the railway's history. The original working agreement which the men signed individually, provided a wage of 22½¢ per hour, raised to 25¢ per hour after six months of service. On August 28th 1909, the commissioners raised this stipend to 25¢ for all employees, effective October 1st, but the men objected and wanted the new rate to take effect August 15th instead, threatening to walk off the job unless their demands were met. There being no union for the workers, Superintendent McCauley had the upper hand and promptly suspended two motormen and one conductor indefinitely. Three other men immediately resigned. With 250 applicants waiting for jobs, this situation posed no threat to the Superintendent. McCauley then went about swearing in all motormen and conductors as special constables, thus giving them authority to arrest drunk and disorderly passengers, and giving himself full authority to dismiss men should they violate the law respecting constables, whether due to excessive enthusiasm or drinking on duty.[22]

New Lines for the Growing System

Construction of new trackage proceeded at a rapid pace on the Calgary Electric throughout the first four months of its life, and lines were constructed both in the down-town core and in residential areas to the east, to the west and to the south. The uncertainty of being able to provide regular service during this construction period due to "the somewhat jumbled condition of the tracks" strengthened Superintendent McCauley in his determination not to publish a schedule of routes or times.[23] Effective Friday October 29th 1909,[24] however, the Calgary streetcar system began operating on its first temporary but published timetable.

The east-west route, designated the Red Line, operated from Hillhurst beginning at 6:20 AM and every ten minutes thereafter until the arrival of the last run of the day at 12 PM; departures from East Calgary began at 6:25 AM and terminated at 11:55 PM. Hillhurst loop was located on 10th Street NW and 5th Avenue NW at the foot of the hill, and Red Line cars operated from this point south on 10th Street NW-SE, across Louise Bridge to 9th Street SW, south to 8th Avenue SW, then east through the city centre to 6th Street SE, south again to 9th Avenue SE and east to the loop on 15th Avenue SE at Cushing Brothers' factory. It took a streetcar twenty-five minutes to run one way over this Red Line.

The White Line cars on the north-south route running between the Mission and Langevin bridges left both termini at 6:15 AM and every fifteen minutes throughout the day

until 11:45 PM, when the last car arrived at each terminal point. Southbound cars left 4th Street SE and proceeded along 4th Avenue SE to Centre Street, south to 8th Avenue SW, west to 1st Street SW, south to 17th Avenue SW, west to 4th Street SW and south to the Mission Bridge. The cars actually turned back at the Blue Rock Hotel just north of 26th Avenue SW and the Mission Bridge. Northbound cars returned over the same route to 8th Avenue SW but continued east on 8th Avenue SW-SE to 4th Street SE, then turned north to 4th Avenue and the Langevin Bridge.

The Belt Line or Blue Line described a circuitous route from Centre and 8th Avenue to 1st Street SW, south to 12th Avenue SW, west to 14th Street SW, south to 17th Avenue SW, east to 2nd Street SE, north to 8th Avenue SE and west to Centre Street. Cars operated both ways on the belt offering fifteen-minute service from 6:20 AM to 11:35 PM. It took a car thirty minutes to complete a circuit.

These routes covered most of Calgary of that day and generally provided service from a residential area into the city centre, with the exception of the east end of the Red Line, which served an industrial development comprising

Cushing Brothers' factory and the CPR, and St. George's Island Park. The park attracted many passengers, and special cars from the 14th Street SW area directly to the park were common throughout the summer of 1910.

In the months that followed, Superintendent McCauley arranged schedules to provide the most effective service possible on a system which was subjected to the pressures of a rapidly-growing city. One annoyance was occasional power shortages and failures, which from time to time slowed or curtailed service unexpectedly. Another was the operating restrictions imposed by single track sections, requiring strategic placing of turn-outs and passing tracks to accommodate the efficient movement of cars. Already the capacity of the twelve cars was being taxed; in early December, therefore, the commissioners recommended the purchase of six additional cars, to be five feet longer than those in service and to be equipped with air brakes. The increased size of the cars, and the heavier grades which would be encountered in an extended system, necessitated the addition of this safety feature.[25]

More Rolling Stock

At the end of December 1909, tenders for the additional cars were awarded. The Ottawa Car Company Ltd. was to build three car bodies while the Preston Car & Coach

Below: A busy scene in front of the Hudson's Bay Company store at 8th Avenue and Centre Street about 1912. Arc lamps along the thoroughfare were soon to replaced with incandescent street lights. (Glenbow Archives NA-644-9)

Above: Another view of 8th Avenue sw looking eastward from 1st Street sw. The motorman of car 8 awaits his conductor's proceed signal, as two fashionably-attired ladies amble across the Avenue, 1909-10.

The white indicator above the front window tells us the car is on the "North-South" White Line. It will make a left turn into 1st Street sw. (Glenbow Archives NA-1009-17)

Company would construct the other three. The Canadian General Electric Company of Peterborough would supply air brakes for three of the cars, while the Canadian Westinghouse Company of Hamilton would provide air brakes for the other three units,[26] as well as controllers and electrical equipment (excluding motors) for all six cars. A letter which followed the telegram informing Preston that it had been awarded the tender to provide three of the additional cars, advised of negative citizen reaction to the seats and to the inadequate heating and lighting in the original Preston-built trams, as well as the poor riding qualities of the Bemis trucks which had been installed on the four Preston cars already in service on the Calgary Electric. Over the signature of R.R. Jamieson, who was chairman of the Commission and also mayor, the letter stipulated that the new cars were to have cluster lights, Brill trucks, and Westinghouse brakes and controllers.[27] No motors were ordered at this time for any of the six new cars; Superintendent McCauley planned to operate most cars on the system with two motors instead of four, hence, the new cars would utilize motors removed from cars already in service.[28]

Mr. McCauley's report to the commissioners covering 1909 operations dwelt extensively on the necessity for a rate reduction from the municipal power department. He noted that the utility received 3¾¢ per kilowatt-hour for power distributed to commercial and residential users, from which it underwrote line construction expenses, transformer losses, as well as installation and reading of meters and maintenance. The street railway was charged 3½¢ per kwh though it provided its own distribution and maintenance. He suggested that 2½¢ per kwh for operating the cars would be a more reasonable price. Electric heaters in the cars drew heavily on power, resulting in high heating costs, so he suggested the installation of more economical steam heaters. Looking ahead, the Superintendent recommended the purchase of smaller cars to operate on light traffic lines, which would result in reduced power consumption costs and still offer frequent service. The six months ending December 31st 1909 realized a total revenue of $57,805 while operating expense amounted to $36,491. After the deduction of interest and fixed charges amounting to $11,489, a net revenue of $10,001 remained at the close of 1909[29] – indeed an encouraging start for the Calgary Electric Railway.

Each month saw a very significant increase in the number of passengers carried – from 101,275 in July to 279,581 in December 1909. The average daily count in December 1909 was 9,019 passengers.[30] The same twelve cars carried increasingly larger loads until June of 1910, when the three new larger Preston-built cars, numbered 16, 17, and 18, joined the fleet.[31] They arrived just in time to help carry the exhibition

traffic, when the average number of passengers carried per day was 30,525.[32] The Ottawa Car Company Ltd. was late in delivering cars 13, 14 and 15, two arriving in December 1910 and the third in January 1911.

By the close of 1910 the streetcars had carried a total of 4,891,384 passengers.[33] Spread over the twelve-month period, the average per month was 407,615 varying from known figures of 301,679 for March[34] to 460,685 for June.[35] Most of this traffic had been carried by the original twelve cars and all of it over the original sixteen miles of track, no extensions having been built during 1910.

Not unexpectedly, the year 1910 proved to be a financial success. Revenues were $213,807 and operating expenses $110,084, leaving a balance of $103,723. After deducting $23,320 for interest on debentures, just over $9000 for sinking fund and $10,634 (5% of gross revenue) for contingent fund, a net surplus of $60,498 remained.[36]

This 1910 surplus was disposed of as follows:[37]

Stores purchased for 1911	$ 4,370
Insurance prepaid for 1911	1,050
City of Calgary – general account	22,500
Loaned to 1911 construction account	15,000
Cash in bank December 31, 1910	17,577

"With a total assessment of $30,000,000 in 1910, the amount of $22,500 paid into the city treasury had the effect of reducing the general taxation by three-quarter mills for the year. In this way the shareholders – that is, the property owners – benefitted according to their interests in the city.

The question as to the disposal of the surplus year by year, whether it will be applied to reduction of general taxation, reduction of car fares, improvement of the service, has not yet been definitely decided, but it has been fully demonstrated that the system is quite able to carry any expenditure on capital account and leave a handsome surplus for other purposes."[38]

Above: A couple stops to observe two streetcars running on the Blue or Belt Line pass in the 2nd Street SE underpass. The Imperial Hotel in the background has a verandah. The low clearance of the underpass is evident as the trolley rope on car 7 (to the right) is dragging on the roadway. This was before trolley retrievers or trolley catchers were mounted on the rear dash to keep the trolley rope taunt as the height of the overhead line changed or as the car rounded a curve. In the two-man car days, it was the job of the conductor (stationed at the rear of the car) to manage the tautness of the trolley rope. At this point, the car is probably stopped for the photograph to be taken and the conductor is otherwise occupied. (Photograph from *The Story of Calgary 1911 & Tuxedo Park Land & General Investment Company Limited, Calgary and Toronto, Canada.* Collection of Colin K. Hatcher.)

Opposite above: Car 8 at the 1st Street SW subway under the CPR tracks, showing the Grain Exchange Building in the background, 1909-10. (Glenbow Archives NA-1009-18)

Opposite Below: Car 7 on 8th Avenue SE looking west from the Post Office at 1st Street SE, 1909-10. (Glenbow Archives NA-1009-14)

A Change of Name

Although no official announcement apparently appeared, the Calgary Electric Railway became known as the Calgary Municipal Railway during 1910. For the balance of the railway's history, rolling stock and letterhead carried the Calgary Municipal name. Curiously, the lettering *Calgary Electric Railway* remained over the doors of the car barn entrance until after the closure of that facility in 1950. Regular fare streetcar tickets retained the Calgary Electric Railway nomenclature until Calgary Transit tickets were introduced in 1946. The Preston-built cars which were delivered during June 1910 were the first cars to carry the new name. Aside from the addition of these new cars, the physical properties of the Calgary Municipal did not grow throughout 1910, but public acceptance of the street railway and the need for its services became established as an integral part of life in the growing city.

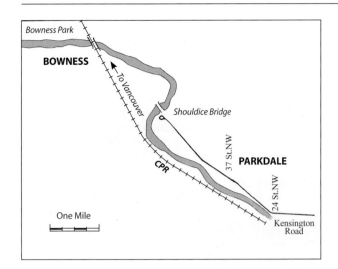

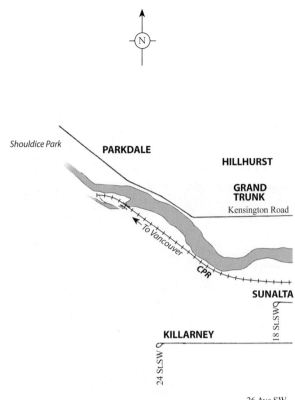

Calgary Municipal Railway
Track Diagram
1912

One Mile

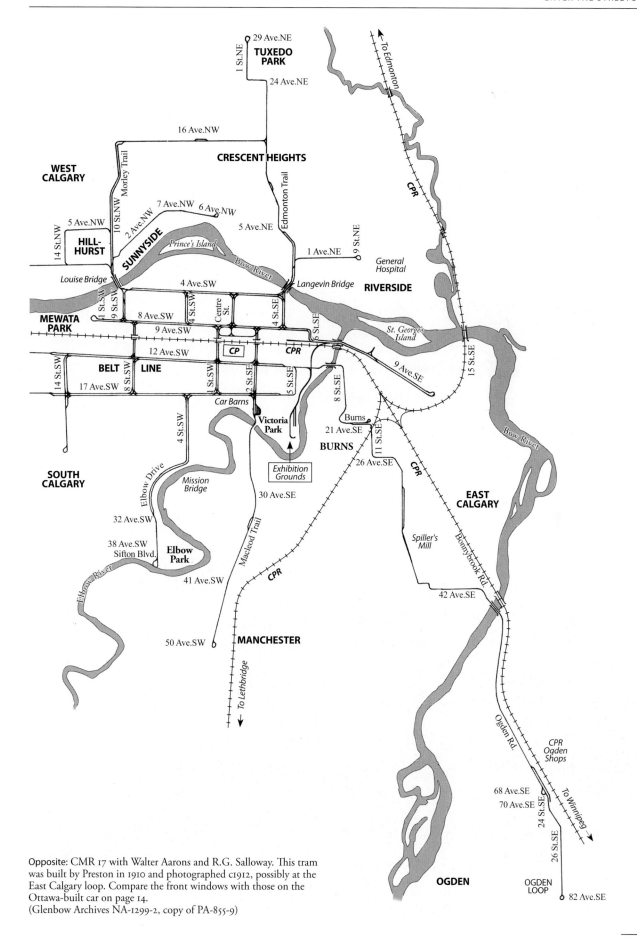

Opposite: CMR 17 with Walter Aarons and R.G. Salloway. This tram was built by Preston in 1910 and photographed c1912, possibly at the East Calgary loop. Compare the front windows with those on the Ottawa-built car on page 14.
(Glenbow Archives NA-1299-2, copy of PA-855-9)

Above: The "Coronation Day" ceremony on the Crescent Heights route, June 22nd 1911. CMR 24 was the first car over the line. Superintendent T.H. McCauley is on the right side of the photo – others in the group include Mayor J.W. Mitchell and G.H. Riley.
(Calgary Transit collection)

Below: Conductors and motormen in their shelter on 8th Avenue SE, c1911. Reuben Buckingham is on the extreme right; others in the photograph were not identified.
(Glenbow Archives NA-3000-1)

CHAPTER FOUR

The System Flourishes

A GREAT DEAL of planning took place throughout 1910 with a view to an early start on construction in 1911. The original trackage and routes were quite level, with the exception of the approaches to the Canadian Pacific Railway underpasses at 2nd Street SE and 1st Street SW; however, any extension north or south involved some very steep grades. Considerable deliberation was devoted to the need to choose a route up the North Hill from the Langevin Bridge and from the Hillhurst loop. Bylaw 1095 provided $484,000 for the constructing, extending and further equipping of the municipal street railway, including extensive track construction which can be followed in detail by comparing the 1909 with the 1912 track diagram. Also included was money for the construction of two bridges over the Elbow River at 12th Avenue SE and at 2nd Street SE, the addition of twelve single-truck passenger cars, the expansion of the shop facilities, electric motors for cars 13 to 18 inclusive, and the purchase of property to provide right-of-way for the railway.[1] This bylaw was voted upon and passed on September 15th 1910 with 970 people casting their ballots in favour and 126 casting against.[2]

The motors for cars 13 to 18 were ordered from Canadian Westinghouse. The experimental operation of double-truck cars with only two motors as an economy measure had proved unsuccessful, particularly under winter operating conditions. Even under ideal operating conditions, double-truck cars with only two motors had difficulty keeping to schedule. Superintendent McCauley also wanted to expand shop and repair facilities to obviate the need to send work out. In his 1910 year end report, he noted that all motor commutators had to be turned at a local machine shop, and that car wheels had to be replaced by arrangement with the CPR, resulting in extensive handling and cartage charges as well as liability to damage in transit. Installation of a lathe, wheel boring machine, wheel press and a pit lift would allow Mr. McCauley's shop staff to do this kind of work at the barns.[3] The Superintendent's desire to get the wheel press equipment was perhaps even more burning after he received the following communication dated May 17th 1911 from the Chairman of the commission – in other words, the Mayor:

"The Commissioners are in receipt of a verbal complaint that the car you are operating on the all night service to East Calgary is blessed with a flat wheel and your department is receiving the blessings, and possibly something else, of the citizens at the annoyance this car causes to them. We would request that you see that another car is placed on this route which will run more smoothly."[4]

The twelve single-truck cars included in Bylaw 1095 were ordered from the Preston Car & Coach Company Limited and assigned numbers 19 through 30 inclusive. They were 32-foot, single-end pay-as-you-enter trams. Interior appointments featured twelve transverse rattan-covered seats with two longitudinal benches at the rear. Other interior appointments were similar to the larger cars already in service.[5] These were the first cars to be delivered in the red and cream paint scheme which later characterized all passenger stock on the Calgary Municipal. Delivery of this series had begun by June 1911,[6] with seven of the dozen ready for service in time for the Fair and for the opening of some of the extended lines.

The first of the extensions to be completed was the Crescent Heights loop line. The last spike was driven on this line on Thursday June 22nd 1911. Mayor J.W. Mitchell, accompanied by G.H. Riley, happened to be making an unofficial tour of the various city work projects when they came upon superintendent McCauley and his crew putting down the last rail, so a timely opportunity was presented for the Mayor to drive the last spike on that part of the line. A touch of regality was added to the occasion, because it was also the day of the coronation of King George V and Queen Mary. Regular fifteen-minute service over the Crescent Heights line was inaugurated on Friday June 30th 1911.[7]

Fair Week, which opened Monday July 3rd, created the need for special car service from various parts of the city directly to the Fair Grounds and twenty-five cars were available to do the job. Direct fifteen-minute service to the Fair Grounds was offered from the Crescent Heights Fire Hall west to 10th Street NW, south over the Louise Bridge to 8th Avenue SW, east to 2nd Street SE, south to 17th Avenue SE, west to 1st Street SW, north to 8th Avenue SW, east to 4th Street SE, north across the Langevin Bridge, through Riverside to the Crescent Heights area. These cars carried a red and white sign. Red Line cars from 10 AM to 5 PM and 7 PM to midnight ran every ten minutes direct to the Fair via 2nd Street SE, transferring through passengers at 8th Avenue SW-SE. Blue Line cars continued on their regular ten-minute schedules but were joined by two extra cars operating around a 17th Avenue SE-SW, 14th Street SW, 12th Avenue SW-SE and 5th Street SE belt. From 10 AM to midnight, White Line cars on their northbound trips continued east on 17th Avenue SW-SE to 2nd Street SE, then turned north to 8th Avenue and on to the Langevin Bridge. Extra cars were also operating around 17th Avenue SE-SW, 1st Street SW, 8th Avenue SW-SE, and 2nd Street SE every ten minutes, providing direct service between the Fair and

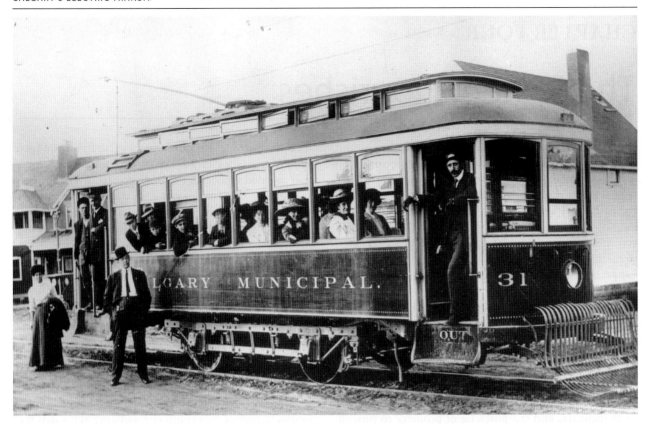

downtown. The following day, operations were eased some-what with the opening of the second track on 8th Avenue sw between 4th Street sw and 9th Street sw, and along 12th Avenue SE-SW.[8] At the close of the Fair Week, operations returned to normal and temporarily only on the Red, White, Blue lines, and the new Red & White Line.

From time to time, service was disrupted or re-routed slightly to accommodate track laying or paving operations. In the west end, Red and Red & White Line cars travelled over newly-laid track on 4th Avenue sw and 4th Street sw, while 9th Street sw and 8th Avenue SE-SW were closed for paving during mid August. With the completion of paving on 9th Street sw and 8th Avenue SE-SW, the Red and Red & White cars resumed service along these thoroughfares. Cars on a new route, designated the Red & Blue Line, serving the recently completed Sunnyside line, remained in service over the 4th Avenue sw/4th Street sw trackage.[9] Later in August, the Shouldice Park line, reaching out to the Bowness Bridge over the Bow River, began offering car service every two hours into downtown Calgary.[10] This route was eight miles long after it was coupled up with the Tuxedo Park extension which opened on September 19th.[11]

Blue Line service throughout most of August, September, and October operated one way only, around the Belt Line trackage, alternating direction from time to time as paving continued. In late September or early October, the 14th Street sw line to South Calgary was completed, and a car began to shuttle along this street between 17th Avenue sw and 26th Avenue sw.

Above: Single-truck "dinky" 31 was well filled with passengers when motorman George Washington posed for the photographer. Records indicate that the picture was taken on the South Calgary-Bankview line late in 1912. S.K. Beal is at the rear door.
(Glenbow Archives NA-1132-1)

Opposite below: A 1912 view of CMR 43 on the Blue Line "Belt Line" route. Neither conductor nor motorman has been identified.
(Glenbow Archives NA-2891-7)

Turning to the eastern part of the city, the Mills Subdivision line, which became commonly known as the Burns Avenue line, opened for service on Wednesday October 18th 1911. The car came from the Burns Avenue area across the new bridge on 12th Avenue SE to 2nd Street SE, turned north to 8th Avenue SE, west to Centre Street, north to 4th Avenue sw, west to 4th Street sw, south to 8th Avenue SE, east to 1st Street sw, south to 12th Avenue SW-SE, and east again to Burns Avenue.[12] This extension soon became a part of the Red & Blue Line running from Burns Avenue to Sunnyside via 2nd Street SE, 8th Avenue SE-SW, 4th Street sw and 4th Avenue sw.

All construction for the year terminated with the publica-tion of a new schedule which became effective on November 16th 1911.[13] The Red Line cars operated every ten minutes with no route change except for the new Hillhurst loop around Riley Park. Cars on the Blue Line or Belt Line ran every seven minutes both ways. The White Line offered a ten-minute service on its route extending north across the Langevin bridge to Riverside and then along 2nd Avenue NE for five blocks to a loop behind the General Hospital.

In the south the route was extended from the Mission bridge to Glencoe, a distance of about half a mile. The Red & White Belt Line offered fifteen-minute service to Crescent Heights one way only (westbound on 8th Avenue sw). Twenty-minute service was available on the Red & Blue Line from Burns Avenue to Sunnyside via 8th Avenue se-sw, 4th Street sw and 4th Avenue sw. The Bankview or South Calgary/5th Street se line left the 14th Street sw and 26th Avenue sw loop every half-hour. The Parkview car offered twenty-minute service from the 2nd Street se Bridge near the car barns to 8th Avenue se, Centre Street se, 4th Avenue sw, 4th Street sw, 8th Avenue sw-se to 2nd Street se and south to the bridge. Tuxedo–Bowness Bridge–Shouldice cars continued to operate on a schedule of about every two hours.

Car lines on steep grades offered the potential for an exciting and sometimes harrowing experience for passengers riding downhill on a streetcar which for a variety of reasons didn't always respond to the motorman's brake. Such an experience occurred for a carload of passengers on CMR number 20 going down the Edmonton Grade on its way to Shouldice one snowy Sunday afternoon in November. When it became evident that the car was not responding to the brake, several passengers leaped out of the rapidly-moving vehicle and rolled over in the snow. As it turned out, the descending tram struck car number 30 on the Crescent

Heights line at the bottom of the hill, resulting in slight damage to both units but no apparent injuries to any passengers.[14] Superintendent McCauley immediately ordered that no car follow within five minutes of another on this grade, with the intent that further accidents of this nature be prevented.[15]

Transportation during this era was not an easy matter. Paved streets were few, making the experience of moving from place to place slow and difficult. As the residential areas extended further away from the core of the city, a number of external pressures in the form of citizen petitions, real estate development proposals and industrial location concessions provided some serious and thought-provoking challenges for Council. Many of these related to the routing of the street railway, which in turn influenced the direction of population growth. The Hillhurst area benefitted by a rather unusual petition received by the commissioners early in 1911, signed by the presidents of two football leagues, one lacrosse league and two cricket associations, asking for an extension of the street railway to the Hillhurst Athletic Grounds. It suggested that track be laid on Victoria Road from Morleyville Road to 14th Street nw and on 14th Street nw from Victoria Road to Kensington Avenue, and then noted that this extension would serve that population of the city lying west of 14th Street in what is known as Upper Hillhurst and Houndsfield Heights. Mr. McCauley favoured

Above: Tuxedo Park Pavilion was to be a centrepiece for the new Tuxedo Park residential project. The streetcar line circled the pavilion. At the time, this development was on the outskirts of Calgary. It was an early suburban community. The streetcar line leading into Calgary centre would be an enticement to home buyers.
(From the Canadian Estates Company promotional booklet, Colin K. Hatcher collection)

the extension, and stated that some two extra miles of rail and fittings had been purchased under Bylaw 1095 for such an occasion as this.[16] On Wednesday July 26th 1911, Red Line cars began operating over this extension.[17]

Two of several real estate firms presented proposals to Council and won their cases to get car service extended into their developments. The first of these was approved by Council on April 3rd 1911. In this exchange, the Canadian Estates Company Limited, developer of Tuxedo Park, agreed to build the streetcar line and waterworks system into its development free of expense to the City of Calgary, with the exception that, when the waterworks produced a reasonable annual revenue from the consumers, the company be reimbursed the cost of such extensions without interest. The railway, however, became the absolute property of the city as soon as its construction was completed.[18] The city also received a park around which the streetcar line looped. The Tuxedo Park car line was opened for operations as part of the Calgary Municipal Railway on September 19th 1911.

To The West – Bowness

The second real estate scheme was presented by John Hextall, owner of Bowness Park. Apparently Mr. Hextall had been working for some time to entice the city of extend the car line to Bowness, where he had extensive residential properties for sale, but council did not seriously consider it until Mr. Hextall offered to open to the public his $55,000 steel bridge over the Bow River.[19] His final offer included public use of the bridge. In addition, he turned over two islands in the Bow River containing a total of 86.3 acres

which could be used for park purposes, as well as a creek 1¼ miles long between the islands and the mainland where boating and fishing could be carried on. He also agreed to provide the necessary track to build from the Shouldice Park terminal to Bowness Park. In return, Mr. Hextall asked that one mile of line be completed in the fall of 1911 and the balance by June 30th 1912, and that seven return car trips be made each day at specified hours from Centre Street and 8th Avenue SW. As soon as twenty families had taken up residence at Bowness, cars were to operate continuously throughout the day between 6:30 AM and 11 PM.[20] The line was completed in due time, and Bowness Park became a very popular feature of the Calgary Municipal Railway for two or three generations of Calgarians.

Southeast – to Ogden

The extension and operations of the street railway (in addition to the extension of water, sewer and electric power facilities) to the site of the proposed CPR shops weighed favourably for the city (over Bassano and Medicine Hat) in inducing the Canadian Pacific Railway Company to locate its western shops in Calgary. After the passing of Bylaw

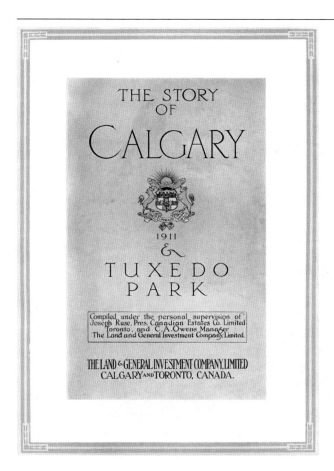

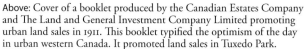

Above: Cover of a booklet produced by the Canadian Estates Company and The Land and General Investment Company Limited promoting urban land sales in 1911. This booklet typified the optimism of the day in urban western Canada. It promoted land sales in Tuxedo Park.

Above: This text comes directly from the booklet produced by the Canadian Estates Company and The Land and General Investment Company Limited
(Both photos: Colin K. Hatcher collection)

1230,[21] the Calgary Municipal Railway built a single track line to the railway shops, named "Ogden Shops" after Isaac Gouverneur Ogden the CPR's first auditor. A regular all-day service to the community of Ogden was provided, as well as a special service each morning and evening to transport about 500 workers to and from the shops. While the city generally gained a great deal from having the Ogden Shops built nearby, the street railway experienced considerable financial difficulty providing the Ogden special service throughout most of its life, as several cars and trailers had to be ordered solely for this service, and they remained idle throughout the day on the siding at Ogden.

The Ogden line was opened for service with the first official run via 12th Avenue SE and Burns Avenue on Tuesday December 31st 1912. Mayor Mitchell, Mayor-elect Sinott, officers of the CPR and city officials participated in the first run, which also featured a tour of the railway's Ogden facilities.[22] Tours of the shops were apparently offered to the public for a day or two after the opening of the new car line and attracted many eager citizens.[23] Since the CMR was short of rolling stock when the Ogden line was completed, the CPR operated an employees' commuter train to supplement streetcar service between Calgary and Ogden. By

Thursday January 3rd 1913, Ogden and the extreme southeast portion of the city had the luxury of regular street car service with cars leaving Centre Street and 8th Avenue SE at 6:30 AM and continuing hourly throughout the day.[24] For almost a full year, all service to and from Ogden operated via 12th Avenue SE and Burns Avenue. Then on Wednesday December 17th 1913, in-bound cars from Ogden began using the CPR overhead bridge via 20th Street SE, 9th Avenue SE, 8th Avenue SE-SW, 1st Street SW and back out to Ogden via the original 12th Avenue SE and Burns Avenue line.[25]

The regular Ogden car service ran a half mile past the shops loop to the city limits at 82nd Avenue SE and 26th Street SE. The operation of that extension was approved by a vote of the rate payers (233 for and 40 against) on condition that a suburban railway company, chartered as the South East Calgary Corporation, pay for the extension as part of its intention to construct and operate a suburban loop line.[26] The city agreed to operate that part of the line from Ogden Shops to the city limits with the intention of meeting the proposed South East Calgary Corporation cars at that point. The proposed SECC line struck out south and east of Ogden Shops for a distance of about three miles, and then formed a three-mile-long by one-mile-wide rectangle through and

Above: George Adie, motorman and Billy Spranklin, conductor halted their Crescent Heights car on the Morley Trail hill. View taken about 1912. (George Adie collection)

Below: Calgary's Scenic Car, a later view than shown on page 40. By now, wooden fender, awning, and air brake equipment had been installed, but the car still carried the number 50, dating the picture as 1912. The following year the "50" was replaced by a "25¢" sign. The car is parked facing north on a dead-end siding on Centre Street. It will back south toward 9th Avenue s to where it will switch over to the northbound track on Centre Street, then proceed on its journey. (Glenbow Archives NA-924-1, copy of PD-11-19)

around land owned largely by D.W. Trotter, who also happened to be Managing Director of the project.[27] As agreed, the Calgary Municipal Railway built the SECC track from Ogden Shops loop to the city limits, and continued to operate the regular Ogden service over it until 1924 when the loop was moved back to 74th Avenue SE and 26th Street SE,[28] thus saving the running of about 4000 feet each trip. The South East Calgary Corporation never did build its electric line beyond the city limits.

Proposals from other chartered electric railway concerns, such as the Alberta Interurban Railway and the Chestermere Calgary Suburban Railway Company, to share in building connections to or operations over the Calgary Municipal, were wisely refused. Neither of these two corporations ever operated any transportation services, although the Alberta Interurban – also known as Alberta Electric, which had an extensive charter to build and operate lines to Banff, Medicine Hat and into the Lethbridge area[29] – was anxious to negotiate with Calgary City Council to reclaim property along the banks of the Bow River to allow it access to its proposed terminal east of Centre Street. The Alberta Interurban anticipated main revenues from freight services, bringing produce from the surrounding farming communities into the Calgary City Market at 4th Street SE and 4th Avenue SE.[30] In September 1912, the city sold thirteen acres in Breckenridge Industrial Subdivision to the Alberta Interurban Railway as a site for its car barns.[31] However, Bylaw 1405[32] requesting the voters' permission for the Alberta Interurban to enter the city on certain streets and to operate its cars over these streets was defeated on December 20th 1912 by a 2 to 1 vote.[33] In the months following, the Alberta Interurban experienced difficulty raising capital funds, and following the deaths of two of its prime promoters, Messrs. Breckenridge and Drummond, it faded into oblivion.[34]

With this flurry of activity on the horizon in 1911, City Council foresaw the need for further expansion of the Calgary Municipal Railway. Bylaw 1200, presented to and approved by the rate payers on October 3rd 1911, included track extensions, double-tracking and the purchase of additional passenger equipment.[35] After tenders were called and received, the building of six 32-foot single-truck cars and six 41'6" double-truck cars was awarded to the Preston Car & Coach Company; the construction of six 46'6" double-truck cars was awarded to the Ottawa Car Company Ltd. The double-truck cars were to be equipped with Brill 27-G-1 trucks and the single-truck cars with Brill 21-E trucks and General Electric 80A 40 HP motors. A 5000-gallon sprinkler, the second one for the CMR, was ordered from Preston, to be equipped with Brill 27-G-1 trucks. The sprinkler bid was slightly higher from Preston than from Ottawa, but an interchange of parts with the existing Preston-built sprinkler was regarded as important. Preston also won the award for the building of a scenic car.[36]

There must have been some change in fulfilling these tenders, however, as the six single-truck cars were delivered with Taylor trucks, and there is a strong suspicion that the sprinkler was delivered with Bemis trucks. All cars with the exception of the single-truck units were equipped with air brakes; air brakes were also purchased for installation on cars 1 to 12. Council later approved the purchase of twelve sets of Westinghouse 4-motor equipment for all of the new double-truck cars.[37] The smaller Preston-built cars were numbered 37 to 42, while the larger Ottawa-constructed vehicles bore numbers 43 to 48 inclusive. The single-truck cars fell into sequence immediately after the earlier series of single-truck cars and were numbered 31 to 36 inclusive.

Apparently, in discussing the streetcars to be purchased under Bylaw 1200, one of the aldermen spoke strongly against having any more small "dinkey" streetcars ordered for the system. Commissioner Graves pointed out the economic advantages of operating these cars on suburban lines where frequency of service could be maintained with a lighter tram requiring less power. Another alderman noted that he would rather have a short wait for a short car than a longer wait for a longer car![38] In that day, the annual power expense for the CMR was almost equal to its wage expenditures, so wise power utilization was a very important factor in keeping the railway on the black side of the ledger.

All tenders for track, ties, poles and electrical fixtures called for in Bylaw 1200 were awarded at the November 21st 1911 Council meeting, with a March 15th 1912 delivery underlined.[39]

The Ottawa Car Company notified the Calgary Municipal Railway by December 15th 1911 that the six cars (43 to 48) for which it had been awarded tenders in October 1911 were completed and on their way to Calgary.[40] Ottawa must have been concerned about its tardy delivery of cars 13, 14, and 15, ordered late in 1909 and not delivered until late 1910 and early 1911. This tardy delivery influenced Calgary Municipal's turning to Preston for the construction of cars 19 to 30 in 1910, and CMR's continuing with Preston with the orders for cars 31 to 36. In thus standardizing single-truck cars, Calgary's practice was consistent with its action in ordering its second sprinkler from Preston in spite of a lower bid from Ottawa for this unit. At any rate, with winter tightening its grip over Calgary, these new cars were quickly put into service to maintain or increase service on most routes.

The first of the 1912 extensions opened on Monday May 13th 1912, when cars with Orange & Blue signs on them began to operate every eight minutes over a belt line, west on 8th Avenue SW to 8th Street SW, 17th Avenue SW and 1st Street SW.[41] Effective Tuesday May 28th 1912, car service was extended to Manchester on a half-hourly basis from 6:30 AM going east on 8th Avenue SE, south on 2nd Street SE and Macleod Trail to the Manchester loop, returning via 17th Avenue SE-SW, 1st Street SW and 8th Avenue SW. The cars carried the sign *MANCHESTER* on them.[42] With the addition of a turn-out on the south end of this line, service was soon offered every twenty minutes. The third phase of the 1912 program was the completion of double track along 4th Avenue SE-SW. By the end of June, Sunnyside cars were operating via 4th Avenue SW and Centre Street, and Crescent Heights cars via 4th Avenue SW and 4th Street SW.[43]

The Pride of the System

The scenic car ordered in the fall of 1911, appeared for the first time on Calgary streets on Thursday July 4th 1912, just in time to help celebrate the third anniversary of the opening of the Calgary Municipal Railway. The new scenic car made its inaugural run by travelling from the Exhibition Grounds at about 6:45 PM to East Calgary, Hillhurst and then back to the Exhibition Grounds. In charge was Inspector Decker and Conductor Clarke. Passengers included Superintendent McCauley, Assistant Superintendent Comba, the Navassarx Ladies Band and several principals from the various amusement enterprises at the Fair.[44] The car made its inaugural trip without its striped canvas top, front fender and air brakes, a subtle indication that Mr. McCauley was very anxious to introduce Calgary Municipal's finest. Built by Preston Car & Coach Company, it was 44 feet long and could seat 50 passengers on varnished wood-slat seats, elevated in stepped tiers and divided by a centre aisle. The white car body, accentuated with thin cherry and gold lines, featured a lavishly-flared front dash, bronze entrance gates, as well as bronze railings around the rear platform. The seven panels on each side were of British bevel plate glass mirrors. The city crest tastefully appeared in gold on either side of the front dash above the numerals "50", thought to have been the original road number of the car. Speculation is heightened by the fact that the inscription "25¢" soon displaced the numerals "50" on the dash, and possibly explains why the number 50 was assigned out of sequence to a 1913 Ottawa-built passenger car. The scenic car was duly described by a *The Calgary Herald* editorial writer as looking "something like Noah's ark on a trip to fairyland".[45] The fare was 25 cents and the tram, sometimes referred to as the "Rubberneck Car", operated on the following schedule and routes:

10:00 AM and 2:00 PM –

From 8th Avenue and Centre street via 4th Street east, through Riverside to Crescent Heights, Mountainview and the North Hill City, crossing the Bow river over the Langevin and Louise bridges, through Hillhurst to 8th avenue, 8th Street west, 17th avenue, 1st Street West to Centre Street.

11:00 AM and 5:00 PM –

From Centre street and 8th Avenue to the manufacturing section of East Calgary, the Mounted Police barracks and St. George's Island via 8th avenue, returning via 4th street east to 4th avenue to 9th street west, thence to Sunnyside and Crescent Heights hill from which a view of the city and Rocky Mountains can be had, returning via 8th Avenue.

3:00 PM and 7:30 PM –

From Centre street and 8th avenue around Belt Line, 2nd street east, 17th avenue viewing the exhibition grounds, St. Mary's Roman Catholic church, Holy Cross Hospital, Shriner's temple, Mount Royal residential section, 14th street west, 12th avenue, 1st street west, 8th avenue, 9th

street west to Hillhurst, Riley Park, the Bow river, returning via 4th avenue and Centre street.

4:00 PM –

From Centre street and 8th avenue to Elbow Park, via 2nd street east, 17th avenue, 4th street west, viewing the Elbow river and classy residential section of Elbow Park, returning via 17th avenue, 8th street west, 4th avenue and Centre street.

Tickets are being arranged so that reservations may be made. Fare for one-hour trip, 25 cents cash.[46]

(*The Calgary Herald*, Monday July 15th 1912, p. 16)

"...We Like It Because It Pays..."

After three years of operation, the Calgary Municipal Railway continued to show substantial net profits paid back to the city, after operating expenses, fixed charges, interest, sinking fund and 5% of gross revenue for contingent, accident insurance and renewal account were paid out or set aside. The following table shows the growth over three years:[47]

	Repaid to city	Cars operated	Miles of track	Employees
July 1909	$ 29,435	2	3	16
June 1910	87,206	15	16½	92
June 1911	101,000	2	26½	102
June 1912		48	53	236

The Calgary Herald editorialized: "... with the growth of the city the street railway should have many more pleasant birthdays. We are all props of the streetcar; it has become as much a necessity as bread or boots. We like its mellow fog horn, its bells and its earthquake effects as it meanders up and down the street, but most of all we like it because it pays. ..."[48]

As incongruous as it may seem amid the feverish pace of developing car lines, one section of Calgary actually put forth a petition to refuse the proposal to build a car line. Marked by favourable grades, easy connections with existing trackage and reasonable population density, the proposed Mount Royal line had plenty of potential to

Opposite, upper: CMR 50 in 1912 on the Sunnyside Loop. This was an excellent spot from which sightseers could view the panorama of the city in leisurely fashion.
(Glenbow Archives NA-2553-4)

Opposite, lower: This is a typical 1920s pocket-sized schedule card issued to advertise departures and routes of the scenic car. On the reverse (not shown), a description of the car notes that it carried an average of 30,000 passengers per season. Each card carried two advertisements; in this case, one for a nationally-known jeweller and, on the reverse, one for a local photographer.
(Colin K. Hatcher collection)

THE CALGARY SCENIC CAR
Operated by The Calgary Municipal Railway

TIME TABLE OF WEEK DAY TRIPS

Leaving Centre Street.

11 a.m.—East Calgary, through the manufacturing section of city, including the Imperial Oil Co.'s refinery and the C.P.R. Ogden Shops.

1.30 p.m.—South Calgary (Highest view point of city and view of Rocky Mountains) and Crescent Heights. This trip shows the South and North sections of Calgary.

5.00 p.m.—Elbow Park—along the Elbow River—Calgary's residential section, and Sunnyside—along the Bow River.

3.00 p.m. } Bowness Park, Calgary's popular pleasure
7.00 p.m. } resort, eighteen miles of Western scenery
9.00 p.m. } along the Bow River.

Special trips for Sundays and Holidays, ask the announcer.

The management reserves the right to alter time table without notice.

CALGARY MUNICIPAL RAILWAY
R. A. Brown, Supt.

Above: The Shouldice Bridge over the Bow River, formerly owned by J. Hextall, developer of Bowness. Car and trailer were loaded with picnickers headed for the Park, August 1947. (W.C. Whittaker)

Below: Trailer car 203 is coupled to a motor car, most likely car 63, as it stands ready to proceed northbound on 2nd Street SE immediately south of the 17th Avenue SE intersection. Note the bell for conductor to signal motorman on lead car.
(Rich Krisak collection)

Opposite: A view along the right-of-way beside the banks of the Bow River. The car is approaching the city from Bowness Park, July 1949. (Foster M. Palmer)

offer a service and still bring in a monetary return to the city. The people of Mount Royal, however, protested successive proposals for lines on 7th Street, 8th Street, and finally 10th Street sw.[49] It appeared that the residents of this prosperous neighbourhood preferred to walk or rely on personal means of transportation rather than use the streetcar. Consequently; the paving of 10th Street sw went ahead without street railway tracks. A few months later, still anxious to tap the potential revenue from this area, Superintendent McCauley proposed motor buses, which he called "trackless motors". The idea of an electric "trackless motor" was several decades in the future for Calgary, and while Mr. McCauley was to become known widely as an innovative Superintendent, this particular innovation did not become a reality during his tenure on the system.[50] Suffice it to say that Mr. McCauley was about twenty years ahead of his time.

Operations of the Killarney or Glengarry line along 17th Avenue sw west of 14th Street sw began sometime during the fall of 1912, but the routing and scheduling of this extension in its early days is speculative. The same speculation applies to the Sunalta extension on 12th Avenue sw. Both lines likely operated a stub shuttle service from their respective terminals to 14th Street sw, where transfers were effected to cars on the Blue line.

In November 1912, Bylaw 1399 was passed, providing for the purchase of 24 new streetcars – twelve 41'6" cars, twelve 46'6" cars and six 44'6" trailers. Council recommended the purchase of all these units from the Ottawa Car Company Ltd. and directed that the motor cars be equipped with Brill 27-G-1 trucks, with Westinghouse motors and air brakes.[51] The trailers were also to be equipped with the Brill trucks;

they were not powered, but their brakes were tied in with the master car's air brake system. They featured centre doors so that a streetcar and trailer train required only three men; conductor and motorman on the lead car and conductor only on the trailer. The Bylaw also provided for an electric sweeper to be ordered from Ottawa and designated "A".

While the trailers were purchased specifically for use on the Ogden line, they were also used frequently for holiday and charter services to Shouldice Park and St. George's Island Park, and in later years to Bowness Park. The delivery of these trailers in time for the 1913 exhibition traffic marked the cessation of the CPR shop workers' commuter train service between Calgary and Ogden. Superintendent McCauley noted, however, that street railway revenues would not increase significantly with the full operation of the Ogden special service, because previously when the men got off the Ogden train, they boarded street cars in downtown Calgary to get them the rest of the way home. Thus, the street railway was already the recipient of the fares from most of the workers.[52]

Sometime during 1912, the schedule of cars operating into Tuxedo Park was improved over the original "every two-hour" service. It appears that a transfer car connected at the Edmonton Trail and 16th Avenue NE with the Crescent Heights cars which operated every fifteen minutes, and thus provided fifteen-minute service between this point and the Tuxedo Park terminus. This service, appreciated by Tuxedo Park residents, was in effect until the winter of 1912-1913, when the Crescent Heights car service was stepped up to a ten-minute service. The Tuxedo Park car could not make the round trip quickly enough to make the connection every ten minutes, with the result that people were left

Above: Motor unit 13 hauls trailer 201 along 2nd Street E near 12th Avenue SE. Photo taken in August 1947. (W.C. Whittaker)

Below: The first trip of the Scenic Car, Thursday, July 4th 1912. The Navassarxs Ladies Band made the inaugural journey of the mirror-panelled vehicle a memorable event. (Glenbow Archives NA-2553-5)

Opposite: CMR 65 and 205 just after crossing Shouldice Bridge heading towards Bowness. Note that the lead car carries no roller sign, but has a fixed destination board below the front headlight. " ... the trailers and many of the other cars were taken out of service during the depression's depths and were stored at the back of the overhaul barn. With the onset of World War II and the gasoline rationing, traffic increased again and these cars were gradually reconditioned and returned to service. One of my fondest memories is of waiting with my Father one sunny morning in the fall of 1941 and finding our transportation was to be car 65 and a trailer (I think 205) on its first run after a complete overhaul as a set. They gleamed in the sun and reeked of new paint smell; we sat at the back of 65 where I could watch the coupler action and swing of the trailer around the curves. Car 65 blew its circuit breaker in the short sharp hill just east of the Elbow River Bridge but recovered and there was no further trouble."
– Correspondence Browning to Hatcher July 30th 1984.
(W.C. Whittaker)

waiting for undue lengths of time in severe weather conditions for transfers to and from the Tuxedo Park car.[53] The interim solution was to set up the Tuxedo Park car service so that it connected with every alternate Crescent Heights car. These Crescent Heights cars carried a sign indicating that they were TUXEDO PARK TRANSFER cars,[54] so Tuxedo Park passengers could readily identify a Crescent Heights car downtown which would connect directly with a Tuxedo Park car. In addition to the transfer service, it appeared that special cars in the morning and probably in the evening ran a through service from Tuxedo Park loop to downtown.

On Monday morning, March 17th 1913, at about 8:30 AM, single-truck "dinkey" type car 24, a Tuxedo Park Special, heavily loaded on its way downtown, ran out of control on the Edmonton Trail (4th Street NE) hill, jumped the tracks, struck a pole and turned over on its side. For a few moments pandemonium was prevalent as people scrambled to get out of the wrecked car. The oil stove on the front platform set the wood on fire, but this was quickly doused by the timely arrival of the fire-fighting apparatus. No one was killed in the accident but about twenty passengers were injured. The motorman was exonerated from all blame by Superintendent McCauley, who noted that the accident was unavoidable.[55] It was the second mishap near this point involving a downbound Tuxedo Park car. Very shortly after the accident, crews began working on the curve to realign it from a radius of 156 feet to a radius of 350 feet.[56]

Meanwhile, at the west end of the city and on the westernmost extremity of the street railway, the Bowness line was ready for regular operation on March 1st 1913, as the Bowness bridge had just been prepared for streetcar operation. The regular five-cent fare applied on car service to Shouldice Park, but as soon as the car crossed the bridge,

the conductor passed through the car with a hand-held fare box and a second fare was collected. On the trip back to Calgary, passengers paid a fare upon boarding and the second fare was collected again when the car crossed the bridge.[57] The cars operated on the following schedule which was part of the agreement with J. Hextall, the developer of Bowness Park:[58]

Leave Centre Street		Leave Bowness	
7:15 AM			8:00 AM
	8:45 AM		9:30 AM
	11:45 AM		12:30 PM
	1:15 PM		2:00 PM
	5:45 PM		6:30 PM
	7:15 PM		11:00 PM

On Sundays in the summer of 1913, large cars were operating fully loaded and in pairs out to Bowness. Once the cars crossed the Bowness bridge they responded very sluggishly to the controller, as the power on that far end of the line was very weak. This created problems with the scheduling.[59]

The Grand Trunk loop line and the Capitol Hill stub line were added to the north west end of the system during 1913. Service on the Capitol Hill line began on Wednesday December 3rd 1913. Capitol Hill cars connected with Crescent Heights cars at 16th Avenue NW and 10th Street NW, and shuttled from this point via 10th Street NW to 20th Avenue NW and then west on 20th Avenue NW to the loop at 15th Street NW every twenty minutes.[60] The Grand Trunk or Parkdale-Hillhurst cars connected with the Red Line cars and operated a circuit beginning at Kensington Road and 14th Street NW, north on 14th Street NW, west along 8th and 7th avenues NW to 24th Street NW, south to Kensington Road and east to 14th Street NW. The car ran the

Above: Car 25 followed by an unknown car travels east toward the city having crossed the CPR overhead bridge in East Calgary between Portland Street and 15th Street se. The cars are returning from Ogden to the carbarn following their morning runs to Ogden. This portion of the line was opened in December 1913 and since it avoided all level crossings with the steam railways, it soon became the preferred route of Ogden cars travelling to and from the city.
(John F. Bromley collection)

Opposite, lower: Car 64, one of the few regular service cars without a Hunter destination sign, travels with its trailer along 12th Avenue SE having just crossed the Elbow River Bridge. Since it carries no form of route identification, it could be operating in charter service. Judging by the short shadows, it could also be a Saturday mid-day inbound run from Ogden Shops. "Victoria Public School (located near the 12th Avenue SE bridge over the Elbow River) organized field days held at Hidden Valley Park on the way to Bowness. Our transportation was nearly always chartered streetcar and trailer combinations, usually two sets, returning from their morning Ogden run. They laid over at the loop marked 37 Street W on the 1946 map until we reboarded in the afternoon. After dropping us off at Victoria School, they continued on to Ogden to service the five o'clock run from there." – Correspondence Browning to Hatcher July 30th 1984. (Percy W. Browning)

Above: The Scenic Car – its mirrors temporarily hidden behind large banners – and two motor-trailer pairs were chartered on Wednesday, May 5th 1915 by the Hudson's Bay Company for The Bay Employees' Picnic. View taken near Shouldice Park.
(Glenbow Archives NA-2037-11)

circuit on a twenty-minute schedule, meeting every second Red Line car up to 11:30 PM. The service which began during November 1913 was not expected to pay for itself until more residents moved into the area it served.[61]

Some interesting events were evident in the deliberations which finally resulted in the building of the South Calgary loop line. An extension had been build west of 14th Street SW along 32nd Avenue SW during September 1913. When this construction got underway the residents of 26th Avenue SW protested because their extension had been authorized in an earlier bylaw. Superintendent McCauley countered by suggesting the building of the 26th Avenue SW line and a line on 20th Street SW to connect the above two extensions, thus forming a loop line. Since the 20th Street SW line had not been approved in a bylaw, it would have to be constructed with funds withdrawn from the contingent fund.[62] The final decision was to go ahead with a line on 26th Avenue SW to 20th Street SW, then south on 20th

Street SW to 34th Avenue SW and east to 14th Street SW.[63] The 20th Street SW track was to be regarded as temporary trackage.[64] This decision involved taking up the tracks just completed on 32nd Avenue SW, the removal of which was estimated to cost $250, plus the finding of $750 to build the 20th Street line. It was expected that the operation of a loop line instead of two stub lines off 14th Street SW would give better car service and eliminate one car per day. This would save about $29 per day or $10,000 per year;[65] hence, the initial outlay of $750 plus track removal expenses would be quickly recovered.

With the completion of the South Calgary loop and the 17th Avenue SW extension west to Glengarry at 28th Street SW, the two lines on December 3rd 1913 replaced the Orange & Blue 8th Street Belt Line. South Calgary cars left 26th Avenue SW every twenty minutes and ran downtown via 20th Street SW, 34th Avenue SW, 14th Street SW, 17th Avenue SW, 1st Street SW to 8th Avenue SW. They returned via 8th Street SW, 17th Avenue SW, 14th Street SW, 26th Avenue SW to 20th Street SW. The Glengarry cars ran east from their loop along 17th Avenue SW to 8th Street SW, where they turned north to 8th avenue SW, to 1st Street SW and then back along 17th Avenue SW, thus looping through the downtown area in the opposite direction to the South Calgary cars.[66] South Calgary cars carried a *SOUTH CALGARY* destination sign with blue and yellow discs on the linen,

Looking north from 9th Avenue sw on 1st Street sw about 1918. Note light-coloured Hudson's Bay Co. store at 7th Avenue sw (behind tram) and the turreted Liggetts Drug Store building which was later replaced by the expanded Hudson's Bay store. (Glenbow Archives ND-8-267)

Above: In this early 1920s panoramic view looking northwest from the Noble Hotel, a streetcar is loading passengers at 1st Street sw at the intersection of 12th Avenue sw. The CPR overpass over 1st Street sw is at the right of the photograph behind the streetcar. The buildings to the upper left are located in the warehouse district immediately south of the CPR main line tracks.
(Provincial Archives of Alberta, H.Pollard collection TN 1420.)

Below: Car 34 draws up to a stop at 1st Street sw on 8th Avenue sw. It has a two-coloured disk on the roof at the front, an early route indicator for the Sunnyside – Burns Avenue cars. The era is about 1912. The seasonal card was published by Pacific Novelty Co. of San Francisco, California.
(Colin K. Hatcher collection)

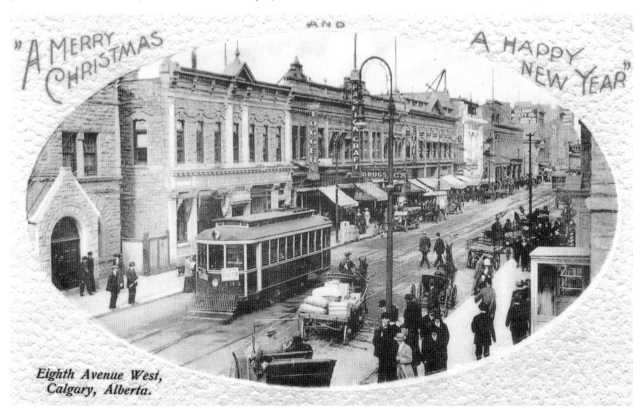

while the 17th Avenue sw cars carried *KILLARNEY* signs with the blue and yellow colours.[67]

A proposal which drew a lot of public attention during 1913 was that for a line to Shaganappi Park and Spruce Cliff. A real estate development firm proposed the car line extension to City Council, and after some discussion it finally passed favourably early in September 1913.[68] The terms of the agreement generally stated that the property holders were to pay the entire cost of construction, plus the deficit incurred on operation until the line could sustain itself or until the end of a four-year period. At the end of that time the city would refund to the property owners the cost of construction.[69] The issue was a hot one. The Calgary Board of Trade was strongly opposed to the move and put its case before the public. The rate payers voted on the issue on Thursday October 30th 1913, and out of the 858 votes cast, 665 spoke out against the extension.[70] In view of the optimism of the day, the citizens' decision to reject the Shaganappi-Spruce Cliff proposal was a wise one, justified by the turn of events over the next few months. The rejection of this proposal marked the end of expansion on the Calgary Municipal Railway for a number of years.

Above: T.H. McCauley in his 1910 Model T Ford on Centre Street overlooking the Bow River. Note the rubber bulb horn and the carbide container on the running board for the headlights. Tail light and side lamps were fuelled with coal oil. (H.W. McCauley collection)

Left: CMR 23 operating on the Crescent Heights line and carrying the "Tuxedo Park Transfer" sign pauses at the passing track on 16th Avenue nw between Centre Street and 2nd Street sw early in 1912. Conductor on the left is Reuben Buckingham, while Jack Plews (motorman) is to the right. (Glenbow Archives NA-2891-4)

Opposite: Same view as page 44 about ten years later. The clustered streetlamps have been replaced and The Bay store is being extended southward. (Canadian National 31830)

CHAPTER FIVE

Innovative Change

THE CALGARY MUNICIPAL grew rapidly during the closing months of 1913. The delivery of thirty streetcars including six trailers was completed, many new extensions were operating and increased service on the main lines was being offered. Until the opening of these new extensions in 1913, the streetcars appeared to be continually trying to keep up to a demand for service, but at some point during the year, the services on the railway began to out-run that demand, particularly on the outlying lines. Ridership was up and so were revenues; however, more cars were running over longer distances, generally with fewer passengers per car. Expenses, therefore, rose more sharply than revenues, with the result that the previous highly-encouraging profit picture began to fade. An indication of this situation appeared in the November 1913 monthly statement issued by Mr. McCauley, where net profit was shown at $1115 for the month as opposed to the November 1912 net profit of $7456. Earnings were up $5000 over those of November 1912, but wages paid out to motormen and conductors totalled $6000 more for the month. In addition, the amount set aside for interest and sinking fund rose some $3000 over the November 1912 figure to $10, 861.[1]

Mr. McCauley, accustomed to operating "a tight ship", began to scrutinize operations even more closely with a view to reducing expenditures. It became evident that the market had been saturated and a substantial increase in revenue was not in prospect.

The first months of 1914 brought with them heavy snow storms and drifting snow. This was the first winter that the Bowness and Parkdale-Hillhurst (Grand Trunk) lines had been operative, and the system's lone single-truck sweeper worked hard to keep these new outlying extensions clear. Other areas of the system affected by excessive drifting were the North Hill and Bridgeland (Riverside) loop areas where Crescent Heights cars were completely stopped and White Line cars were unable to proceed into the turning loop. Two storms struck in as many days early in February 1914,[2] making reliable service difficult on all parts of the system and stopping it completely in the previously-noted areas. These weather conditions adversely affected revenues, because fares were not collected, while expenses increased as crews worked through the night in an attempt to keep the lines open. Unfortunately, even after winter passed, monthly reports continued to show a further falling-off in gross revenues compared with the corresponding months of 1913.

The first hint at one-man operation came in June 1914 when Superintendent McCauley suggested that cars on the Grand Trunk loop and the Capitol Hill stub operate with one man acting both as motorman and conductor, in an attempt to reduce the operating deficit on these two lines. This recommendation came in the wake of the following operating deficits during the month of May 1914 on each of the respective lines: Ogden, $2461; Bowness, $1634; Grand Trunk, $579; Capitol Hill, $562; Tuxedo Park, $360; Sunalta, $240.[3] The one-man cars actually began service on the Grand Trunk and Capitol Hill lines on June 16th 1914. T.C. Scatcherd was the first night motor-conductor on the Capitol Hill one-man car.[4]

In May 1913, Bylaw 1535 had been passed authorizing extensive double-tracking and concrete sub-base for existing street railway tracks, the extension of many lines and the purchase of six additional 41'6" streetcars.[5] Most of the expenditures authorized under this Bylaw were made during 1913, but there was not sufficient money to complete all the double track and concrete sub-base construction; so on June 26th 1914, Bylaw 1704 was presented to the ratepayers and passed.[6] This Bylaw authorized the additional expenditure of $90,000 to complete all the double-tracking and concrete sub-base work authorized under bylaws 1171, 1535 and 1304, which had not previously been completed.

However, the work approved by this authorization was only barely started when world conditions took a turn for the worse. With the out-break of World War I in August 1914, all improvement works and capital expenditures on the Calgary Municipal Railway came to a sudden and abrupt halt. Only part of the double-tracking program had been completed, and the order for the six new cars was cancelled after only one of those cars had been delivered.

Frequency and quality of service on the Calgary Municipal was threatened even more. The city itself suddenly stopped expanding, unemployment was becoming prevalent, and fewer riders resulted in fewer fares being dropped into the fare boxes. Mr. McCauley presented a series of route changes and another one-man car proposal in September. One-man cars were introduced to the Tuxedo Park route and motormen operated cars by themselves on the Manchester run from the cemetery to the south end of the line. In a further effort to trim expenses, the Grand Trunk, Capitol Hill and Sunalta stubs ceased operating after 7 PM daily, while all service ceased at 11:30 PM daily. Belt Line service was reduced by taking one car off each way but increasing the speed of the remaining cars. Bowness cars terminated at 14th Street

Opposite: Another angle on the same day as the view on page 47, showing steelwork rising to the sixth storey of the Hudson's Bay store. Tram patrons are pushing their way in through the McCauley door, while the "bobby" keeps a watchful eye on things from the centre of the 8th Avenue sw intersection.
(Canadian National 31834)

Above: As described on page 79, the Calgary Municipal Railway in the early 1920s needed expanded repair facilities to handle its fleet of over eighty passenger cars and work cars. This illustrates the interior of the additional facility, a former stable and hay loft located on the property adjacent to the carbarns. Hydraulic press equipment is illustrated in a bay beside the track on which car 10 stands. (Calgary Transit collection)

sw to connect with Red Line cars hourly, and the Ogden service operated hourly only between Ogden and 2nd Street SE instead of running through on 12th Avenue SE-SW to 1st Street SW. During the ensuing six-month period, car men and car barn staff agreed to work only nine hours daily in a six-day week, so that no men would be left without a job as a result of the changes.[7] Finally, service on the Bankview line was altered on November 19th to run into the city via 14th Street SW, 12th Avenue SW, 8th Street SW, 8th Avenue SW and 1st Street SW. Cars returned west via 12th Avenue SW and 14th Street SW.[8]

Early in 1915 it became apparent that the railway's usual good annual financial position was being threatened for the first time since its inception. The adjustment of power charges had enabled the street railway utility to show a surplus of approximately $10,000 for its 1914 operations.[9] Another accounting adjustment involving the Ogden line brought the street railway even further away from an impending deficit position, while offering a truer financial picture of street railway operations. This amounted to charging interest and sinking fund on the Ogden line against general taxation, a procedure from which the light, power and waterworks departments also benefitted, as the provi-

sion of all of these services to the Ogden shops area had been regarded as a bonus to encourage the growth of the City of Calgary rather than to provide services to an existing population in that area. The reduction of depreciation charges from 7½% to 5% on the Ogden line because of reduced car service, and the resulting reduction of wear and tear on the tracks also contributed to the general surplus position of the street railway for its 1914 operations.[10] City Council approved these changes on recommendation of the auditor on Tuesday February 16th 1915.[11]

The requirement to provide certain previously-agreed-upon services to Bowness and Ogden, both some considerable distance beyond the heavily-populated area of the city, and an obligation to supply free return transfers to passengers travelling to the public market at 4th Avenue SE and 4th Street SE, enabled Superintendent McCauley to be very vocal about the fact that the street railway was bearing the burdens of other civic departments by providing these bonus services. This concern led to the already-noted changes in charges against the Ogden line, but Superintendent McCauley was challenged by Superintendent Reader of the Parks Department who was responsible for the operation of some eighteen skating rinks

Above left: The original 1909 barns building extends across the left background of the photograph. The 1913 addition housing offices and staff meeting facilities was located in section to the right of the photograph. The building faces onto 2nd Street SE.
(Glenbow Archives PA-1689-13)

Above right: The carbarn complex included the maintenance building acquired by the street railway department in the early 1920s. That building is pictured in the centre of the photograph. The streetcar tracks swing to the right to go across the Elbow River on the 2nd Street SE bridge, and straight through then left to go into the carbarn yards. The south LRT line follows a tangent along the east side of 2nd Street SE now, with the Macleod Trail occupying the space at this location where the carbarns once stood.
(Glenbow Archives PA-1689-12)

Below: The shop derrick, which was used for general maintenance and in-shop transportation. For a period it was used as a locomotive to haul similar trailer flatcars.
(Foster M. Palmer)

as well as a mile-and-a-half skating course on the Elbow River. In the summer season the Parks Department had the responsibility for providing amusement services and band concerts – notably at St. George's Island Park. Mr. Reader noted that all of these services were provided through funding from his department, but that the street railway gained considerable revenue, particularly from passengers going to the Elbow River skating course and the Hillhurst skating rink in winter and to the St. George's Island band concerts in summer.[12] The precise results of a meeting between Mr. McCauley and Mr. Reader are unknown, but a decision was made soon after to hand over Bowness Park to the street railway so that it could develop the area and increase the potential for the Bowness line to pay for itself, especially during the summer season, by transporting large numbers

Above: T.C. Scatcherd, conductor is standing on the step and C.S. Newcombe, motorman stands in front of car 70 on the "Crescent Heights-Sunnyside-Burns Avenue" route. (T.C.Scatcherd collection)

of people to and from the park.[13] By mid-April 1915, the City Commissioners began to call for tenders to make Bowness Park an amusement centre that same summer. Facilities contemplated included boating facilities, refreshment and camping facilities and a dancing pavilion. City Engineer Craig also prepared plans for a small dam to provide a sheltered waterway for boating and canoeing.[14] So began the street railway's major role, spearheaded by an energetic Superintendent McCauley, in the operation of a summer amusement park, a role for which it became well and favourably known in Southern Alberta. Thus, instead of being a struggling money-losing line, the Bowness line became a true "bonus" line, by generating considerable additional income each year for the street railway.

Having been successful in initiating expense-saving accounting changes, and then convincing Council to accept his proposal for the development of Bowness Park to improve revenues, Mr. McCauley continued to search for ways to improve the overall efficiency of car service. Sometimes efficiency meant a reduction in service; such a change came on Sunday January 17th 1915, with the reduction of all Sunday car service to half of that regularly offered Monday through Saturday. Up until this time all regular services had been identical seven days per week. The new Sunday Service was outlined as follows:[15]

Blue Line cars – Will leave 8th Avenue and Centre Street. Eastbound every 10 minutes, from 7:15 AM until 11:45 PM, and every 10 minutes from 14th Street W. from 7:30 AM, running one way only. East on 12th Ave.

Red Line cars – Will leave East Calgary loop at 7:20 AM and every 20 minutes until 11:20 PM and Riley Park at 7:30 AM and every 20 minutes until 11:30 PM.

Red and Blue Line cars – Will leave Burns avenue loop at 7:20 AM and every 20 minutes until 11:20 PM and Sunnyside Loop at 7:30 AM and every 20 minutes until 11:30 PM.

Manchester and Tuxedo line – Will leave Manchester at 7:30 AM and every hour until 11:30 PM, and Queen's corner at 7:45 AM and every hour to Tuxedo until 10:45 PM. From Tuxedo at 8 AM, and every hour until 11 PM, and from Queen's corner to Manchester 8:15 AM and every hour until 11:15.

Bankview cars – Will leave Bankview at 7:40 AM and every 40 minutes until 11:40 PM, and 8th Avenue and 1st Street w. at 7:20 AM and every 40 minutes until 11:20 PM.

Glengarry cars – Will leave Glengarry Loop at 7:40 AM and every 40 minutes until 11:40 PM and 8th Avenue and 1st Street W. at 7:20 AM and every 40 minutes until 11:20 PM.

Bowness and Ogden car – Will leave Ogden at 9 AM and every 2 hours until 11 PM and will leave 1st Street w. and 8th Avenue at 8:30 AM and every two hours for Ogden until 10:30 PM.

Bowness car will leave Bowness at 8 AM and every 2 hours until 10 PM and 1st Street w. and 8th Avenue at 7:30 AM and every two hours for Bowness until 9:30 PM.

(*The Calgary Herald*, Friday January 15th 1915, p. 13)

A further move to improve operating efficiency resulted in some major route alterations between April and June 1915. With the completion of a new track connection at 4th Street sw and 12th Avenue sw, White Line cars began to operate on an improved 7½ minute schedule north on 4th Street sw to 12th Avenue sw, 1st Street sw and 8th Avenue sw. Every second White Line car coming from Elbow Park ran through to Riverside via Centre Street, 4th Avenue SE, 4th Street SE and the General Hospital loop on 2nd Avenue NE, but the other White Line cars short-turned downtown via 2nd Street SE, 9th Avenue SE, Centre Street and 8th Avenue sw, utilizing a newly-installed cross-over on 8th Avenue sw just west of Centre Street. A total of six cars was required to maintain this service, with four running through to Riverside and two short-turning downtown.

Superintendent McCauley then took two cars off the Blue Line, leaving it with a fifteen-minute service each way. One of these cars was assigned to a new quarter-hourly Sunalta service which ran east from the Sunalta loop along 12th Avenue sw, scheduled between Blue Line cars to maintain a 7½ minute 12th Avenue sw service as far as 1st Street sw. Here, the Sunalta car turned north to 8th Avenue sw-se and then on to return to the Sunalta loop at 18th Street sw.[16] Thus, Sunalta residents received direct service into downtown Calgary throughout the day, to replace the former stub line transfer service.

The other Blue Line car went to the Bankview (South Calgary) run, reducing that route's headway from twenty to fifteen minutes so that the Bankview cars alternated with Blue Line cars to maintain a 7½ minute service between 14th Street sw and 4th Street sw along 17th Avenue sw. At the latter intersection, the Bankview cars turned north to operate over the new 4th Street sw trackage to 12th Avenue sw and looped through the downtown area via 12th Avenue sw-se, 2nd Street se, 8th Avenue se-sw, 1st Street sw and returned to Bankview via the inbound route.[17]

Another series of changes became effective on Monday August 23rd 1915, when the Killarney cars began to run on a fifteen-minute service through to Riverside via 17th Avenue sw and 4th Street sw, following the same route as the White Line cars formerly did into Riverside. All White Line cars short-turned in the downtown area, providing a ten minute service, to and from Elbow Park. Bankview cars, also known as South Calgary or Orange & Blue Line cars, continued to offer a fifteen-minute service to the city centre via 14th Street sw, 17th Avenue sw, 8th Street sw, 8th Avenue sw, 1st Street sw and back via 17th Avenue sw. The Sunalta loop service remained unchanged except that it turned back through the downtown area via 1st Street sw, 8th Avenue sw-se, 2nd Street se, 9th Avenue se, Centre Street, 8th Avenue sw, 1st Street sw and back to Sunalta

along 12th Avenue sw.[18] One car was dropped from the Red line. This did not, however, affect this route's ten-minute service nor was that route changed. Blue Line service continued both ways every fifteen minutes over an unchanged route. The schedule on the Red & Blue line, the Red & White Line and the Manchester-Tuxedo Park line remained unchanged. The Bowness and Ogden lines were coupled offering through hourly service. Cars came in from Bowness along 8th Avenue sw-se and went on to Ogden via 2nd Street se and 12th Avenue se. Superintendent McCauley expected that these changes would result in a saving of $50 per day.

Complaints were received almost immediately concerning the coupling of the Bowness and Ogden runs, largely because the last car to Bowness left the city at 11:15 PM and was thus very inconvenient for theatre goers.[19] At the Ogden end, people complained of the cars running too fast in order to keep to schedule over the long route, even though the cars were apparently capable of a maximum speed of only 25 miles per hour. The complaints resulted in another schedule alteration which became effective October 4th 1915. Ogden cars continued to offer hourly service, but they turned back from 8th Avenue se to 2nd Street se, returning to Ogden

Right: Not off the track! CMR 64 on a little-used curve at 24th Street NW and Kensington Road – a pastoral scene in 1949 that would hardly be recognizable today. Note the Inspector's automobile in the background.
(Foster M. Palmer)

Above: On September 15th 1944 the motor-conductor on car 69 is turning the track switch with the switch-iron extended through the floor of the car. The car is on route 7 South Calgary and is about to turn from 1st Street sw onto 12th Avenue sw. In the background is the Isis Theatre. Compare this view with the panoramic view on page 45. (CRHA - R.F. Corley fonds)

via 12th Avenue SE.[20] The Bowness service became only a token one as follows:[21]

Leave Centre Street + 8th Avenue	14th Street NW + Centre Avenue	Bowness	Arrive Centre Street + 8th Avenue SW
7:15 AM (Red Line transfer car)	7:30 AM	8:00 AM	8:30 AM
8:15 AM (Red Line transfer car)	8:30 AM	9:00 AM	9:30 AM
12:15 PM (Red Line transfer car)	12:30 PM	1:00 PM	1:30 PM
4:15 PM (Direct service)	-	4:45 PM	5:15 PM
5:15 PM (Direct service)	-	5:45 PM	6:15 PM
6:15 PM (Direct service)	-	7:00 PM	7:30 PM
11:15 PM (Direct service)	-	11:45 PM	12:15 PM

The Calgary Herald, Thursday September 15th 1915, p. 10.

Passengers going to Bowness from downtown at 7:15 AM, 8:15 AM and 12:15 PM boarded a Red Line transfer car which connected at 14th Street NW and Centre Avenue (Kensington Road) with the Grand Trunk car at 7:30 AM, 8:30 AM and 12:30 PM respectively, which went to Bowness via 14th Street NW, 8th and 7th avenues NW, 24th Street NW, and on to Kensington Road. These cars after picking up passengers in the Bowness area, returned directly to 14th Street NW and Kensington Road, where they transferred their passengers to a Red Line car which carried them on downtown.

Grand Trunk cars connected with Red Line cars at 14th Street NW and Kensington Road, then ran north on 14th Street NW, west on 8th and 7th avenues NW to 24th Street NW, then south to Kensington Road and then west to a loop (Parkdale loop) at about 34th Street NW and back to the Red Line transfer point. Cars left the Parkdale loop at 6:45 AM, 7:15 AM, 8:15 AM, 9:15 AM, 9:45 AM, 10:15 AM, 10:45 AM, 11:15 AM, 11:45 AM, 12:15 PM, 1:15 PM, 1:45 PM and every half hour through to 7:15 PM. This was the last trip until the last car returning from Bowness went through at 11:55 PM. On Saturdays, half-hourly service continued on the Grand Trunk-Parkdale loop until 10:15 PM.

Capitol Hill transfer cars operated every hour, Sunday excepted, from 6:10 AM to 7:10 PM and on Saturdays from 6:10 AM to 10:10 PM.

On the day the new Grand Trunk-Bowness line schedules were introduced (Monday, October 4th 1915), considerable confusion ensued. The 8 AM car leaving Bowness arrived at 14th Street NW transfer point fifteen minutes late, packed full of irate passengers and going backwards! Apparently the passengers forced the motorman to run the car all the way downtown, presumably after it had turned around on the wye at Kensington Road and 14th Street NW, as several passengers waiting to board the car expecting it to go north on 14th Street into Grand Trunk began to walk. The newspaper article described the incident as a "small sized riot" and noted that threats were being made for a vigilance committee from the district to go down some night and tear out the tracks leading to Bowness until the city authorities saw fit to give the taxpayers inside the city limits a service at least as good as that accorded to the residents living outside the city at Bowness.[22]

Two days later, it was announced that the Grand Trunk car would make the trip around the loop in the morning in the opposite direction to that taken previously, so that residents of the Grand Trunk area could catch the car as it returned from Bowness and not have to walk the five blocks to Kensington Road. In summary then, the morning run was eastbound on 7th and 8th avenues NW while the afternoon run was westbound on 8th and 7th avenues NW.[23]

In order to appease the irate residents, Superintendent McCauley even met with them on Wednesday October 12th at Parkdale Church. The meeting agreed upon a half-hourly schedule for Grand Trunk cars between 6 AM and 9 AM eastbound on 7th and 8th avenues NW. Service was then suspended until 2 PM when cars ran in the opposite direction on the loop. He noted that the noon car to Bowness was available for Grand Trunk residents and the 11:15 PM Bowness car would travel over the Grand Trunk loop at a passenger's request. An additional evening car was scheduled for 10 PM as well as an earlier Red Line car over the loop to take workers out to the Ogden shops. It appeared that Mr. McCauley successfully appeased the residents, as they gained a regular half-hourly service in the morning, but lost regular mid-morning and noon hour service. They also gained a better Ogden service and two trips in the late evening.[24] With the Grand Trunk car providing regular half-hourly service, it would appear that Bowness morning and noon-hour cars, whose schedules remained unchanged, now provided through service to downtown at least until

Below: Car 64 and its trailer are in service to East Calgary on the Blue Line. The dual air tanks on car 64 signal the presence of a train air brake system necessary for those cars in trailer-hauling service. The semi-convertibele feature of this streetcar is well illustrated as all but one of the side sashes has been lowered. The rear entrance indicates two-man car operation, placing the photo date before 1917. The car appears to be laying over or waiting for a scheduled departure. (Colin K. Hatcher collection)

November 15th 1915 when it was announced that the 12:15 PM Red Line car would transfer passengers to the Bowness car[25] at 14th Street NW, instead of running an extra car from the city centre. One might assume from this announcement that the Grand Trunk car was left parked at 14th Street NW all morning, then completed the 12:15 PM Bowness trip before beginning its afternoon circuit on the Grand Trunk-Parkdale run.

For the Calgary Municipal, the year 1915 could well be regarded as one of experiment and change insofar as routes were concerned. On Monday November 29th the third change of the year for main line services became effective as follows:[26]

Red Line – Hillhurst (West Calgary) to downtown only every 15 minutes.

White Line – Elbow Part to East Calgary every 10 minutes.

Orange and Blue – South Calgary (Bankview) to Riverside every 30 minutes.

Arrow – Killarney (Glengarry) to Riverside every 30 minutes. Between the hours of 6 and 9 AM, 12 and 2 PM, and 5 and 8 PM, extra service from Killarney and South Calgary short-turned in the downtown area to offer fifteen minute service into the south west areas while regularly assigned cars on both lines combined offered fifteen minute service all day into Riverside.

Blue Line – 10 minute service both ways connecting with the White Line cars at 4th Avenue.

Sunalta – Direct service into downtown every 30 minutes from 7:30 AM to 7:30 PM.

(*The Calgary Herald*, November 27th 1915, p. 9)

Confusion and unhappiness seemed to follow in the wake of most route and schedule changes and in this instance Killarney residents expressed dissatisfaction with the new service. If they happened to work in the northeast section of the city, they were still left with only half-hour service, as all the extra cars turned back to Killarney from downtown. They also complained about the crowded conditions prevailing on the small single-truck cars assigned as extras.[27] No apparent changes were made at this time to counter the concerns expressed by the passengers of these districts, as an intensive car-assignment and ridership study of the evening rush-hour situation had taken place in February 1914. It illustrated that regularly-assigned short double-truck cars alternating with single-truck extras were capable of handling the traffic.[28]

The above-noted route and schedule changes and the introduction of limited one-man car service were efforts by Mr. McCauley to save money while he developed the park at Bowness, in an effort to stave off the threat of operating the street railway at a loss.

The Sarcee Story

Another revenue-producing possibility which generated considerable discussion during 1915 was the building of a tram line to the Sarcee Military Reserve just outside the south-western city limits. Sarcee was a large military training ground, housing 10,000 soldiers under canvas from May to October. It was occasioned, of course, by the recruiting and training efforts of World War I, and while it was not unusual for the men to march the eight miles in parade formation between the campground and the city centre on formal occasions, a car line would have the potential

Opposite: CMR 7, Route "A" Grand Trunk, turning off 24th Street NW onto Kensington Road, August 1947. The origin of the name "Grand Trunk" remains a mystery. The Grand Trunk area was in the northwest part of the city, while the Grand Trunk Pacific Railway, which built into the city from Edmonton via Ogden and the southeast, had its terminal at 6th Street SE, and never ventured further west. Apparently, plans existed for a westward extension that was, of course, never built. (W.C. Whittaker)

Above: Three pairs of motor-trailer trains at the streetcar terminal, Sarcee Military Camp. (Glenbow Archives NA-1044-10)

to generate considerable revenue from casual civilian and military passenger traffic and from the haulage of supplies into the camp.

Superintendent McCauley was at first reticent, and Council in 1915 voted against building the line for fear that the capital outlay would never be regained.[29] A few months later, however, Mr. McCauley reversed his stance. With the support of the Retailers' Association,[30] the City Commissioners, on Saturday April 15th 1916, formally adopted the recommendation to build a temporary line to Sarcee via 17th Avenue SW, 28th Street SW and south-westerly along the gravity water line and a telephone pole line to the north-east corner of the Sarcee Reserve. This was at the intersection of Richmond Road and 37th Street SW at the city limits. Most of the right-of-way was across city-owned lands except for a short cut across some CPR property. The cost of construction was estimated to be $6700, this amount to be recovered from revenues generated by the operation of the line.[31] This route was favoured over an extension of the South Calgary line because the operation of trailer cars to Sarcee was foreseen. Such cars could not be pulled up the 14th Street SW hill, but could be handled on the 17th Avenue SW hill.[32]

Considerable deliberation preceded the building of this extension. The City Solicitor had suggested that Council could change the route of a 3000 ft. car line proposed for 29th Street SW (as authorized in Bylaw 1399 and passed by the citizens on December 23rd 1912 but never constructed), to laying that amount of track on 28th Street SW, if it were in the interests of the city and the street railway. That bylaw, however, did not authorize Council to order construction of the car line beyond that point to the Sarcee Reserve. Since the rails and fixtures on hand had been purchased for construction under previously-approved bylaws and stored pending more optimistic economic conditions, the use of this stored track and fixtures on the Sarcee line beyond the point approved in Bylaw 1399, therefore had to be regarded as a temporary expedient.[33]

The inaugural trip over the Sarcee line occurred on Friday May 19th 1916.[34] Round trip tickets sold for 25¢. One way passengers paid 15¢ or three regular tickets. A third fare option allowed passengers to ride from the camp to the 17th Avenue SW loop for 10¢ or two tickets. Payment of a third 5¢ fare or one ticket at the 17th Avenue SW loop allowed the passenger to ride all the way into city centre.[35] The 25¢ return fare was expected to attract many riders, as a private "jitney" service the previous year had charged 25¢ each way from the camp just to the end of the South Calgary carline. Passengers then paid the regular streetcar fare to ride into the city, resulting in a return trip that could cost as much as 60¢. Rainy weather, moreover, was not conducive to handling passengers or supplies in heavily loaded motor or horse-drawn vehicles over the muddy roads of the day. It could be said that the profitable but unreliable jitney service prompted Superintendent McCauley to favour building the line, as streetcars could operate under almost any weather conditions. The new service featured a transfer car running all day between the Sarcee loop and the Killarney loop at 17th Avenue SW and 28th Street SW until 4:30 PM, after which cars ran directly in to the Centre Street / 9th Avenue loop. The through service was also available on Wednesday and Saturday early afternoons, and throughout the day on Sundays and holidays.[36] On Sundays, Calgarians were encouraged to attend church parade with the 10,000 soldiers at the camp, and special cars left 8th Avenue SW and 1st Street SW half-hourly beginning at 8:30 AM.[37]

Superintendent McCauley capitalized on the opportunity to haul freight into Camp Sarcee. Loaded with food and wood, an average of ten cars daily were operated into the site during July 1916, and the service realized $1700 to $2000 monthly for the street railway. The resourcefulness and imagination of the superintendent manifested itself in the rolling stock and storage facilities for this service. Some cars were constructed so that the bodies could be taken off the trucks and later used as waiting shelters. Dump cars were modified and pressed into service, and storage sheds at Sarcee were constructed of scrap lumber.[38] It was reported that a further extension had been built from the Sarcee loop to the south end of the camp, ostensibly for freight service but occasionally used for passenger service.[39]

Above: Centre-cab work car "B", a home-built product of 1913 vintage carrying rails in August 1947. It is believed that the rails came from the Manchester line which was abandoned in that year. (W.C. Whittaker)

Opposite below: Almost at the end of the line. Motor flat "G" waits as workmen repair street paving between the rails on August 3rd 1950. (Foster M. Palmer)

During the first few weeks of its operation, the Sarcee line had paid for itself, and to help celebrate its success, Superintendent McCauley had, by mid-August, proposed that Council reduce the fare to 10¢ each way.[40] Furthermore, the line was regarded as a money-maker for the system, since it contributed to the showing of a general street railway surplus of $13,976 for the month of August 1916, compared to a deficit of $4,036 for the same month in 1915.[41] Operations continued until the camp closed for the year in the late fall, and reports indicated that the line cleared $27,000, thus preventing a loss at the year end for the street railway.[42]

The Sarcee line's second year began on Sunday May 13th 1917, featuring through service from Centre Street and 8th Avenue every 1½ hours from 10 AM to 11:30 PM. Cars left the Sarcee loop for the return trip 45 minutes later. Sunday fare was 10¢ or two tickets each way.[43] An additional Sunday car at 7:30 AM began operating from downtown on July 29th. Monday through Saturday, Sarcee cars left 8th Avenue sw and 1st Street sw at 7:30 AM, 11:15 AM, 4:15 PM, 5 PM, 5:45 PM, 6:30 PM, 8:45 PM and 11:30 PM, also leaving Sarcee loop for the return trip 45 minutes later in each case.[44] By the end of July, Monday through Saturday car service had been increased by two trips daily, one at 2:30 PM and another at 10 PM[45] and a weekday fare reduction each way[46] brought midweek fares into line with the Sunday fares. It could be concluded from this latest course of events that the Sarcee line continued to be a highly profitable venture throughout 1917.

On Tuesday May 7th 1918[47], regular service between Calgary and Sarcee began again, with cars leaving 1st Street sw and 8th Avenue sw at 6:45 AM, 8 AM, 12 noon, 3 PM, 4:30 PM, 6 PM, 7:30 PM, 10 PM and 11:30 PM. As in previous seasons, the one way trip took 45 minutes, except for the

early morning trip which was allowed only forty minutes. Recollections are that car 18 usually held this assignment, and that to maintain its schedule it rolled and pitched in a very nautical fashion over the less-than-adequate temporary track. With the proceeds coming in at $100 per day up to $250 on a heavy day, Mr. McCauley again approached the commissioners and Council to reduce the fare, this time to one regular fare each way for the uniformed soldiers.[48]

The final days of 1918 marked the end of World War I and the future of the temporary Sarcee line was consequently in doubt. Some consideration was given to building a permanent line to the Sarcee Military Hospital, in conjunction with the Federal Government, but the proposal never did materialize[49] and the big trailer cars ground laboriously up the 17th Avenue hill for the last time late in the fall of 1918.

In January 1919, Council decided not to renew the lease on the CPR land over which the car line ran, and so it followed that the Sarcee line was abandoned, its rails used in the construction and improvement of other parts of the system.[50] It has been reported, however, that part of the line remained intact into 1919 and that "dinkey" car number 22 was fitted for double-end operation to transport returned veterans between the camp and the Colonel Walker school in east Calgary, but this service was apparently short-lived.[51]

Glengarry residents, having waited from 1913 to 1916 to get a Calgary car line extended through their community, were not about to allow the city to abandon the Sarcee line all the way back to the 17th Avenue sw loop. Even while the line was operating, several unsuccessful representations were made to Council for regular service through the Glengarry area, so it came as no surprise when, on August 15th 1919, City Commissioners recommended the building of a permanent loop line through the area, on 29th Street sw from

17th Avenue sw to 23rd Avenue sw, east to 26th Street sw[52] and north to 17th Avenue sw. The Commissioners also recommended the double-tracking of 17th Avenue sw from the top of the hill at 24th Street sw to 26th Street sw. The proposal was accepted by Council on August 18th 1919[53], and the Sarcee line on 28th Street sw was taken up, marking the close of an interesting make-shift but very profitable venture for the Calgary Municipal Railway.

Parcel Freight Service

The rather curious freight operation, which was a feature of the Sarcee line during its latter months, continued to flourish for some years afterwards on the Bowness and Odgen lines, utilizing car 300. This vehicle began life as passenger car 8, the last of the original order of passenger cars delivered by the Ottawa Car Company in August 1909. In 1917, car 8 was regularly assigned to Ogden, and happened to be among the ranks of the rapidly-dwindling fleet of unconverted two-man cars. The car caught fire at the car barns on Sunday afternoon, June 10th 1917[54], apparently due to worn out or faulty wiring. Shortly thereafter, it was announced that the car would be rebuilt into a combination passenger-freight vehicle for service on the Ogden, Bowness and Sarcee lines. Approval to rebuild the car was given on Saturday July 17th 1917, as a one-man car had apparently been assigned to transport about 3000 lbs of milk daily from Bowness at 10¢ per 100 pounds or 12½¢ per 100 pounds if the empties were returned.[55] Finally in May 1918, Superintendent McCauley announced that streetcar 8 had indeed been rebuilt into the planned passenger-freight vehicle. The new combination car carried the number 300, featuring an arched roof, a forward

passenger compartment with four windows per side, and a freight section with a sliding door immediately ahead of the rear platform on the right side. The car went into service on May 20th 1918 operating from a freight loading and storage dock near the car barns.

A minimum charge of 10¢ per parcel prevailed, with additional charges of 10¢ to 25¢ per 100 pounds.[56] Schedule and route changes over the years are somewhat obscure, but it is known that a loading platform was built mid-way between Bowness loop and the siding west of the Bow River. This point became known among the street railway men as Milk Siding, and car 300 took on milk cans at this platform and delivered them to a truck at 4th Avenue se near 4th Street se. The electric car provided this service until the extension of improved and paved roads made it easier for motor vehicles to provide the same service. Sometime between 1932 and 1934, the combination car reverted back to its original function as a passenger car, assuming unit number 36, and characterized by its square-car windows, wide window posts, arched roof and wide letterboard.

One Man Operation

Without doubt, the most significant and innovative change on the Calgary Municipal Railway during this period was the introduction of, and complete conversion to, one-man operation. We have seen how Superintendent McCauley first introduced the concept in 1914 as an expense-reducing measure on the Grand Trunk and Capitol Hill lines, extending it further to include Tuxedo Park and the south end of the Manchester route. Cars assigned to all of these services, with the possible exception of the Manchester line,

Above: The first single-truck one-man car equipped with the McCauley front door. Also note the "back-up" fender under the rear platform. The number of this pioneer unit has not been ascertained. (Calgary Transit collection)

Below: Car 8, a 1913 product of the Ottawa Car Co. and originally car 78 on Calgary Municipal Railway's roster, stands outside the carbarn following an overhaul and a fresh coat of paint. The photograph was taken in the 1938 - 1941 period. Note the brass handrail in the second

window. It extends past the first window to the exit door to steady passengers while they wait near the door for the car to come to a stop. This was a common fixture in the McCauley one-man cars. (Percy W. Browning)

Opposite: Interior view of one of the large wooden trams, showing light shades and air baffles on the ceiling and the McCauley door on the front platform. (Anthony Clegg)

were single-truck trams (otherwise known as "dinkey" cars). The door side of the rear platform was simply sheathed and windowed in a fashion identical to the blind side, leaving only the front door available for passengers. Additional seating was provided on the rear platform. There appeared to be no publicized resistance to this move, probably because people in these outlying areas were open to any suggestions which would prevent increased fares or the possibility of curtailed service. The Manchester-Tuxedo Park cars, which operated on the outer extremities with only one man, had no structural changes at all, other than the placing of a fare box on the front platform. One can only speculate on how passengers were prevented from boarding the cars at the rear door when no conductor was on board.

Twelve one-man cars appeared on the Blue Line on Saturday July 1st 1916, and assisted in carrying a system total of 100,000 passengers that day, while the normal Saturday rate was about 40,000 passengers.[57] Since reference was made to the possibility of installing air brakes on these one-man cars, a safety feature common to all the system's double-truck cars, it follows that these twelve units were likely all "dinkey" cars. Consideration was being given to running the cars with long platforms forward, but this never materialized, because the Lethbridge Municipal Railway had already applied for a patent for this innovation, and the Calgary system would have been obliged to pay royalties to Lethbridge for each car so converted in Calgary. There was also concern that the long platform forward would present operating problems when meeting opposing cars on the curves.[58] This gradual introduction of the operation of one-man cars was officially recognized when the railway in its 1916 wage agreement offered an extra

5¢ per hour to men operating these cars into the city centre, an area bounded by 8th Avenue SE-SW, 8th Street SW, 17th Avenue SW-SE, and 2nd Street SE. This meant that a man with a minimum of three years service required to operate a one-man car within these boundaries was paid 40¢ per hour. The railway also agreed to pay each employee 50¢ to attend the monthly lectures on street railway practice, which were very important due to the gradual introduction of one-man cars. In addition, the employees received "time and a half" on six specified holidays and double time on Christmas and New Year's Day.[59]

The McCauley Front Door and Other Improvements

The first one-man car featuring the Calgary-type door in the right front dash appeared on Friday January 12th 1917.[60] Unfortunately, the unit number of this single-truck tram remains a mystery, but its unique, rather ungainly appearance embodied many safety principles patented by Mr. McCauley. The corner front door offered the distinct advantage that the boarding passenger was always in sight of the motor-conductor. It also encouraged more efficient operation because embarking passengers could board through the corner door while disembarking passengers used the original front side door. Removal of all the transverse seats in favour of longitudinal seats facilitated movement of passengers inside the car. Since the motor-conductor, as he became known on the Calgary system, was to be the lone crewman on the car, Mr. McCauley developed a number of features which would allow him to perform as many of his functions as possible without leaving the platform.

Above: Southbound car 76 stops to pick up passengers at the Garnet Block at 304-10th Street NW in the community of Sunnyside. This location on route 4 Crescent Heights is one block west of the northwest LRT Sunnyside station. The motor-conductor assists a passenger to lift a baby carriage onto the car. (CRHA – R.F. Corley fonds)

Below: A Red Line car on 8th Avenue sw at 1st Street sw en route to its eastern terminal at Burns Avenue in the early 1920s. Note part of the Canadian Northern Railway sign above the rear part of the tram roof and the stonefaced Liggetts Drug Store at the extreme right, later site of the Hudson's Bay Company's expanded store. Compare with similar views on page 48. (Glenbow Archives NC-26-91)

Calgary never used any electric track switches, so a system was developed whereby a pair of switch bars were installed in every car, one on each side of the platform. The motor-conductor simply lined the car up so that the switch turning point was directly under the switch bar hole in the car floor, then dropped the bar through the hole and turned the switch point without having to leave the car. Clerestory ventilating windows were activated by a lever on the front platform, as was the safety catch for the emergency door at the rear. Rear platform passengers could also activate the unlocking device, but such action would break a light bulb purposely set up to deter passenger from unnecessarily opening the emergency exit. Baffles were installed on the interior ceilings of the cars to better direct the flow of fresh air from the vents and to prevent the lights from reflecting off the front windows into the eyes of the motor-conductor. The front bulkhead separating the front platform from the body of the car was removed but the rear platform bulkhead remained, allowing that area to become a separate smoking compartment, a feature which greatly assisted with public acceptance of the one-man car.

A modified hand-brake in the form of a wheel required less effort on the part of the motor-conductor to bring the car to a stop. When he kicked out the "dog" to release the brake, a spring-loaded device rewound the brake so that the brake chain remained taut without actually applying the brake shoes to the wheels. The only pressure required on the brake wheel to retard or stop the car was that required to actually apply the brake, rather than having the motor-conductor completely rewind the brake handle on each application. Apparently eighty pounds of energy was kept on the brake chain at all times with this device. In addition, a rear fender was installed on each of these cars in order to ensure safe back-up movements.[61] Initially, six single-truck cars were converted in the above manner, and were used on the Blue Line and other less-heavily-travelled runs. The first double-truck one-man cars also started out on the Blue line, and on Wednesday April 11th, were reported to have effectively handled unusually large crowds to the horse show at the Stampede Grounds. With the introduction of the double-truck cars on the Blue Line, the single-truck one-man trams were relegated to extra and rush hour assignments.[62]

Sunday April 22nd 1917 marked the first time that all cars in operation on the system were one-man cars, thus effecting a saving of $160 for the day. This was a rare occurrence, however, until after all the mechanical and political implications were resolved and the system was ready for full daily one-man car operation. By April 25th regular daily service was being provided by one-man cars on the Blue line, the Manchester-Tuxedo line and the Red Line (Burns Avenue-West Calgary). The car shop staff had organized themselves to turn out three cars per week, and at that time the first of the big twelve-window cars regularly assigned to the White Line was being modified.[63]

While the actual mechanical changes were progressing at the shops without any apparent difficulty, Superintendent McCauley and Commission Graves found themselves busily interpreting the advantages of the one-man cars to the general public. They had succeeded in convincing the Council of the Board of Trade to publicly support the change.[64] The executive of the Council of Women met with them, and Superintendent McCauley arranged to hold a one-man car at 12th Avenue and 1st Street West so that the group could inspect the modified vehicle and give their suggestions after hearing the railway's presentation. The ladies expressed concern that baby carriages were forbidden on the cars but it was noted that this had always been a policy; however, collapsible go-carts were permitted on board. Another concern expressed by the women's group concerned a rumour that Mr. McCauley would make $100,000 from the City of Calgary, but he did note that he trusted the city would reimburse him for expenses incurred in the development of the features. Superintendent McCauley went on to stress the safety features of the car, dwelling on the fact that the motor-conductor could always see people boarding and alighting, and that he did not have to rely on the judgement of the conductor to start or stop the car. In other words, the motor-conductor had complete charge of all the processes concerning the operation of his car. He also noted that it would be more difficult for passengers to pass the fare box without depositing their fares because they would be doing so in full view of all of the passengers. In answer to a question about the motor-conductor becoming ill, Superintendent McCauley stated that this type of situation would be visible to the passengers who could pull the emergency door lever on the rear platform. This move would result in the opening of the emergency exit and the automatic application of the air brakes. The ladies suggested the need for a hand-railing at the front of the car under the windows, which could be grasped when the car started. They also recommended that the transverse seating arrangement be restored. After Mr. Graves outlined the financial advantages of the one-man car, the ladies of the executive of the Council of Women voted unanimously in favour of one-man operation.[65]

Support for the one-man car was slowly showing through the original skepticism on the part of both crewmen and passengers, but an unfortunate and untimely accident on Sunday May 6th 1917 involving a two-man Red & White Line Crescent Heights car downbound on the 10th Street NW hill slowed public acceptance quite considerably. The car's front truck left the rails, sending its front end careening off to the side of the road, striking an automobile and fatally injuring one of its occupants. The rear truck remained on the rails.[66] The jury's recommendation was the strict enforcement of the posted and well-known 4 MPH speed limit on this hill.[67] While the accident had no relationship to the number of crew manning the car, it did contribute to considerable public reticence toward the idea of operating one-man cars on the hill routes.

Finally in August 1917,[68] the commissioners requested Council's permission to operate one-man cars on the Crescent

Above: CMR 60 heading for Ogden on August 8th 1950 at the corner of 8th Avenue and Centre Street. The roof façade had been removed from the former Hudson's Bay store, occupied by the Royal Bank, but Ashdowns was still in the same location. Only the eastbound track on 8th Avenue s is still in service. Following the abandonment of the Bowness streetcar service in April 1950 the tracks on Centre Street s were taken out of service and the two remaining streetcar routes (Ogden "O" and Burns Avenue "8") looped from 12th Avenue se/sw through downtown via 1st Street sw, 8th Avenue s and 2nd Street se. As a result, most of the intersection at Centre Street and all of the westbound track along 8th Avenue s west of 2nd Street se was paved over, leaving only

the 8th Avenue s eastbound trackage in place between 1st Avenue sw and 2nd Street se. Both tracks on 8th Avenue se east of 2nd Street se were left in place to accommodate the inbound and outbound Ogden streetcars.
(CRHA Archives – E.A. Toohey collection 50-288, courtesy S.S. Worthen)

Below: CMR 59 passes under the CPR on 1st Street sw with the elegant Palliser Hotel in the background during 1947.
(W.C. Whittaker)

Heights line, simply because there was a shortage of manpower allegedly caused by the harvest. By October the shortage was still highly evident, and on Monday October 15th 1917, City Council put its final stamp of approval on one-man operations in Calgary with a scant 5 to 4 vote in favour.[69]

One week later, on October 22nd 1917, all cars on the Ogden line operated with one-man, thus marking the complete conversion to one-man car operation on the Calgary Municipal.[70]

The die had been cast and Superintendent McCauley had succeeded in making the Calgary Municipal the first major streetcar system in Canada to become totally operated with one-man cars. Other major Canadian systems carefully observed the Calgary model and began to move toward adopting it for themselves. The McCauley corner front door patent, however, was not as successful as hoped. Regina was the only other system to use it extensively. While the small cars which were traded to Saskatoon in 1919 had the McCauley front door, that feature was dispensed with at an early date by the Saskatoon Municipal system. Two Saint John, New Brunswick cars and some Quebec City and Moose Jaw cars were equipped with the feature, but again only for a short period of time.[71]

Right: Page eight from a twenty-page timetable issued in June 1941 shows the schedule for Route 5 Belt Line cars. These cars travelled west on 8th Avenue sw, south on 1st Street sw, west on 12th Avenue sw, south on 14th Street sw, east on 17th Avenue sw, north on 2nd Street se to 8th Avenue sw. Route 5 Belt Line cars also travelled around the same circuit in the opposite direction.

Below: The system's double-truck locomotive-type snow fighter was also built by Ottawa. It was commonly referred to as "Mary Ann" and saw 22 years of service on the Calgary street railway. (Glenbow Archives NA-647-3)

Route No. 5
BELT LINE—Each Way

South on 1st Street West to 12th Avenue, west on 12th Avenue to 14th Street West, south on 14th Street to 17th Avenue, east on 17th Avenue to 2nd Street East, north on 2nd Street East to 8th Avenue, and west on 8th Avenue

West on 8th Ave and East on 17th Ave.		East on 8th Ave. and West on 17th Ave.	
1st St. W. & 8th Ave.	14th St. W. & 17th Ave.	Centre St. & 8th Ave.	14th St. W. & 17th Ave.
6.20 a.m	6.30 a.m.	6.05 a.m.	6.20 a.m.
6.40	6.50	6.25	6.40
7.00	7.10	6.45	7.00
7.15	7.25	7.05	7.20
7.35	7.45	7.20	7.35
7.55	8.05	7.40	7.55
8.15	8.25	8.00	8.15
8.35	8.45	8.20	8.35
8.55	9.05	8.40	8.55
9.20	9.30	9.05	9.20
9.40	9.50	9.25	9.40
10.00	10.10	9.45	10.00
10.20	10.30	10.05	10.20
10.40	10.50	10.25	10.40
11.00	11.10	10.45	11.00
11.20	11.30	11.05	11.20
11.40	11.50	11.25	11.40
12.00 noon	12.10 p.m.	11.45	12.00 noon
12.15 p.m.	12.25	12.05 p.m.	12.20 p.m.
12.35	12.45	12.20	12.35
12.55	1.05	12.40	12.55
1.15	1.25	1.00	1.15
1.35	1.45	1.20	1.35
1.55	2.05	1.40	1.55
2.20	2.30	2.05	2.20
2.40	2.50	2.25	2.40
3.00	3.10	2.45	3.00
3.20	3.30	3.05	3.20
3.40	3.50	3.25	3.40
4.00	4.10	3.45	4.00
4.15	4.25	4.05	4.20
4.35	4.45	4.20	4.35
4.55	5.05	4.40	4.55
5.15	5.25	5.00	5.15
5.35	5.45	5.20	5.35
5.55	6.05	5.40	5.55
6.15	6.25	6.00	6.15
6.35	6.45	6.20	6.35
6.55	7.05	6.40	6.55
7.20	7.30	7.05	7.20

and every twenty minutes up to

| 11.40 | 11.50 | 11.25 | 11.40 |

OWL CARS

12.05 a.m.
12.35
1.15

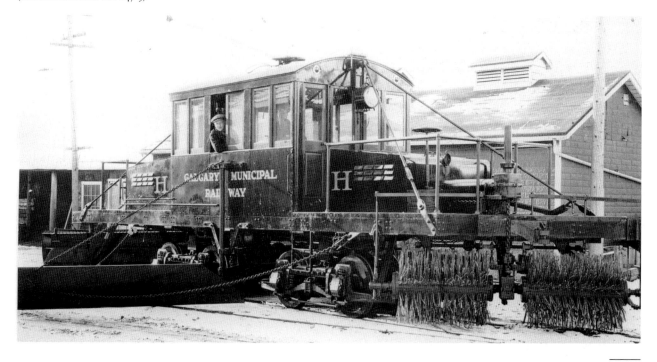

Above: Car 47, eastbound on route 8 and signed for Burns Avenue, approaches Centre Street from the Sunnyside cut immediately north of the Centre Street bridge.

Below: Car 78 (second) is just east of the Alberta Stock Yards building on the Ogden line. In the background is the site of the old brickworks. (Both photos: Percy W. Browning)

CHAPTER SIX

Adjustment, Expansion and Rehabilitation

THE YEARS 1918 and 1919 brought continuing challenges to Superintendent McCauley as the Calgary Municipal Railway attempted to keep abreast of mounting expenses, deteriorating equipment, and increased service demands. The Ogden line was a particular "thorn in the side" financially, and neither he nor his successors were ever able to get that service to break even. Considerable time and effort went into an examination of the possibility of relocating the Ogden line to shorten the distance travelled by the cars. This proposal became embroiled in several technicalities, the largest of which was the need to purchase the right-of-way, but such an expenditure would never have been recoverable through the time saved on operating over a shorter distance. Nevertheless, two short-line proposals were considered. One proposal would have seen the line branch off at the curve west of the overhead bridge, run parallel to the Canadian Pacific Railway main line and join the original car line again before it crossed the Bow River at Bonnybrook Road and 34th Avenue SE.[1] A second suggestion was to strike out on a tangent in a south-easterly direction from the 11th Street SE and 26th Avenue SE intersection to join the line again at Bonnybrook Road and 34th Avenue SE.[2]

In order to obtain the latter of these proposed routes, the city was faced with a $15,750 land expropriation expense in addition to the cost of actually relocating the line, so the commissioners were considering an approach to the Public Utilities Commission to have that body fix the price of the land. They also felt that the owners of unsubdivided property should be obligated by law to make grants of land for street, avenue or lane purposes similar to that which required owners of subdivided property to make such grants free of charge.[3] In addition to the high cost of land, Council received a protest through a legal firm representing the Calgary & Western Land Company, as that company had donated certain parts of the original Ogden right-of-way and had sold land on the strength of that line's location.[4] As further studies suggested that the Ogden line re-alignment would save only three minutes per trip, the re-alignment proposals were dropped and workmen began to make repairs to the existing Ogden line in the form of improved grading, tie replacement, rail alignment and snow fence protection.[5] Thwarted in efforts to improve the service and cut expenses, the only alternative left was to raise the fares, and that was done in the form of abolishing the yellow workman's tickets. Sale of the yellow tickets arbitrar-

ily ceased effective July 20th 1918, although they continued to be accepted on the cars during the following week.[6] This move was expected to increase the street railway revenues by about $15,000 per year.[7]

The first "organized withdrawal of service" on the CMR occurred at 11 AM on Saturday October 19th 1918, when the employees of the street railway went out in sympathy with the CPR express handlers[8] who had been on strike for some days before that. The cars remained idle until the following Tuesday October 22nd, when the CPR strike was settled. The union of CMR workers had been in existence for only three years, but at this time had taken its first solid stance. Until 1915, the employees had signed individual contracts with the Superintendent after he had met with them as a group to reach wage settlements. Efforts to thwart these settlements manifested themselves in several attempts to form a union, but Superintendent McCauley continued to convince the men to stay with the Calgary Municipal Railway Social, Insurance and Sick Benefit Association. Club and games room space was made available for this group at the car barns. In September 1915, however, several employees had formed Division 583 of the Amalgamated Association of Street Electric Railway-Motor Coach Employees of America.[9] Its early membership was small, but in 1917 City Council agreed to hear grievance and negotiation committees from both union and non-union men.[10] The sympathy walk-out in 1918 indicated that the union was gaining strength among the street railway workers.

The labour troubles cost the railway about $4000 in lost revenue,[11] but the very serious influenza epidemic of 1918 reduced revenues even further immediately after the shutdown. The situation became so serious that the Department of Health ordered street railway patrons to wear masks covering the nose and mouth while riding on the cars, under pain of possible arrest. Motor-conductors sold the masks and were instructed to refuse passengers who attempted to travel without wearing them.[12] The crisis eventually passed, and operations began to return to normal, but the shutdown and the epidemic together had so reduced the revenue of the railway for the months of October, November, and December 1918 that it appeared the system was facing a deficit of some $25,000 on the year's operation.[13]

Although revenue had dropped sharply in the final three months of 1918, total gross revenue and ridership figures for the year were beginning to approach those of the great 1913 peak. This meant that all the cars were being heavily

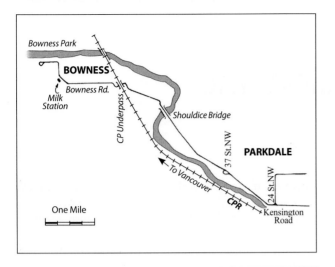

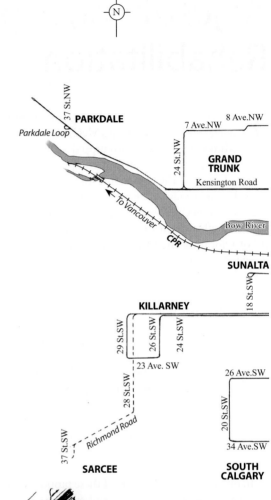

Calgary Municipal Railway
Track Diagram
1919 - 1921

One Mile

Illustration by Robert J. Sandusky

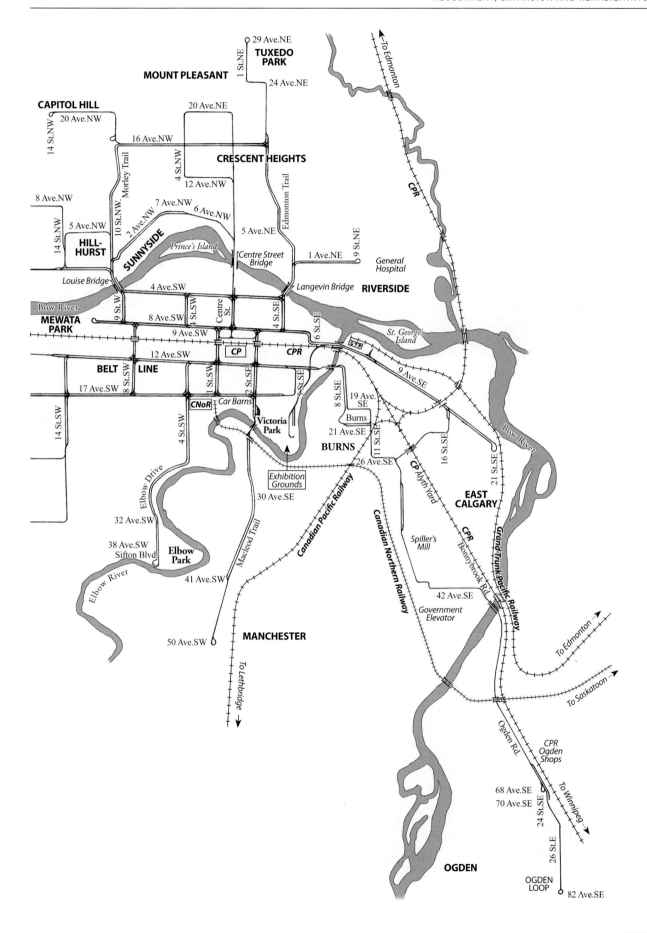

Above: The sign hanging from the overhead span wire reminds all vehicular traffic that the area is a hospital zone. Car 28 has just turned from 12th Avenue sw onto 4th Street sw on its journey to Elbow Park. On the right side of the photo is Central Park and out of sight on the left is the Colonel Belcher Hospital. Judging from the short shadows, the streetcar could be a Saturday noon car coming in from Ogden carrying workmen to their homes along the Elbow Park line. This was the era of a five-and-a-half day work week. (Rich Krisak collection)

Below: In service in Saskatoon as a new car, number 24 was traded to Calgary in 1919 and retained the same number in its new home. (Saskatoon Public Library – Local History Room)

used and no extra equipment was available to augment the service. The alternative left to Superintendent McCauley was to introduce a system of skip-stops which was applied to the South Calgary and Killarney routes. Cars on these routes stopped to let down or take up passengers only at a few specified major stops between the downtown area and 14th Street sw and 17th Avenue sw. After passing this intersection, the cars did stop at all intersections on signal. This system went into general use on Monday February 17th 1919 between the hours of 5 PM and 6:30 PM.[14] A sign indicating the points at which the car stopped appeared on the front fender at the appropriate time of the day. The skip-stop system as used in this instance was a feature of several North American street railway systems at that time.

Centre Street North became a significant car line during 1919. Its story goes back almost to the initial years of development on the Calgary Municipal Railway, when it was noted by the City Engineer's Department, and concurred with by Superintendent McCauley, that Centre Street provided the best grade into the North Hill area. The events leading to the development of the Centre Street Bridge – which would allow access to this ideal grade – are many, but early in 1917 the present structure was opened, and a single track-car line was extended from 4th Avenue north on Centre Street to the bridge. This short piece of track was estimated to cost about $2000 and was to be charged against the railway's capital account. On leaving the bridge, the single track line continued in a north-westerly direction along a grade on the north bank of the Bow River to connect with the Sunnyside line at a point west of the loop, as it approached Sunnyside below the loop. This portion was estimated to cost $3500 and was to be paid for from surplus revenue.[15] So began an often-interrupted operation of the Sunnyside cars across Centre Street Bridge into the city. Cars bound for Sunnyside continued to use the original route via Louise Bridge. The Sunnyside loop line was to be plagued with unstable track and roadbed throughout its existence as the north bank contained several springs leading into the river. In fact the first disruption of service due to movement of the roadbed came in July 1917, when the north approach to the Centre Street Bridge collapsed.[16] The Sunnyside loop line was part of the westerly leg of the Burns Avenue line until Monday August 23rd 1917, when it was connected with the Riverside line.[17] It was not until September 1919 that final authorization went through Council for a single track line to be built up Centre Street across 16th Avenue NE-NW north to 20th Avenue NE-NW, then west to 4th Street NW, south on that street to 12th Avenue NW, then east to Centre Street. This arrangement avoided the necessity to purchase expensive special trackwork for the intersection at 16th Avenue NE-NW, and was expected to handle a reasonable volume of traffic.[18] No time was wasted in construction, as service on the new White & Yellow Line commenced on Wednesday afternoon, November 19th 1919 on a fifteen-minute schedule from 6:30 AM to 11:30 PM. The first cars over the new route were greeted by the happy faces of North Hill residents who happened to spot them downtown, and from many housewives who were attracted to their front doors to see them rumble past their homes. In typical Calgary street railway fashion, there were no formalities surrounding the launching of the new service. No bottles of wine were dashed against the prows of the cars as they moved out from the barns. The cars, routinely dispatched by Mr. Charles Comba, General Foreman, under the care of motormen Armitage and Burn, set out on their new assignment carrying white and yellow arrows pointing skyward as their distinctive route markers. After returning from their first trip to 20th Avenue NE-NW, they turned from Centre Street into 8th Avenue SE to loop via 2nd Street SE, 9th Avenue SE and then north again on Centre Street to complete their first regular trip.[19]

The opening of the Centre Street North line caused considerable controversy among residents of Tuxedo Park, as plans were announced that Centre Street would be used as a trunk line to replace the Edmonton Trail, 24th Avenue NE and 1st Street NE line. Tuxedo Park residents had already spoken out very vehemently against the new Rosedale loop line as they felt that this area was always getting excellent car service and that the opening of the Centre Street Bridge should have had as its priority the provision of better service to Tuxedo Park by continuing north on Centre Street to 34th Avenue NE-NW.[20] It was not unusual to have fifty people packed into a community meeting place called Ranch House, located at the original Tuxedo Park loop, on Saturday evenings as the controversy raged on. Some residents were pressing for extension of the Centre Street line while residents several blocks east of Centre Street wanted to see an extension of the line on the Edmonton Trail. Since the Tuxedo Park car line was built by the Canadian Estates Company, that firm had to be consulted, complicating the situation even further.

Confusion surrounds even the final outcome of the controversy. A special committee report dated December 20th 1919 and accepted by City Council on December 22nd 1919, reads as follows:

"A: Extension of the present Centre Street Car Line from 20th Avenue terminus, at present to 32nd Avenue North, or as far beyond 32nd Avenue North as may be necessary in order to affect a terminus. The line to be operated, if possible, by double control cars.

"B: The Canadian Estates Company be requested to permit the removal of the line on 1st Street NE to Centre Street in order to carry out the above recommendation, and that the present line from 24th Avenue NE be taken up and relaid on the Edmonton Trail to 27th avenue NE. A regular service to be maintained on this extension and operated as the Tuxedo-Manchester Line."[21]

It is clearly evident that the construction outlined in Section A was completed. It seems likely, however, that Section B was never acted upon, but instead the original

Above: CMR 16 on 2nd Street SE enters the subway under the CPR main line on August 16th 1950. This was the only car on the Calgary system rebuilt with the long platform at the front end, obviating the need for a McCauley door. Note the Imperial Hotel, the CPR freight office buildings to the right and the trolley coach overhead. (CRHA Archives - E.A. Toohey collection 50-290, courtesy S.S. Worthen)

Below: Car 82 returns to the carbarn from a morning Ogden run. (Percy W. Browning)

Opposite below: Car 36, rebuilt from passenger-express car 300 which was originally first car number 8, appears on September 9th 1944 on 17th Avenue SE at 2nd Street SE operating on the Manchester - Bridgeland route 9. (Rich Krisak)

Tuxedo Park line remained intact and a one block extension connected the new Centre Street North line with 1st Street NE along 29th Avenue NE. A schedule and route change effective Thursday November 11th 1920, substantiates this possibility. Manchester cars became part of the White & Yellow Line operating on a half-hourly service, while the Tuxedo Park cars continued to operate under the Blue & White star sign, also on a half-hour service, over a large belt formed by 8th Avenue SE, Centre Street north to 32nd Avenue NE, where they looped and returned south on Centre Street to 29th Avenue NE and east to 1st Street NE and return via 24th Avenue NE, Edmonton Trail, 4th Street SE and 8th Avenue SE to Centre Street.[22]

During the time that the North Hill controversy and route changes were taking place, some very significant changes were occurring down at the carbarns. Increased ridership, coupled with extended routes, created a need a need for more and larger cars on the system, but inflation had almost doubled the price of a new car between 1913 and 1919 to about $15,750 per unit. So Calgary seized upon an opportunity to exchange cars with the Saskatoon Municipal Railway when that system required some more versatile equipment to replace six fine double-truck, double-end, Preston-built trams of 1913 vintage. These cars were restricted in their assignment in Saskatoon because they were too heavy to travel over some of the bridges in that city. Mr. McCauley inspected the cars, and after consultation with the commissioners the following recommendations were presented to Council:

"That Saskatoon supplies the city with six double-truck cars, three fully equipped with four motors and two controllers on each and three with two motors and one controller on each as inspected by Mr. McCauley, for seven Calgary single-truck cars, fully equipped, painted and suitable for one-man operation. Each party to pay the freight on the car it receives."[23]

The seven "dinkey" cars which went to Saskatoon were 19, 20, 21, 24, 28, 33 and apparently 31 (see Roster). All of these cars were shipped before the year end; three Saskatoon cars were on hand in Calgary by late November 1919, while the remaining three cars arrived early in 1920.[24]

Shortly after the Saskatoon trade had been concluded, Superintendent McCauley left for eastern Canadian and US centres in search of additional cars. On November 10th 1919, Council authorized the purchase of four cars to cost between $4000 and $6500 plus freight.[25] A December 6th decision authorized Superintendent McCauley to purchase two additional cars, making a total of six.[26, 27] Official records do not record the builders of these cars nor the system from which they came. They were delivered to Calgary from New York State[28], and were commonly known among Calgarians as the New York cars. Essentially, there were three classes of cars represented in this group, with one class being larger cars than the others. At the time of delivery they were all double-end, but characterized by shorter platforms than those on the Saskatoon Preston-built cars. Some of them even ran in Calgary as double-end cars, a feature which was a rarity

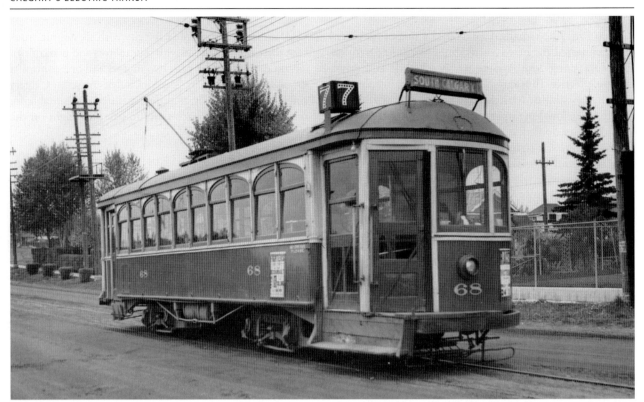

Above: Car 68 was rebuilt after the accident described below, and saw service almost to the end of street railway operations. The tram was photographed in June 1946 on 20th Street sw near 34th Avenue sw. (W.C. Whittaker)

on the CMR. Upon delivery early in 1920, these cars were assigned consecutive numbers from 78 to 83 inclusive. There are strong indications, and it is generally agreed, that 78 and 79 were Wason-built, while some evidence indicates that 82 and 83 were the products of Newburyport. Speculation and opinion is divided between these two builders for cars 80 and 81,[29] although another possibility suggests that these two units were Brill products.

Calgary's first car numbered 78, a 1913 Ottawa-built street car, became second car 8 to replace the gap left when the 1909 Ottawa-built short car was destroyed by fire on June 10th 1917 and subsequently rebuilt and renumbered in 1918 to combine 300. The only one of the six cars ordered from Preston that was actually delivered had been numbered 79. This original 79 became second 31 taking the number of the 7th "dinkey" traded to Saskatoon; thus all the numerical gaps in the roster were completely filled.

The busy, colourful expansion which characterized the years 1918 and 1919 on the Calgary Municipal were marred by two serious setbacks. On Wednesday evening, May 1st 1918 the big White Line trolley number 60 was destroyed by fire as it stood on the loop at 21st Street SE. It had just discharged its passengers when the fire, blamed on a carelessly tossed cigarette, blazed up between the coal box and the partition at the front of the car. Motor-conductor McHenry tried to extinguish the blaze but it very quickly got out of control. The seats, roof and windows of the car were completely destroyed.[30] Since the need for cars was pressing and

the shop was successfully rebuilding car 8 into combine 300, car 60 emerged several weeks later with wood-slatted seats and an arched roof.

Car 68 Goes Shopping

Another extremely unfortunate mishap occurred on Monday December 15th 1919, when South Calgary car 68, the first car on the line for the day, came hurtling down the 14th Street sw hill, lurched into the open switch leading into 17th Avenue sw, fell over on its side and crashed into Crooks' Drug Store, fatally injuring one of its passengers, a Mr. R.D. McWilliams. Several other passengers and the motor-conductor were injured, but not seriously. The interior of the store was a complete shambles and the car itself wrecked.

Car 68 with about fifteen passengers aboard, had started carefully down the first slope of the treacherous 14th Street sw hill. The rails, covered with hoar frost, were very slippery. With sand being freely applied, Motor-conductor William J. Walker sensed that he was gaining momentum even with a heavier brake application. The car slowed insignificantly on the short bench between the two hills, but as it went into the second slope, it became obvious to the motor-conductor that his car was out of control. His only hope for avoiding disaster depended on the position of the switch at the bottom of the hill. As a safety precaution, all motor-conductors were ordered to turn the switch to line the track straight through on 14th Street sw after they had turned the corner onto 17th Avenue sw. A sign was posted to that effect at the intersection, but it was not unusual for a passenger to take the switch iron and open the switch as a courtesy to

Above: The scene at 14th Street and 17th Avenue sw on Monday December 15th 1919, showing workmen from flatcar "G" preparing to remove tram 68 from Crook's Drug Store. Sign on the post at right side of photo states: "Notice to Street Car Operators:
This switch must always be left turned back to straight track after run-

ning over it. By Order." (Glenbow Archives ND-8-362)

Below: The scene of destruction inside Crook's Drug Store. (Glenbow Archives ND-8-363)

Above: Calgary's second tram numbered 78 on 9th Avenue SE, October 15th 1945. This was one of the cars purchased second-hand from US lines in 1919-20. In the background is the CPR overpass for the line to Edmonton. The car is pausing at 16th Street SE as the motorman turns the track switch from inside the car to direct the car onto 16th Street SE toward the CPR Alyth overpass and on to Ogden. (Glenbow Archives NA-2935-4)

Opposite: CMR 20, the first of the six ex-Saskatoon cars to go into service on the Calgary Municipal Railway, November 1919. George Gush, in charge of trolley maintenance, is on the front step. The six cars from Saskatoon were given the same numbers as previously carried by the "dinkies"; number "31" was left unassigned for the time being. (Glenbow Archives NA-2891-8)

the motor-conductor. On this occasion Mr. Walker could only hope that none of the waiting passengers had extended their usual courtesy, but the switch had been opened and the worst did indeed happen. No one had been seen near the switch, except for the cleaning man who had gone about his usual task of sweeping out the intersection before the approach of the first car of the day. He emphatically noted that the switch was lined straight through the intersection when he cleaned it out, and denied just as emphatically that he had turned it.[31]

The City Commissioners agreed to pay $3000 to Mr. Crooks to compensate for the loss of his stock, and to carry out repairs to the building under the supervision of the City Engineer, on the understanding that no claim be made against the city for damage to the building. The Commissioners also noted that the above work was to be done without the city admitting to any liability for the accident, and solely for the purpose of enabling Mr. Crooks to resume his drug business in the building at the earliest possible moment.[32]

Immediately following the accident, the switch was spiked closed permanently, and thereafter all South Calgary cars travelled into the city via 14th Street sw and 12th Avenue sw.[33] Car 68 reappeared on its South Calgary assignment some time later with an arch roof, a construction technique that characterized all cars rebuilt in the Calgary shops.

The closing months of 1919 were eventful, and much of the work of operating the system in this period fell upon General Foreman Charles Comba, as Superintendent McCauley spent a considerable portion of this time inspecting second-hand street cars, some of which were subsequently delivered to Calgary. The events of these two months wore heavily on Mr. McCauley, particularly the December accident, and so it was not surprising that, when an invitation was extended to manage the New Brunswick Light & Power Company in Saint John at some considerable increase in salary, he consented to go. Mr. McCauley turned in his resignation on Monday January 19th 1920,[34] requesting that it be effective February 15th. So concluded the successful formative and developmental years of the Calgary Municipal Railway. Thomas McCauley was moving on, but he was leaving behind him a system envied by several others across North America, because it had earned more money than it had expended for most of the first ten years of its life. This enviable position had been achieved through Mr. McCauley's rugged determination to initiate, develop and complete projects such as the one-man car program, Bowness Park and the temporary Sarcee line.

A New Regime

R.A. Brown, City Electrical Engineer, became the Superintendent of the Municipal Railway at this time, in addition to his electrical department duties. He was given authority to appoint a Traffic Manager to attend to day-to-day administration of the railway, and Charles Comba was appointed to act as Assistant Manager or Traffic Manager to Mr. Brown.

At the beginning of 1920, the railway had reached a point where much of the trackage and equipment required extensive refurbishing. With these kinds of expenditures looming and the need to increase revenues to keep up with increased normal costs, Mr. Brown recommended a fare increase which became effective on Monday June 28th 1920. Cash fares rose to 10¢, adult tickets to twenty for one dollar, four for 25¢ or two for 15¢.[35] Children's fares remained at eight for 25¢.[36] In mid-August, speculation was that books of twenty tickets for one dollar were to be replaced by books at eighteen for one dollar. The speculation turned out to be correct, and as of midnight Tuesday August 17th 1920 passengers received only eighteen tickets instead of twenty tickets for their dollar.[37] When the announcement for the increase was made a few days earlier, streetcar tickets became "best sellers". Patrons purchased 8,000 books on the Sunday and Monday; another 4,000 books were sold on the Tuesday.[38]

On Monday September 20th 1920, the regular Ogden cars returned to their former hourly service. Eight months earlier, the headway had been reduced to forty minutes, but it was not at all profitable.[39] Ogden residents again began to pressure Council to build a more direct line; but that issue had been settled two years earlier when the city was unable to obtain the right-of-way at a reasonable price. This was the first service reduction initiated by Mr. Brown, and

was followed on November 10th 1920 with adjustments to the Manchester, Centre Street North and Tuxedo Park services. These have already been described in the discussion about changes to the track plan for Centre Street North and Tuxedo Park in late 1919.

The installation of a new track intersection at Centre Street and 8th Avenue s disrupted service slightly for a few days in mid-October. The new switches allowed cars northbound on Centre Street to turn west onto 8th Avenue SE/SW; cars approaching Centre Street along 8th Avenue s in either direction could turn south into Centre Street, a facility which greatly simplified short-turn operations in the downtown area, principally because the new arrangement eliminated the cross-over on 8th Avenue SW west of Centre Street. Cars were still unable to travel north on Centre Street across 8th Avenue s without operating on the southbound or west track after crossing 8th Avenue s, a practice followed by the White & Yellow Line cars until they began to run through to Manchester, at which time they returned to Centre Street via 2nd Street SE and 8th Avenue SE, instead of 9th Avenue SE. Approaching Centre Street in this manner, cars could run northbound on the east track and gain access to the single track across the bridge by way of a cross-over just north of 4th Avenue.

For several years the single track on the Centre Street hill between the turnout into the Sunnyside cut and the turnout onto 12th Avenue NW was protected by hand-operated red light signals. In addition to the signal lights mounted on a pole at these turnouts, there was also a heavy-duty electric light switch. If the section was clear, no red light showed.

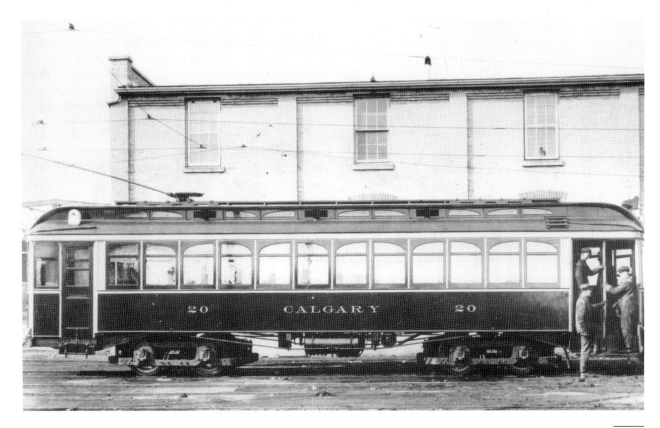

Above: One of the units constructed in Calgary from one-and-a-half single-truck "dinkies" in 1924. It is shown here at a passing siding on the Bowness line.

Below: One of the original Preston-built trams mounted on Bemis trucks. Photograph taken at the 8th Avenue NW / 7th Avenue NW "S"–curve (Grand Trunk route) after the car had been converted for one-man operation.
(Photos above and below: W.C. Whittaker)

Opposite: The new Louise Bridge over the Bow River. Note the centre-of-the-road lamp standards and the ornate trolley-wire brackets. (Glenbow Archives ND-8-332)

An approaching motor-conductor could then proceed, but upon entering the section would stop and turn on the switch which activated the red signal lights at both the Sunnyside cut turnout and the 12th Avenue NW turnout past the top of the hill. This indicated to any other tram traffic approaching from either the top or the bottom of the hill that a car was already on or approaching the hill. On reaching the other end of the section, the motor-conductor turned the switch off which turned off the red lights at both ends, thus indicating to approaching traffic that the hill was clear of tram traffic. Apparently at about the same time a similar system protected movements on the Bowness line.[40]

Mr. Brown secured for the Calgary Municipal Railway a large brick stable located in the immediate carbarn area. Originally the lower floor was a stable and the upper floor a hayloft. The interior was completely reconstructed using reclaimed lumber; windows were enlarged, resulting in a building well-suited for shop purposes. The building was heated by steam piped in from a municipal power plant located some 2000 feet away. All of the shop machinery from the carbarn was moved into the shop building. The building contained an enclosed paint shop, a machine shop with a blacksmith's corner, a large wheel lathe, a hydraulic press, a machinist's lathe, a pipe and bolt cutter, an emery wheel stand, a drill press, a hacksaw and a babbitting bench. There was also an extensive carpenter shop, a truck repair shop, air compressor and controller repair benches. Another section was devoted to armature repairs. Mr. Brown also had built a coal, sand and wood storage building with sand drying facilities and a sand tower just off 2nd Street SE to service cars particularly during winter operations.

In 1924, material was purchased for the construction of passing tracks on the Centre Street North line and on the Bowness line.[41] By 1929, most of the Centre Street line was double-tracked, the section to 12th Avenue N being completed in 1928 and to 20th Avenue N in 1929. The 1929 extension included the installation of a double track wye at 16th Avenue N and Centre Street.[42]

In the meantime the new Louise Bridge had opened in late 1921, and the new double track car line and intersection at 9th Street SW and 4th Avenue SW facilitated operations at a longtime bottleneck where four routes – the Red, Red & Blue, Red & White and Bowness lines – crossed the Bow River. Additional changes took place on the CMR at East Calgary during 1926 in the form of track relocation. This involved the removal of double track along 9th Avenue SE from 17th Street SE to 22nd Street SE, and the construction of five blocks of single track down 17th Street SE to 30th Avenue SE. This change occurred as a result of requests from residents living south of Colonel Walker School to have a car line through their neighbourhood[43] to serve a denser population than that along 9th Avenue SE, and to give better access to the CPR Alyth yard office and roundhouse.

Riding habits of the early 1920s tended to make many of the remaining eleven single-truck cars on the CMR roster obsolete. With the exception of regular assignments to the Sunalta, Capitol Hill and Grand Trunk routes, the single-truck cars appeared on other routes only as rush hour extras. They proved to be very inadequate for this kind of service as overcrowding always occurred; thus they became even more unpopular with passengers. Calgary Municipal solved this problem in a very unusual manner. Six of the single-truck cars, numbers 25, 29, 30, 32, 34 and 36 were taken out of service in 1924 and rebuilt into four large double-truck cars[44] carrying unit numbers 25, 29, 30 and 32. All of these cars featured long platforms at both ends, so it seems likely that

Above: Car 67 – the first Calgary tram to be extensively reconditioned under the 1927 refurbishing programme – was outshopped early in September with new lighting fixtures, pneumatic rear door, and under-the-platform lifeguard fender. The gentlemen inspecting the remodeled car have not been identified.
(Glenbow Archives NA-2891-52, copied from PA-1689-7)

Below: Calgary Municipal 81 – one of the trams purchased from the USA in 1919-20. Neither carbuilder nor former operators of these trolleys is a matter of record. The car is travelling into the barns via 2nd Street SE at 17th Avenue SE at the entrance to the Stampede Grounds. (Robert W. Gibson collection)

Above: Trailer car 201 waits behind its motor car for a signal to proceed. This is a rare blind-side (non-door side) photograph of a trailer. Note the smoke jack for the Peter Smith coal heater. Since these cars were not powered, the coal heater was the only source of heat in Calgary's cold winter months.
(Rich Krisak collection)

the original long rear platforms from the "dinkies" became the long front platforms in the rebuilding process. Their new long rear platforms could have been made up from those of cars 34 and 36, the shorn off rear platform of car 26 which then became an auxiliary car, and the combined front platforms of cars 34 and 36. In essence then, no single-truck cars were scrapped in this program. Four additional motors, Standard 0-50 trucks,[45] and Canadian Allis Chalmers type AA7B air brakes were purchased for these rebuilds.[46] Each car in this series had its own operating characteristics, but they were apparently not very popular with the motor-conductors. They did, however, remain in service throughout the balance of the street railway's history and were dispatched for both regular and extra assignments over most routes, illustrating their versatility and improvement over the single-truck cars from which they were built. On the other hand, all of the five remaining "dinkey" cars – 22, 23, 26, 27 and 35 – were retired or derelict by the early 1940s.

A further rolling stock refurbishing program was initiated with the out-shopping of car 67 in August 1927.[47] Cars affected by this program emerged from the CMR shops with new dome light fixtures, a new type of headlight, improved folding front entrance-exit steps, pneumatic rear exit door, and a standard lifeguard fitted under the front platform. The commissioners planned to refurbish one car per month to these specifications until all regularly-assigned cars had

been so fitted. However, only nine cars – numbers 1, 2, 29, 67, 68, 69, 70, 71, and 72 – benefitted from this program. Selected features, chiefly the under-platform lifeguards, were applied to many other cars on the system. When cars 16 and 36 underwent major shopping and subsequent rebuilding during the 1930s, they appeared with both the pneumatic rear door and the new lifeguard features.

The 1920s were regarded as a period of growth and prosperity in this continent's economic history. All was not well and prosperous for street railways, however, as declining patronage meant less revenue while expenses continued to rise. In Calgary it was evidenced by the growing number of private automobiles which were gradually luring people away from the streetcars. During this period Superintendent Brown had suggested the possibility of installing a car track on 7th Avenue SE-SW to carry streetcar and automobile traffic in one direction only – while 8th Avenue SE-SW would carry traffic in the opposite direction – as increased automobile traffic on 8th Avenue SE-SW was interfering with the streetcar schedules.[48] Mr. Brown, however, was half a century ahead of the times and nothing was done in this matter.

During 1924, a number of route changes were proposed – some of which were put into effect. On March 21st a new schedule and route plan, designed to reduce the mounting deficit, was announced – changes that were to come into effect on April 7th 1924.[49] Practically all of the revisions

Above: CMR's second No. 8 – originally first No. 78. The view is at the Twelfth Avenue Bridge over the Elbow River as the car heads towards the Burns Avenue terminal. Note the double trolley wire – there was double track at both ends of the single track span.
(Both photos: W.C. Whittaker)

Below: One of Calgary's Canadian Car & Foundry-built steel trams in June 1946. Note the wire mesh window guards and the roller bearing trucks. The car is proceeding north on 2nd Street SE at the intersection of 17th Avenue SE. It is going into service from the carbarn onto the Belt Line route 5. Note the tower of fire station No. 2 above the building housing the Coffee Cabin. The tower appears in LRT photos at Stampede station.

Above: Sometime in the late 1930s, car 92 passes under the CPR tracks on its way to Bowness. (Fred Murdoch photo, collection of Percy W. Browning).

consisted of reduced schedules and longer headways, and in some cases even the complete elimination of off-peak operation on some of the outlying routes. As might be expected, the citizens did not take kindly to these changes and public opinion was against these the proposals, even though *The Morning Albertan* editorially supported the moves which were endorsed by the City Council. Pressure groups worked to have service restored to former levels, and operation of some of the main lines was altered again effective Wednesday April 16th.

The month of April 1924 was certainly a period of trial and error for the Calgary Municipal Railway, as it attempted to stem the ebb tide of ridership and surpluses.

By the 1920s, the steadily-aging trackwork required considerable sums of money each year for major rehabilitation programs. Extensive repairs were carried out along 17th Avenue sw between 8th Street sw and 14th Street sw. 8th Avenue se-sw, from 2nd Street se to 4th Street sw, was completely refurbished with new road bed, concrete base, ties and rails in 1927, while Centre Street from 9th Avenue South to 7th Avenue North including the intersection was completely renewed in 1929. After 1925, passenger riding began to rise again, and the need for new equipment became evident. In June 1928 one large double-truck sweeper-plow was ordered from the Ottawa Car Manufacturing Company, to be equipped with four General Electric 65HP motors, at a cost of $18,960.

Modern Steel Trams

In June 1928, three new cars were ordered from the Canadian Car & Foundry Company of Montreal. These passenger cars were priced at $20,534 each[50], compared with the $8000 cost of a similar-sized wooden car in 1912. They resembled in size and exterior appearance the 2850 – 2874 class trailer cars of the Montreal Tramways Company, except the Calgary cars were fully equipped motor cars. Furthermore, the Calgary cars did have distinctive features; a rear smoking compartment separated from the rest of the car by a double-swing door, brown leather-covered seat cushions, the notched letterboard which housed the destination sign immediately above the motor-conductor's front window, the winter installation of the Peter Smith forced air coal heater, and the unmistakable sound of an air whistle. The words *CALGARY MUNICIPAL RY.* appeared on the letterboard on each side of the car, centered above the body windows. The exterior finish was standard Calgary red and cream with pin stripe lines set a few inches away from the edges of the steel sheathing. Unit numbers were centered below the headlight and trolley catcher at front and rear respectively, and below the second and eleventh body window on each side. The cars were delivered with three route number indicators identical to those used on Montreal street cars, one mounted on the lower right front window, another in the upper part of the first window on

Above: Car 85 stops on 8th Avenue sw in front of the T. Eaton department store at the 3rd Street sw corner to pick up a passenger with a baby carriage. The car routes are posted at the left edge of the photo. The car is travelling east on route 1 to East Calgary.
(CRHA – R.F. Corley fonds)

Below: On a busy morning on 8th Avenue at Centre Street, car 88 signed for Bowness route "B" passes eastbound. It will loop via 2nd Street se, 9th Avenue se and Centre Street, then return to 8th Avenue s via the trackage it is about to cross. The date is June 9th 1949.
(Foster M. Palmer)

the right side and yet another in the upper part of the right rear platform window. These route indicators were used for only a few years until Calgary developed its own style of roof-mounted route indicators and applied them to these cars. The Calgary shops added roof-mounted headlight brackets to selected cars in this series to permit their operation on the outlying line to Bowness, and in later years, on the Grand Trunk extension.

The three cars, delivered in November 1928, were numbered 84, 85, and 86. They first saw trial-run service in Calgary on Tuesday November 13th 1928 when one of them went out on the North Hill (Crescent Heights) run with Mayor F.E. Osborne, Commissioner A.G. Graves, Superintendent R.A. Brown and Assistant Superintendent Charles Comba aboard. That same evening, following the Council meeting, the members of City Council and City Hall staff on duty were treated to a trip in one of the new cars, with Mr. Comba at the controls.[51] These cars were subsequently assigned to regular service, one on the Red Line, one on the White Line and one on the Red & White Line. T.C. Scatcherd had the enviable privilege to be among the first regular operators of the new car assigned to the Elbow Park (White Line).[52]

Comfortable, clean interiors and fine riding qualities made these cars an instant hit with Calgarians. Light coloured agasote headlinings and five dome-covered lighting fixtures provided plenty of interior illumination. Woodwork was of birch and stained cherry. The main body of the cars could seat 45 passengers, while the smoking compartment could seat eight, for a total seating capacity of 53 people.

From an operating point of view the cars had the very latest safety devices of the day applied to them. The doors, for example, could only be opened after the application of the air brake. In turn, the interconnection of the air brake and the door-opening motors prevented the release of the brake as long as any door remained open. An open treadle exit door activated the motor-conductor's signal lamp in front of him, indicating that power could not be applied to the motors through the controller. The controller featured a dead-man safety device whereby release of the controller handle and the dead-man foot pedal automatically cut off power, sanded the track, applied the brake and released the pressure on the door mechanism.[53]

In May 1929 the City Commissioners recommended the purchase of six additional identical cars, because passenger riding has increased by 9.3% and revenue by 11.6% over the previous year. Council agreed, and as a result cars 87 through 92 were ordered from the Canadian Car & Foundry Company at a contracted price of $22,560 each.[54] The cars were complete and delivered in October 1929 and represented the final purchase of railway rolling stock for the Calgary Municipal Railway.

Below: Front entrance arrangement with motorman's seat and controls in Calgary's 84 to 92 class trams. Shown from left to right are manual brake wheel, controller with dead man's handle feature, reverse key, air brake and door-control valves, rear door indicator lamp, air gauge, fare box and Montreal-style route indicator guide.
(Glenbow Archives NA-2891-18 left, Glenbow Archives NA-2891-15 right)

Below: The back end of these cars featured a small enclosed Smoking Room beside the rear treadle exit. This smoking compartment was a popular feature on Calgary's one-man streetcars. Many a Calgary boy considered he became a man the day he could sit in the Smoking Room and listen to the opinions of his elders. All seats in these cars were comfortably padded and upholstered with leather.

Above: Double-end cars were a rarity in Calgary, but single-truck "dinky" 22 was maintained for emergency shuttle services. It was photographed August 11th 1939 beside the carbarn.
(CRHA - R.F. Corley fonds)

Below: The first bus on the Calgary Municipal was a Leyland 4-speed gear shift vehicle. It was photographed in 1935 on Talon Avenue with driver Ken Gush.
(Glenbow Archives NA-1131-1)

CHAPTER SEVEN

Deterioration of the Railway

DELIVERY OF CALGARY'S last new cars coincided with the advent of severe economic conditions on the North American continent, bringing a sharp decline in passenger riding. Fortunately, many of the physical properties of the CMR had undergone considerable refurbishing under the pressure of the greatly-increasing traffic demands of the late 1920s, and the railway was in fairly good shape.

The streetcar system, however, suffered two unfortunate mishaps at this time. Two streetcars, numbers 16 and 91, while parked at the car barns in April 1930, caught fire and were extensively damaged inside. The fire spread to three other cars parked nearby, numbers 8, 10 and 25. Car 91 had only been in service a few months at the time of the outbreak and required a complete interior refit. It is suspected that car 10 was scrapped as a result of this incident. Car 16 was completely rebuilt with an arched roof and turned end for end, so that the long end was forward, thus eliminating the need for the front dash door typical of most Calgary wooden one-man cars. It was also equipped with a treadle rear exit and under-platform lifeguard. Cars 25 and 8 were only slightly damaged and were immediately restored to operating condition.[1] It was the second time that a car carrying the unit number 8 had been involved in a fire.

The second setback came during November 1930, when rain and subsequent frost caused between $80,00 and $100,000 damage to track and roadbed.[2] The Elbow Park track and pavement had to be repaired all the way along 4th Street sw from 12th Avenue sw to the Mission Bridge and around the 29th Avenue sw curve south to the loop. Other damaged areas included 14th Street sw from 12th to 17th avenues sw; 8th Avenue sw between 4th Street sw and 6th Street sw, and between 8th and 9th Streets sw; 9th Street sw from 8th Avenue sw to 4th Avenue sw; and on 12th Avenue sw from 6th Street sw to 14th Street sw. These repairs were approved in lieu of installing trackless trolleys or purchasing gasoline-powered buses because of the lower cost involved.[3]

In order to experiment with the feasibility of bus service, however, the City of Calgary signed an agreement with the Brewster Transportation Company Limited to operate motorbuses instead of streetcars on the Elbow Park line for a minimum period of two weeks and a maximum period of four weeks beginning on March 1st 1931.[4] The experiment must have been somewhat of a success, as later in 1931, the street railway began to supply bus service into Mount Royal with rented buses, and in February 1932 Council approved the purchase of two Leyland buses[5] for the Mount Royal service; these vehicles were numbered 300 and 301. It was about this time that street car 300 was taken out of service as the milk and express car, converted back to a full passenger car and assigned the number 36.

With the advent of the buses, men had to be trained to operate them. Tommy Kent, Ken Gush and Dick Steele[6] were the first CMR employees to learn the new skills required for driving these vehicles, which ushered in a new era in public transportation.

Mount Royal residents responded well to the new bus service, in strong contrast to their 1913 refusal to allow a car line to loop through the neighbourhood. In fact, the new buses were such a novelty that they filled up with passengers bound for points closer to the city centre than Mount Royal, leaving Mount Royal residents to complain that they couldn't even board a bus going to their neighbourhood. This forced the CMR to charge an extra fare to ride on them, a practice that continued until June 1938.[7] The enthusiastic reception of the buses was a fortunate turn of events at a time when other transit services were tapering off, resulting in personnel layoffs. The City arranged to have regular motor-conductors lay off two days per month to provide the spare men with work, and all regularly-employed shop men were retained by working out a system of short time.[8] Several cars were taken out of service, among them the scenic car, which no longer drew many sightseeing passengers.

Shifting of the roadbed on the private right-of-way in the Sunnyside cut west of Centre Street Bridge continued to be a common problem in 1930. An advertisement in *The Morning Albertan* advised Sunnyside car patrons that a transfer car was operating from 4th Street NW and 7th Avenue NW down to 10th Street NW and 2nd Avenue NW, to meet the regular Sunnyside car which was forced to turn on the Hillhurst Loop and return to Burns Avenue via 4th Avenue sw, 4th Street sw, 8th Avenue sw-se, and 2nd Street se. This service was to begin on Monday June 9th 1930, and continue for a three-day period.[9] The transfer car is believed to have been double-ended single-truck car 22, held in reserve for just this type of emergency service.

Although unpaved, this private right-of-way was used from time to time by the occasional automobile. Streetcar operators had but 45 minutes to cover the Burns Avenue-Sunnyside run, so didn't waste any time, particularly on the cut where there was little traffic nor any car stops. Ken Gush recalls that he used to pay a boy 5¢ to stoke the coke stove when operated on this line, but one night, motor-conductor Don MacDonald took advantage of the private right-of-way with no traffic to stoke his own stove. While he was bending over attending it with his car running, he ran into an automobile stuck in the mud in the cut.[10]

Above: Car 85 assigned to route 5 Belt Line travels east on 12th Avenue sw at 4th Street sw in August of 1945.
(A.H. Coverdale)

Opposite: A group of motor-conductors on the Calgary Municipal Railway c1930. Identified are: Front row: Slim Gillespie, unknown, Dick Speers, unknown, George Green and Frank Ashley. Second row: John MacQueen, unknown, unknown, Angus MacKay, Ken Gush, unknown, and Clarence Harkley.
(Glenbow Archives PA-1689-19)

Further slides occurred in the fall of 1930 and the early months of 1931, as the toe of the shifting, light, sandy soil, aided by springs in the hillside, continued to press further across the cut. Following each slip, the car line was relocated slightly closer to the outer edge until finally it became evident that a considerable sum would have to be expended to repair the retaining wall sufficiently to prevent the toe of the slide from forcing its way across the car line.[11] Even after major retaining wall work, the cut still shifted and countless times the City Engineer recommended its abandonment. Finally 540 residents of the area petitioned for abandonment, while three residents were opposed; and the urgings of the City Engineer were heeded.[12] The Sunnyside cut was abandoned at the close of service on Wednesday June 28th 1944,[13] and a shuttle bus operated from 10th Street NW into Sunnyside to connect with the Sunnyside cars which turned back on the West Calgary loop. Subsequently a turnaround was built at the bottom of the Sunnyside hill at 7th Avenue NW and 4A Street NW to permit the regular street cars to double back from their approach to the neighbourhood. Following the abandonment of the cut, cars from Burns Avenue approached the downtown and Sunnyside area via 12th Avenue sw to 1st Street sw; 8th Avenue sw; 4th Street sw; 4th Avenue sw and 10th Street sw. The cars returned to Burns Avenue via the same route until reaching 1st Street

sw where they continued east on 8th Avenue sw-se to turn south at 2nd Street se.

As the economically-depressed decade wore on, track rehabilitation continued to be required. In 1933, it was found necessary to replace the original west track on the Centre Street Bridge which had been placed there in 1916, as water was leaking through during rain or thaw and threatening to damage the concrete on the bridge. Cost of this work was minimal as ties and rail were on hand and installation could be done by relief labour. At the same time, approval was given to relay the tracks north of the Langevin Bridge to 1st Avenue NE.[14]

The 1930s marked the end of operation of two street railways on the Canadian prairies – Moose Jaw and Brandon – but the larger municipally-owned systems, although seriously affected, continued to "weather the storm". The Calgary Municipal had a strong financial base and for some time was able to stave off the need for lower fares to attract passengers. Superintendent Brown, in a report to Mayor Davison and Commissioner Riley, pointed out that during the depression, the street railway was not able to pay all operating expenses, fixed charges, taxes and still show a small profit. Mr. Brown noted that throughout its history, the system had contributed a total of $560,450 by way of taxation to the General Account and paid on behalf of the General Account (in fulfillment of the Ogden street car contract), an amount of $484,373. The street railway also paid out $579,000 for construction, repair and maintenance of paved streets over which the car lines operated – a sum which would otherwise have been paid for by General Account.

By quoting these figures, Mr. Brown's intention was to convince Council to give the street railway system relief from paying taxes to the General Account instead of changing the fare structure. He noted that paying passengers decreased 32% from the peak of 1914 to the 1933 level, but the fares had increased only 29.5%. A lowering of fares would only decrease revenues, in Mr. Brown's opinion. He recommended maintaining the fare structure but monitoring the results of other street railway systems which had reduced fares.[15] He also noted that the track-miles per capita in Calgary were greater than on any other street railway system on record. This meant that much track mileage was serving sparsely-populated areas, an unprofitable venture necessitating 15-to-20 minute headways and resulting in lost passengers. In Mr. Brown's words:

"This is unsatisfactory from the rider's point of view and results in many of our prospective passengers being picked up by automobiles. There is no doubt that the private automobile is here to stay and the person who cares little for expense and uses his automobile from choice has probably been lost to us for good except during the very inclement weather when the operation of the private automobile is difficult and unsatisfactory. So instead of ranting over this lost revenue we believe it better to appeal by way of good service to the class of people to whom the difference between 5.6¢ and 5.0¢ means much."[16]

The Chairman of the Special Street Railway Investigation Committee recommended the following as a result of Mr. Brown's report:[17]

a) The $30,000 contribution made by the street railway to the depreciation account be reduced to $12,000 for 1934.

b) The request to drop the 5% tax on gross revenues of the street railway be refused.

c) Fare structure variation to be left to the discretion of the commissioners.

City Council, however, did not agree to the above recommendations, and in November and December 1934, a reduced fare schedule was introduced as a carefully-documented experiment. Adult tickets were available in quantity groups of five for 25¢ or twenty for $1.00. From November 1st to 15th, adult cash fare fares stayed at 10¢, but from November 16th to the close of the experiment on December 31st, the adult fare went to 5¢. Children and student fares remained unchanged. During the first two weeks of the experiment, there was a decrease of 9% in the number of revenue passengers carried over the same period in 1933, and a 6% decrease in revenue. From November 16th to December 31st, there was an increase of 4% in ridership but a decrease of 11½ % in revenue. Over the whole two-month period, only a 1½ % increase in passengers carried was evident while revenue decreased 14% over the same period. The average fare paid before November 1st 1934 was 5.6¢, while

Above: It is Stampede time in Calgary and an air of optimism abounds in this scene as people go about their daily routines. Amid that, streetcar 55 is about to clatter over the 8th Avenue intersection at Centre Street on its way to the carbarns following an early morning assignment. (Foster M. Palmer photo, John F. Bromley collection)

Opposite: 8th Avenue sw showing car 73 turning north into 4th Street sw beside the T.Eaton Co. store, 1929, as an unidentified mother pushes her carriage across the intersection. The car is likely on the Crescent Heights Red & White line. (Canadian National 31829)

it dropped to 4.6¢ during the duration of the experiment.[18] Another fare adjustment took place during this era on the Bowness line. In 1933 and several subsequent summers from May 24th (Victoria Day) – when the Bowness Park opened for the season – until Labour Day early in September, passengers were required to deposit one fare only. The double fare system remained in effect in the September-to-May period and was also reintroduced for the summer months in the late 1930s.

Adventures on the Bowness Line

The ride out to Bowness on a hot summer weekend was as much a part of the experience as the attraction of the park. All afternoon and evening, service was offered every fifteen minutes. The cars travelled in groups or convoys, limited in size by the length of the passing sidings on the line. Two cars hauling trailers plus a single car without a trailer or five single units could be accommodated in each passing siding. Keeping time was not always easy; one troublesome car could throw the whole route off schedule. The task of the Inspector at the Bowness terminal required a lot of patience, good humour and good judgement. J.K. Gush, a retired officer of Calgary Transit, recalled his experience as an inspector or dispatcher at Bowness Park which, on

a fine Sunday, could attract 25,000 people. Twenty-eight streetcars were assigned all day on such a Sunday or holiday to handle the traffic. It was estimated that a big car and its trailer could carry a "crush" load of up to 300 people. On one occasion, he recalled that no cars appeared for some time at the Bowness loop, evidence that there were problems somewhere along the line. Mr. Gush got into his automobile, drove back toward the city and found a number of cars lined up at the CPR underpass. As one car had negotiated its way through the underpass, its trolley had slipped off the wire, jumping up through the spaces between the ties on the railway line above. Since the car could not be moved, and the pole could not be powered, Mr. Gush and some of the motor-conductors in the lineup attempted to remove the pole from the top of the car. In the course of doing so, however, the whistle of an approaching CPR train was heard; the men scrambled from the top of the streetcar in time to see the railway locomotive break off that part of the trolley pole protruding through the ties. The problem of the jammed trolley pole was solved, but the disabled vehicle had to be pushed all the way out to Bowness, then hauled back to the barns.[19] By this time, of course, just about every car on the busy line had come up behind.

Sudden storms on a busy afternoon always tried the patience of the Bowness terminal dispatcher, as hundreds of picnickers quickly packed up their baskets and rushed towards the gates to board the four or five available cars. The good judgement of the dispatcher also came into play on a beautiful weekend evening when people took advantage of the weather to go canoeing on the small lake. As it was the dispatcher's job to decide how many cars he would send back to the barns during the final hours of the evening, he would base his decision on his estimate of the number of canoes still out on the lake. To return too many cars might mean too many passengers to be accommodated on the last car. If he misjudged, and another car had to be called from the barns to take the overload, he was sure of a severe reprimand from a senior street railway officer.[20]

Other Problems

Streetcar motor-conductors seemed to be a target for robberies, especially during the 1930s, as they carried a considerable amount of cash collected from the sale of tickets, as well as a supply of change. The most vulnerable locations for theft were on the outer extremities of the system where there was no street lighting. The usual strategy of the would-be-thief was to pull the trolley pole off the wire, making

the car both dark and immobile. The motor-conductor would be ambushed when he left his car to put the pole back on the wire. This happened one night in 1932 to John MacDonald on the Capitol Hill loop at 20th Avenue NW and 15th Street NW. He found himself confronted by a man wearing a mask over the lower part of his face and holding a gun. Mr. MacDonald recalls that "...he told me that he was in a hurry and to hand over my money. This didn't particularly appeal to me, even if it was the City's money, so I tried to stall and move closer to him at the same time, pretending that I was trying to fix the trolley. Then I took my chance and made a grab for him. That was evidently the wrong move; he shot point blank at my head. He turned and ran into the darkness, just disappeared. The badge saved my life but the bullet creased my skull. There was a lot of blood but I proceeded to crawl to the nearest home in sight; it was the home of Mr. and Mrs. MacLeod. They phoned the police after helping me in. The bandit was never captured."[21] The steel badge on Mr. MacDonald's uniform cap had saved his life. Two weeks later he was back on the job, but for some time after, he and many other night men would barely slow down at these loops, forcing passengers to scramble to get aboard. Another motor-conductor, Sam

Above: Grand Trunk loop line car 55 on Kensington Road, June 19th 1947. (Foster M. Palmer)

Below: On a westbound run to Bowness, car 91 drifts down the west ramp away from the Shouldice Bridge.
(Percy W. Browning)

Opposite: In the mid-1930s car 77 stops on 8th Avenue sw at 1st Street sw in front of the Bank of Montreal building. The Hudson's Bay department store is to the left. The car is westbound on the Crescent Heights Red & White route. Following behind is car 84 which is signed for Elbow Park.
(Colin K. Hatcher collection)

Emery, was held up and shot on the East Calgary loop. He, too, fortunately survived the ordeal.[22]

The depression's economic vacuum created a number of difficulties for the railway. Service was reduced, resulting in a need for fewer men and thus increasing unemployment. Route changes were common during this period, in an attempt to get the best possible use of equipment and manpower. On Monday April 3rd 1933, a new routing system was introduced which altered the Blue line, White line, Killarney and South Calgary tram routes as well as the Mount Royal bus route. The changes left the section of 12th Avenue sw from 8th Street sw to 1st Street sw and 4th Street sw from 17th Avenue sw to 12th Avenue sw without streetcar service. Also, 2nd Street se received considerably less service than previously.[23]

The new routes were economy measures which brought considerable protest from Calgarians. Many noted the service greatly favoured people living west of 1st Street sw. Mr. Brown agreed, since traffic studies had indicated that 75% of the traffic came from points west of 1st Street sw while the remaining 25% was picked up east of 2nd Street se. As occurred in 1924, public reaction forced a return to the original routing shortly after the change went into effect.

Another schedule and route change was presented to Council on March 28th 1934. It proposed the coupling of the Elbow Park and Tuxedo Park service on a ten-minute headway via Centre Street, and eliminating that part of the service east of Centre Street and 16th Avenue NE. Manchester-Riverside was set up as a through route, with twenty-minute regular service and fifteen-minute rush hour service. The Red & Blue Line cars provided a new service

with twenty-minute headway from Sunnyside to Burns Avenue, also stepped up to fifteen-minute service in rush hour. The Killarney route remained unchanged, providing a twenty-minute regular service and a ten-minute rush hour service.

South Calgary cars did not have their route changed, and provided the same headways as the Killarney cars. The Ogden and Bowness routes were unchanged, offering a car every hour. Ogden, however, did get half-hour service between 3:30 PM and 7 PM. The Red Line did not change in routing and offered a fifteen-minute service, as did the Grand Trunk car, except that it offered no service between 9 AM and noon, and finished at 11 PM daily. Bus service was scheduled every half hour on the Mount Royal run and tram service on 12th Avenue NW was replaced by a regular ten-minute bus service between Centre Street and 7th Street NW in Rosedale, operating along 12th and 13th avenues NW.

It was noted that during inclement weather, in the morning, the Rosedale bus would run through 10th Street NW and 16th Avenue NW for the convenience of students at the Technical Institute. The Sunalta route was slated for complete cessation of service.[24]

Two more extensive changes were proposed, one for the Crescent Heights and Blue Line and the other for the Capitol Hill area. The Crescent Heights and Blue lines were combined, with a twenty-minute regular service in each direction. While this was fairly straightforward to passengers, motor-conductors found this situation very confusing as they had to stop and think carefully about where they were going to go in their circuit each time that they went

Bowness Park..

Operated by Calgary Municipal Railway

Bowness Park Officially Opens on Victoria Day, May 24th and closes after Labor Day in September, each year.

CALGARY'S most popular park. It is an ideal place to spend an afternoon, an evening, a day, week or month! This park has many attractions to offer; there is lots to see and do at Bowness: See the Illuminated Fountain in the Lagoon . . . Hear the Orthophonic Concert and News Broadcasts . . . dance in the Pavilion . . . swim in the large Out-door Pool . . . go canoeing or boating . . . play miniature golf . . . have a jolly picnic. Cottages for rent are equipped with electric lights. Pavilions for large picnics.

Especially for the children there is a well-equipped playgrounds . . . swings . . . slides . . . wading pool . . . merry-go-round and confections at the Pavilion.

BOATING . . .

Dancing at BOWNESS PARK

BABY CARRIAGES

Baby carriages are not allowed on street cars between the hours of 4:30 p.m. and 6:30 p.m. Not more than two baby carriages will be allowed on one street car at the same time.

LOST PROPERTY

Make sure you have not left any belongings on this car.

The Department will not be responsible for lost property.

Enquiries regarding lost articles may be made by calling the Lost Property Office, M 1910.

FARE RATES IN EFFECT

Adults—10c cash, 2 tickets, 15c, 4 for 25c.

Students—5c cash, 10 tickets, 25c. (Students' Identification Cards must be presented when purchasing tickets or when requested by operator.)

Children—5c cash, 10 tickets, 25c. (14 years of age and under.)

Dogs—10c cash, or 2 adult street car tickets.

NOTE: Passengers are requested to deposit their own ticket or cash fare in fare box on entering car.

RIDE THE STREET CARS

TO YOUR

. Zoo .

ON ST. GEORGE'S ISLAND

THE FINEST ZOO AND NATURAL HISTORY PARK IN CANADA

While there is no admission fee the Zoological Society needs and welcomes donations.

Visit and Support Your Zoo.

ATTENDANCE PER YEAR APPROXIMATELY 250,000

Above: Advertising for Bowness Park on the Calgary Municipal Street Railway timetable No. 4, January 22nd 1945. (Colin K. Hatcher collection)

Below: The motorman of car 33 pauses for a chat with a colleague before pulling ahead into the loop at Bowness. Note the "CALGARY" lettering on the centre of the carbody. This lettering arrangement was apparently applied to this car and five similar ones after they were delivered to Calgary through a trade with Saskatoon in 1919. During the 1920s other Calgary cars emerged from the paint shop similarly lettered. (Percy W. Browning)

Above: Car 13 on the Calgary Municipal Railway underpass beneath the Canadian Pacific Railway on the streetcar line to Bowness. Photograph taken in August 1947.
(W.C. Whittaker)

through the downtown area. The Capitol Hill area was to get a shuttle car service along 20th Avenue to Centre Street. Rails for 20th Avenue NW from 4th Street NW to 10th Street NW were to be taken from the 3rd Street NE line and 29th Avenue NE connection to Centre Street.

Effective Friday July 6th 1934, most of the changes outlined came into effect, after Council had taken some time to consider the matter. The following deviated from the original proposal: Capitol Hill cars operated on a twenty-minute shuttle service along 20th Avenue NW from 15th Street NW to Centre Street. The rail used to connect the gap between 4th Street NW and 10th Street NW came from tearing up one line of double track on the southernmost portion of the Manchester line. Bridgeland-Riverside did become part of the Manchester route, operating via 2nd Street SE, but Manchester had service every twenty-four minutes, while Bridgeland-Riverside was favoured with twelve-minute service. Sunalta service became a shuttle-only to 12th Avenue SW and 14th Street SW, connecting with Blue Line and South Calgary cars rather than being curtailed completely.[25] Cars 79 and 81 were refitted for double-end operation on the new Capitol Hill line since no loop was ever constructed at Centre Street and 20th Avenue NW.

Several protests grew out of this schedule, notably from areas where services were curtailed, such as the Edmonton Trail-3rd Street NE (Mountainview) area, the 4th Street SW area and the Sunalta area. People in the Capitol Hill district were not happy with their car service either. In September 1934, the Street Railway Committee presented a report to Council suggesting further route revisions, but these recommendations had not been acted upon by mid-January 1935. The Council did authorize the purchase of another bus to ensure the system had sufficient buses to cover emergency and expanded rush-hour services;[26] however, this authorization was apparently not acted upon. A Sunday bus service was implemented between Rosedale and Mount Royal for a trial period beginning Sunday January 27th 1935, and concluding Sunday February 28th.[27, 28, 29]

Suffice it to say that 4th Street NW and 12th Avenue NW had seen the end of streetcar service. Routes were again re-adjusted late in 1934 or 1935, with Capitol Hill cars returning to their original run on 10th Street NW, and White Line cars from Elbow Park operating north on Centre Street to 20th Avenue NW. At this point, alternate White Line cars turned west on 20th Avenue NW to a new loop (Mount Pleasant) constructed at 7th Street NW, while the remaining White Line cars continued north on Centre Street to Tuxedo Park loop at 32nd Avenue NE. Cars bound for the city from Tuxedo Park turned east onto new track on 23rd Avenue NE to the Edmonton Trail, then south on the Trail to 16th Avenue NE; west to Centre Street and on down to Elbow Park. This arrangement was designed to accommodate the Mountainview residents. The construction of the 23rd Avenue NE connection permitted abandonment of track on 29th Avenue NE, 1st Street NE and 24th Avenue NE.

Above: Car 14 followed by a second car discharges passengers at Bowness Park. Once everyone is off the cars they will move forward to the turning loop to await their return to the city centre. The rural nature of this locale is very evident in this photograph. (Percy W. Browning)

Below: At Bowness passengers disembark from car 84. The car is equipped with a roof-mounted headlight, necessary for night service on this outlying line. The open country is very evident in this scene. (John F. Bromley collection)

New Route Identification

At some time during the summer of 1936, Calgary street-cars lost their very characteristic coloured route markers, to be supplanted by a route numbering system. A partial route numbering system had been introduced in 1928 and 1929 with delivery of the new steel cars which did not have any provisions on them for the coloured indicators. At that time, the steel cars carried route number 10 for the east-west line (Red Line), route number 12 for Elbow Park (White Line) and route number 14 for Crescent Heights (Red & White Line). These numbers appeared on the coloured route markers of the old cars. The 1936 system saw the complete demise of the coloured route indicators in favour of a single numeral or letter. The new route symbols were displayed on the trams on two sides of square black boxes – one mounted on the right side of the front platform roof, the other on the left side of the rear platform roof. These "jack o' lantern"-type route indicators were illuminated at night by light shining from within through holes punched in the outline of the appropriate numeral or letter. A route could be readily identified in daylight because the symbol was also painted in white on the black background of the box. The route identifications are illustrated on page 193.

This type of route identification was patterned after those found on the street railway systems of the San Francisco and Los Angeles areas. The route indicator change was Mr. Brown's last significant mark on the Calgary Municipal Railway, because, in 1937, he resigned from his position with the City of Calgary.

Charles Comba was appointed as the Superintendent of the Street Railway Department upon recommendation of the commissioners on June 18th 1937.[30]

Above: Aerial view of the single-tracked 12th Avenue Bridge, showing streetcar 43 on Route 8 heading towards downtown. (Foster M. Palmer)

Below: Student ticket (front and back) courtesy Edmonton Radial Railway Society Fonds Eric Smith. CMR transfer courtesy Edmonton Radial Railway Society Fonds Leslie Corness.

Above: One of the final missions of Calgary's Scenic Car – exhorting patriotic Canadians to invest in Canada Victory Bonds. George Adie was the pilot in charge.
(Glenbow Archives NA-1299-3. copy of 855-10)
(Below: Ed Radcliffe photo, Rich Krisak collection)

Below: It is May 1939 and Calgary is preparing to welcome Their Majesties King George VI and Queen Elizabeth. Each of Calgary's streetcars carried a pair of Union Jack flags mounted on either side of the destination sign. Here car 51, on its route 1 West Calgary assignment, stops on its westbound trip along 8th Avenue s at Centre Street.

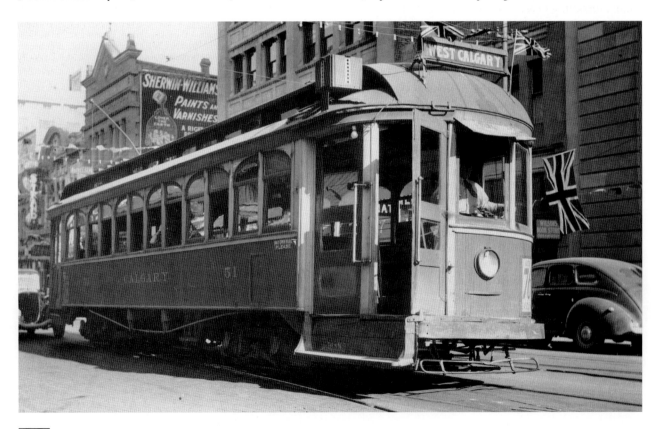

CHAPTER EIGHT

The Final Mobilization

CHARLES COMBA TOOK ON the task of operating the Calgary Municipal street railway on the eve of the system being confronted by a requirement for it to perform at a level never before experienced. For the first time since 1913-14, the regular performance of every available car on the system would be demanded for almost half a decade.

Throughout the 1930s, only the best of the streetcars were kept in operating condition, leaving a considerable lineup of cars which were being held for parts and accessories at a time when the system could ill afford to purchase them. Almost as if in expectation of an emergency, the cars taken out of service were not scrapped, but merely stored unserviceable, with the exception of the single-truck cars numbered 22, 23, 27 and 35. Car 22, a double-ender, had been held for emergency shuttles and was available for service until after 1939. It appears that it was involved in a collision at some point after this time and was never repaired. It eventually became derelict as it sat in the yard without attention, its services no longer required, since a bus could be more readily used in the type of service to which it had previously been assigned.

Car 35, for many years the "anchor" of the Grand Trunk service, became a lunch room for carbarn employees.[1] Cars 23 and 27, never equipped with route box numbers, were taken out of service and used for storage in the carbarn area. Auxiliary number 26, the single-truck car with the shorn-off rear platform, was also removed from service before the 1940s and replaced by car 80.

The visit of Their Majesties King George VI and Queen Elizabeth in May 1939 was celebrated on the CMR by equipping each car in regular service with a pair of Union Jack flags, mounted at the roof on either side of the destination sign. Shortly after the 1939 Royal Visit, World War II broke out. The demand for street railway services suddenly increased, as industrial production developed to meet wartime needs. People turned back to public transportation increasingly as gasoline was rationed and automobile tires became unavailable. The maintenance shops of the Calgary Municipal Railway once again became an active area, as streetcars previously withdrawn from service were rapidly restored to serviceable condition. In March 1943, Superintendent Comba reported to Council that 76 motor cars and four trailers were available[2] and in almost daily use. Seven more motor cars and two more trailers were out of service.[3] By the close of that year, four of these motor cars were back in service with the remaining three scheduled for return to operation early in 1944.[4]

Route changes were very uncommon during the 1940s, but car headways were greatly reduced everywhere on the system. Schedules were adjusted from time to time to accommodate special wartime activities. A loop was installed on the Ogden line at the RCAF Equipment Depot to allow short-turning of cars for better utilization. At one point, consideration was given to the construction of a car line to the Currie Barracks, but this was turned down in favour of a shuttle bus service between the barracks and the number 7 South Calgary car line. The shortage of cars left Mr. Comba to reintroduce the skip-stop system all across the city so that a car could cover each trip in a shorter span of time.

Throughout the war, everything possible was done to keep the cars running at peak efficiency as no new equipment was available. Owl runs up to this time had involved a car on each of the major routes operating until 1 AM, but during the war years, an all-night service was provided by one car from 2 AM to 6 AM operating from East Calgary on the hour, to the North Hill via Centre Street, west via 16th Avenue NW, south via 10th Street NW to 8th Avenue SW and then south to the Belt Line on 8th Street SW to 12th Avenue SW; 14th Street SW; 17th Street SW; 1st Street SW; and then returning to 8th Avenue SW-SE and back to East Calgary.[5] Double fare was charged to riders taking advantage of these after midnight services.

Victory Bonds were commonly promoted across Canada by the local street railway systems. Montreal selected certain regular service passenger cars to be specially painted for these promotions. Toronto had a work car profusely decorated, and Regina cars each carried a V sign on them. In Calgary, the scenic car was given a final lease on life and made its way through the streets carrying Victory Bond banners, with motor-conductor George Adie piloting most of these promotional trips. Victory was celebrated in the streets on Monday May 7th 1945, with the announcement that the war on the European front would officially end on the following day at 9 AM. Calgarians became so vivacious that all streetcars were called into the barns at 4 PM, as disruptions due to wild celebrating had already occurred and street railway officials were concerned that some of the cars might be damaged in the revelry, a situation which they could ill afford to face.

Winter Problems

Calgary's hills and unpredictable climatic conditions made a mockery of the renowned adhesion of the steel wheel to the steel rail. Such problems plagued the system

Opposite, upper: In this c1940 view, the Hudson's Bay store extends the full block and the Bank of Montreal has a new building, while westward, Eaton's three flags are still blowing in the southern breeze. Today, this once-busy thoroughfare is a shopping mall, completely devoid of vehicular traffic.
(Canadian Pacific 6651)

Opposite, lower: This view looks north on 1st Street sw across 8th Avenue sw. A bus occupies the curb lane while a streetcar on route 6 Killarney eases up to the intersection to prepare for its left hand turn into 8th Avenue sw. A route 7 South Calgary car makes a right hand turn off 8th Avenue into 1st Street sw. One of the "20-class" trades from Saskatoon pauses in its left turn into 1st Street sw as it likely prepares to head out to Elbow Park. Compare this view with the one on page 44.
(Canadian Pacific M4094)

Above: CMR 67 ascending the troublesome hill on 14th Street sw south of 17th Avenue sw, May 30th 1948. This was the hill down which tram 68 skid in 1919 and the scene of the 1946 accident where cars 67 and 89 collided.
(W.C. Whittaker)

throughout its life. Motor-conductors found that the best adhesion conditions prevailed just after a heavy rain storm, when all of the grease and grime seemed to get washed off the rails. Hills were always a problem in winter. Ascending cars often backed down to take another run at some hills, and platform men often had difficulty in trying to prevent an overzealous descent. Motor-conductor Jim Hughes told of having to open his controller to half power, then get out of the car to sweep the frost off the rails as he ascended Cemetery Hill on the Manchester run for his first trip out

on a frosty morning. He also recalled how the poplar leaves would fall on the right-of-way of the Elbow Park line, where it skirted the Elbow River bank. They would render the brakes and reverse power completely useless, as the car slithered with locked wheels over leaf-covered rails. A streetcar could glide out of control for two or three blocks under these very dangerous conditions.[6]

Frosty rail problems led to the second accident on the 14th Street sw hill, at 6:30 AM on Tuesday morning January 29th 1946. It was close to a repeat performance of the December 15th 1919 accident, except that motor-conductor Kurtz knew he wouldn't be turning the corner at the bottom of the hill. Mr. Kurtz stopped his car – number 67 – to pick up passengers at 25th Avenue sw, but skidded right past those waiting at 23rd Avenue sw. He realized then that he was about to skid through the 17th Avenue sw intersection. When he saw car 89 on the Belt Line about to turn in front of him, he shouted to his passengers to drop to the floor, and whistled continuously at the Belt Line car. Motor-conductor Brinton on number 89 did not realize that car 67 was out of control, so he proceeded normally into the turn; the cars collided with a terrific thump. Car 89 was thrown over on its side and forced against a steel pole on the corner, which severely damaged its roof.[7] While wooden car 67 was left without a front platform, it remained upright and was pulled back to the shops by the auxiliary car. Steel car 89 was raised up high enough to get a couple of sets of dolly trucks under it, and was hauled to the shops on its side. No. 67 was subsequently repaired and sent back into service but No. 89 never returned to duty. Fortunately, no serious personal injuries resulted from the accident.

Above: On a sunny September 9th 1944, car 29, in service as a southbound extra on route 3, picks up some well-dressed passengers on Centre Street just north of the bridge. Automobiles, in customary fashion, line up behind the stopped streetcar. Extra service, operating on this route as far north as Centre Street and 23rd Avenue, provided 7½-minute service between the hours of 12 noon and 8 PM. The track and overhead connecting at this point is the recently abandoned Sunnyside cut.
(Andrew Merrilees collection,
Ernie Plant/National Archives of Canada/PA174283)

Below: Car 56 travels eastbound on route 9 Riverside along 8th Avenue sw at 1st Street sw past the columns of the Hudson's Bay department store. The car is coming from Sunnyside. Note the automobile behind the streetcar.
(John F. Bromley collection, photographer unknown)

Opposite: A cold March morning as No. 50 heads back from Ogden along 42nd Avenue se. Photo taken near Sixteenth Street se on March 18th 1950. (Robert W. Gibson)

The usual concerns for the ageing streetcar fleet prompted some public consternation about the accident. Many people were suggesting that better equipment such as the steel cars should be assigned to the hill runs.[8] Mr. Comba was quick to point out that all cars in service were mechanically safe. He noted that the light-weight steel cars did not perform at their best on the steep hill runs and as a result, they were always assigned to less undulating routes such as the east-west run and the number 5 Belt Line. Many Calgarians, during the final years of the rail transit system, seemed to take issue with any small faults in the streetcars. There were complaints about the cars equipped with only two steps – trams which had previously been held for extra service but had been pressed into regular use during the war. The system had forty cars with the two-step arrangement; Mr. Comba was reluctant to spend an estimated $12,400 to equip them with the folding three-step feature because many of the cars were due for retirement.[9]

Rails to Rubber

The impending change from rails to rubber tires brought with it a change in management as well. Upon the retirement in 1946 of Mr. Hargreaves, Assistant Superintendent,

C.V.F. Weir was appointed to fill his position.[10] Later in 1946, Mr. Comba retired as Superintendent and Mr. Weir moved up to take his position. Mr. Weir then hired R.H. Wray as his Engineer to work on the planned conversion from streetcars to trolley coaches. The important and once-proud role that the street railway had played in the development of Calgary was diminishing, and the cars became objects of scorn as citizens looked forward to the arrival of buses to replace them. As if to hurry along the change even before the conversion program had begun in earnest, the name Calgary Municipal Railway was dropped in favour of the new corporate title, Calgary Transit System, which was officially adopted by Council on July 19th 1946.[11]

The first major conversion from streetcars to buses came about on June 1st 1947, when trams were retired from route 4 Crescent Heights line. The Capitol Hill tram service which fed into route 4 was also discontinued at this time. Later in June 1947, streetcars were replaced by diesel buses on route 9 to Manchester, but Bridgeland (Riverside) continued to be served by cars which looped in the downtown area.[12]

The closing of the Manchester line brought an end to the only staff signalling system ever in operation in Calgary. In the mid-1930s, one of the double tracks on that line

Opposite, upper: During the last few months of Calgary streetcar operation in 1950, car 42, then the regularly assigned Ogden car, passes the oil storage tanks of Imperial Oil and under the Canadian National Railways approach to Calgary. The line to Ogden passed through open tracts of industrial land but its destination was a residential area just beyond the CPR Ogden shops. (Robert W. Gibson)

Opposite, lower: CMR 45 on Tenth Street NW approaching Louise Bridge over the Bow River, May 30th 1948. Note that the overhead has been installed for the trolley coach operation. During the changeover period the trams operated on one of the same trolley wires. (W.C. Whittaker)

Above: Track in pavement had to be taken out of the pavement to be repaired or replaced. Often that was done by clasping the rail end with a hook-and-chain, then having the work car pull it free. Once streetcar service ended, some of the rail in pavement was simply left in place. (Percy W. Browning)

had been lifted from 40th Avenue SE back to the top of Cemetery Hill, to be used in constructing the 20th Avenue NW line. This left the Manchester line with a long stretch of single track which hampered operations at rush hours, particularly throughout the 1940-46 period. The motor-conductor about to go south from Cemetery Hill, from double track to single track, was required to pick up a wooden staff kept in a locked receptacle at the top of the hill where the double track ended.

He was not permitted to leave the double track section without having this staff in his possession. If the staff was not in the locked box, this indicated that another car was already occupying the section. The southbound car thus had to wait until the opposing car had passed and given up the staff.[13]

Further 1947 conversions included the early August demise of all streetcar service on Centre Street, as far as

Mount Pleasant and Tuxedo Park. The Elbow Park rail route remained in operation until trolley coach overhead was erected on Centre Street, in turn releasing gasoline buses for service on the Elbow Park section. Elbow Park cars ran through to Riverside during this brief period, giving that section of the city ten-minute service for a couple of months.[14] Late in the fall of 1948, car services on routes 5 Belt Line, 6 Killarney and 7 South Calgary were terminated. Effective Sunday October 24th 1948, South Calgary passengers were transferred from the streetcar to a gasoline bus at 14th Street SW and 17th Avenue SW to continue their journeys to South Calgary. The Killarney cars made their final trips west of this intersection on Saturday November 13th 1948, the abandoned portion also being serviced by gasoline buses. Finally, on November 29th 1948, all streetcar service over the Belt Line was withdrawn, and through trolley coach runs began on routes 5, 6 and 7.[15]

The districts of Bowness and Grand Trunk were incorporated into route 1 during the year 1948. Such cars signed West Calgary extended their trips to loop through Grand Trunk via Kensington Road, 14th Street NW, 8th and 7th avenues NW, 24th Street NW, then east on Kensington Road and through to East Calgary. Cars carrying a **B** designation ran from Bowness all the way through to East Calgary. The last streetcars on route 1 ran December 7th 1949;[16] after that date, Bowness cars ceased operation to East Calgary, looping downtown via 2nd Street SE, 9th Avenue SE and Centre Street. Service on Riverside-Sunnyside had terminated one month earlier, the final trips occurring on Saturday evening November 5th 1949.[17] The special Ogden streetcar transferred its passengers to and from a bus at 4th Street SE and 8th Avenue SE.

Above: Canadian Pacific's Calgary station forms a background for tram 50, photographed on Centre Street just north of 9th Avenue, March 18th 1950.
(Robert W. Gibson)

Below: Leaving downtown for Bowness. CMR 55 turns the corner of 9th Avenue and Centre Street, March 18th 1950. CPR offices and baggage-handling facilities are in the background – the railway station is just out of view to the right.
(Robert W. Gibson)

Opposite: The "Last Scheduled Run" on the erstwhile Calgary Municipal Railway – then know as the Calgary Transit System – was handled by Operator R. Thompson with streetcar 14 on December 29th 1950.
(Glenbow Archives NA-2891-9)

Opposite, lower: Bowness Park transfer and card.
(Percy W. Browning collection)

The Last Scheduled Run

The year 1950 marked the termination of streetcar operation in Calgary. Bowness had seen the last of the big summer movements in 1949 as the final run to the Park was made on April 12th 1950.[18] Burns Avenue cars made their last circuit on Friday evening November 11th 1950,[19] leaving only the Ogden route still served by rail.

Calgarians were, on the whole, happy to see the era of the tram quickly passing; but with the departure of the electric cars, an era of skill and pride peculiar only to the streetcar also passed. Going with the cars were the days when a motor-conductor would, in jest, remove his controller handle as he trundled along to wave it out the window at a passing motor-conductor, who picked it out of his startled cohort's hand as they passed. The prankster had to resort to throwing his power breaker off to stop the car, then walk back and pick up his stray controller handle.[20] It seemed, however, that Calgary Transit wished to perpetuate the informal streetcar flavour for as long as possible, as the newer steel cars had found their way into the retirement ranks by early 1950, leaving the older heavy wooden trams to finish up the service. One of the "tricks of the trade" required to keep a car on schedule was the need to load, unload and get away from a car stop as quickly as possible. The wooden cars were devoid of the automatic safety devices linking the door opening and the braking systems. For this reason they were preferred by most motor-conductors over the steel cars which took precious extra seconds at each stop, because the latter could not be moved until all the safety devices had released the brakes. The motor-conductors could be proud of their safety record in avoiding injury to passengers boarding and alighting from the cars – while still keeping to a tight schedule, without having to rely on the automatic safety features available on only a small percentage of the total fleet of cars. Mechanical safety, particularly concerning air brake maintenance, was of prime concern to the shop staff as long as any car was in service.

During the last few years of service, motor-conductors also knew the gears on the cars were getting well worn, leaving plenty of slack as the gear teeth engaged. A motor-conductor who released his brakes, then opened his controller to the first notch, found his car would suddenly bolt forward, leaving standing passengers scrambling for a better grip. In order to avoid this discomfort to passengers, an experienced operator would leave the air brakes on, then open the controller and gingerly release the air brake, resulting in a much smoother start. Under normal operating conditions, such a practice would be frowned upon, as power consumption would be unnecessarily increased.

Rush-hour motor-conductors who pulled trailer cars relied upon a skilful conductor on the trailer to hustle passengers off and on, and then relay a prompt curt signal on the gong indicating that car and trailer could safely proceed. Motor-conductors also learned a great deal about their car so that they could perform small maintenance tasks with-

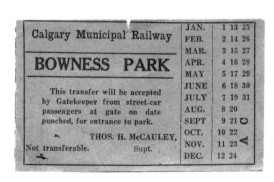

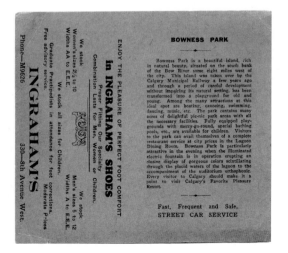

Above: The Alberta Stockyards was a busy place and the location of the wye which allowed Ogden cars to travel back to downtown Calgary via either the CPR overhead bridge or the CPR level crossing near the Burns Avenue streetcar loop. The overhead bridge was the preferred route. Car 16 has just passed the wye and is proceeding from Ogden to the overhead bridge and on to the carbarns following its early morning run to Ogden. Most of the early morning cars laid over at Ogden all day but some always did return to the carbarns to be available for other runs – often school charters – during the day.
(Percy W. Browning)

Below: Car 55 at the Shouldice Siding, just after crossing the Bow River on the Bowness line, March 18th 1950. Note the length of the siding track built to accommodate the long convoys of streetcars travelling in summer to and from Bowness Park.
(Robert W. Gibson)

Opposite: CMR 53 over the pit in the Calgary shops. Note the extra headlight carried by cars on the suburban runs at night.
(Foster M. Palmer)

out calling for a replacement car. They learned very early in their career that to call for a spare car from the shops often meant getting stuck for the remainder of their shift with a more cumbersome car than the one they sent into the shops. They also found, if their car was not equipped with a windshield wiper, that a bar of soap, some chewing tobacco or wet grass rubbed over the outside of their front window pane would make the rain water run evenly down the pane, giving them a better view of the track ahead.

Operating rules were often effectively enforced among the crews by the men themselves. Les Armour recounted an experience he had on the Bowness line one dark night as he waited for his meet at the Shouldice Bridge siding. As his meet approached the siding, it stopped, the motor-conductor got off and walked toward Armour's car. As Armour opened the door to greet his co-worker, his big auxiliary headlight went out, accompanied by the sound of breaking glass. The motor-conductor then admonished Armour for not turning out his big headlight while in the passing siding, walked back to his own car and proceeded on his way. Having to make the balance of the trip to Bowness and back without the use of his big headlight on the unlit right-of-way effectively impressed upon Armour the ruling about extinguishing the bright light when passing a car running in the opposite direction. How the broken light was explained to the shop staff is not known.

Ken Gush tells of a harrowing experience when he stopped his packed White Line car one Sunday afternoon just after picking up the day shift workers from the Holy Cross Hospital. A Blue Line car, stalled part-way around the intersection at 12th Avenue sw and 1st Street sw, had suffered a broken trolley rope. The trolley was off the overhead, the pole extending almost vertically through the maze of intersection wires, with the dangling retriever rope partially wound around a guy wire. Motor-conductor Gush climbed atop the stalled car and, with all his weight, managed to get the pole down so that he could maneuver it back onto the wire. Having successfully accomplished this and still on the roof, he heard the air compressor start up, the front door of the car close, and the car got under way with him riding on the roof, the guy wires slipping quickly past his head. He cautiously crawled along the roof to the front of the car, and pounded on the roof over the operator's head. That worthy gentleman, thinking that the pole had gone off the wire again, responded by making a heavy brake application. Fortunately the roof-mounted destination sign saved Mr. Gush from falling right off the front of the car. After some sharp verbal exchanges with his colleague, which fortunately are no longer a matter of record, motor-conductor Gush walked back some distance to his own car and boarded it to the cheers of his own passengers, most of whom had disembarked from the car to better observe the spectacle.[21]

Almost every motor-conductor could recount the experience of being thrown to the floor of his car from his perch on its wooden stool by an unexpected lurch into an intersection, after passing an unobserved open switch. These situations usually occurred when there were few passengers aboard and the operator was preoccupied counting transfers or change.

Occasionally, passengers received their shares of the action, too, when cars ran into unexpected turns.[22]

On the morning of December 27th 1950, a fire of unknown origin destroyed much of the 1909 carbarn building. Five streetcars, including two steel cars inside the barn, were destroyed. Flames did spread to and destroy another car body, in the course of being dismantled, parked in the yard adjacent to the building. Fortunately, no one was injured. The fire had no impact on operations as only the Ogden line was still being serviced by streetcars, and all of the cars used in that service were out at Ogden at the time of the fire. All other Calgary Transit operations had previously been transferred to the new facilities in Eau Claire.

The terminus for Calgary's rail transit system was finally reached on December 29th 1950, when car 14 made the last official farewell run from Ogden into the city, completing exactly 38 years of service to the Ogden area and 41½ years of service in Calgary. Number 14 had been in service since 1911, and it was appropriate that it should figure in the closing ceremonies, however restrained they might be in contrast with last runs in other cities.

The termination coincided closely with the conclusion of Calgary's 75th Anniversary celebrations. In preparation for the last trip, Mayor D.H. Mackay, City Commissioners and City Council members had themselves photographed standing in front of the 75th Anniversary cake at City Hall. From this point, they took a special bus to Ogden where they boarded car number 14 waiting to take them back into the city. Several notables were also on hand for the run, includ-

Above: Route 6 Killarney car 5 is bound for the city centre as it plies its way eastbound along 17th Avenue sw mid-way between 9th and 8th streets sw.
(W.C. Whittaker)

Below: Little traffic was visible on 34th Avenue sw in June 1946 as South Calgary car 40 leaned heavily into the corner onto 14th Street sw. (W.C. Whittaker)

Opposite: Auxiliary 80, painted a bright silver in contrast to all other Calgary cars, was the only unit in operation in January 1951. Photographed near the carbarns with the Exhibition Grounds grandstand in the background.
(Anthony Clegg)

ing Arthur G. Graves who, as a City Commissioner, rode on the first streetcar in Calgary in 1909. Mr. Graves had actually been a member of City Council when the first bylaw approving the construction of the street railway was passed in 1907. Soon after that time Mr. Graves became a Commissioner responsible for the building and operation of what became the Calgary Municipal Railway. Commissioner Graves could well be regarded as one of the original architects of the railway, and it was to him that men like Thomas H. McCauley, Robert A. Brown and Charles Comba answered as the railway grew and changed with the times. Transit Superintendent R.H. Wray had also arranged for retired Superintendent Charles Comba – who as a motorman had actually operated Calgary's first stretcar on July 5th 1909, to operate the last car for part of the trip into the city. Motor-conductor Bob Thompson had the privilege of running the car for the balance of the trip to 1st Street sw and 8th Avenue sw. Mayor Mackay suggested that everyone get out, circle the car and sing Auld Lang Syne during the 5:15 PM rush hour.

From this corner, number 14 followed the same route as the first 1909 car, to 2nd Street SE and 17th Avenue SE, where the official party transferred from the streetcar to a 48-passenger trolley coach for the trip back to City Hall.[23]

Car 14 continued the short trip down 2nd Street SE to the carbarns, to take its place at the end of the line of darkened, still, silent streetcars. Passenger services on what had once been the Calgary Municipal Railway had ended.

The power was left on over remaining rail lines only long enough to allow the two work cars and the shop derrick to take up the track. Calgary Municipal had built much of its line by putting up the overhead first and then using railway equipment to lay the track. Now the reverse was happening, and after the rails came up, the overhead wires came down.

Epilogue

Streetcars operated in Calgary for a period of just over 41 years. It has been 59 years since the abandonment of streetcar service in Calgary. Those who recall the experience of riding a streetcar as a regular means of getting around in Calgary, and indeed in all Canadian cities, is (with the exception of Toronto) diminishing quickly. The Calgary streetcars, as they were retired, were dismantled from their trucks, and all of their air brake and electrical parts removed. The bodies were offered for sale, and most went to use outside the city as cottages, roadside diners or as farm storage buildings. Sixteen cars found their way to a motel project at Bragg Creek a few miles west of Calgary. Thirteen of those car bodies became cabins for accommodation, while three others were converted into a shower area, a coffee bar and an interdenominational church. Fire of unknown origin destroyed at least one car while it stood off its trucks at the carbarn yard, and on December 27th 1950, five serviceable cars were destroyed when the carbarns were swept by fire. One car, number 14, was held with a view to preservation.

During the summer of 1975, trolley cars commenced operating over a 3300-foot private right-of-way. The route connected Heritage Park with the intersection of Heritage Drive and 14th Street sw and to the parking lot near that point.

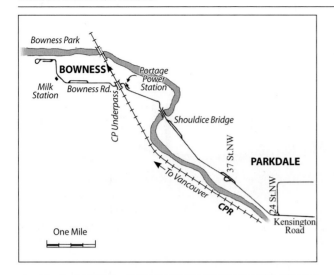

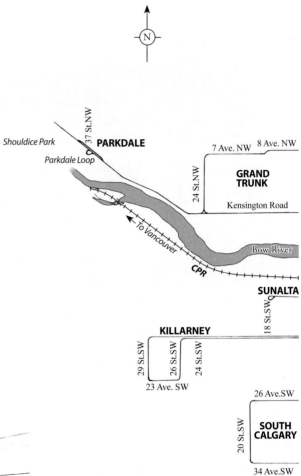

Calgary Municipal Railway
Track Diagram
1946

One Mile

date built _____
date abandoned - - - - - - - - -

Left: Helpful motorman gets forgotten
on car roof. See text, page 109.
(Illustration by Robert J. Sandusky)

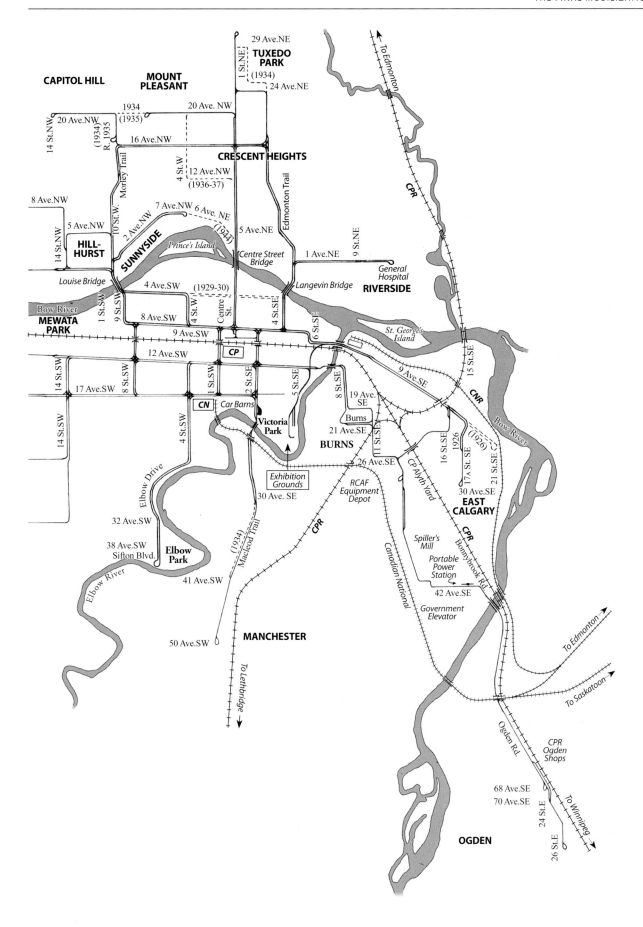

Above: Southbound route 7 South Calgary car 3 pauses at the bottom of the 14th Street sw hill at the intersection of 17th Avenue sw. (W.C. Whittaker)

Below: Car 39 runs along 2nd Street se at 17th Avenue se on its way to the carbarns. This car was part of the 37 – 42 series built by Preston in 1912. These cars and the other 41'6" cars on the roster were known on the system as "short cars". They were generally assigned to route 4

Crescent Heights, route 5 Belt Line, route 6 Killarney and route 7 South Calgary.
(W.C. Whittaker photo, collection of John F. Bromley)

Opposite: In this blind side view of car 19, the tram is at a loop and likely in Ogden service although no route identification is posted in the photographer's view.
(W.C. Whittaker photo, John F. Bromley collection)

Service on the line was inaugurated by No. 14, a full-sized replica of Calgary's last streetcar. The replica was built in the Heritage Park workshops from builders' plans prepared for the original No. 14. Car 7, which had been taken to the Ghost Dam as a cottage upon its retirement in 1947, also found its way back to Calgary to be used in the Heritage Park trolley construction program. The Ottawa-built car 14, which performed the final streetcar run in Calgary, was officially retained as a relic following the cessation of service in December 1950. It was stored for many years in the yard of the Calgary Brewing Company, but was removed in the 1960s and used for promotional purposes. Old age and neglect took their toll, and by the time Heritage Park took over the body of No. 14, it was beyond restoration.

The replica uses the original car's frame. It is mounted on a pair of trucks purchased from the Toronto Transit Commission. Since the Heritage Park line is a stub line, second No. 14 is a double-ended car. There were plans to build a replica of the Calgary Scenic Car, but Heritage Park instead leased ex-Montreal observation car No. 3 from Exporail, the Canadian Railroad Historical Association's collection at St. Constant, Quebec. That car was fitted with decorative mirrors in the side panels to emulate the original Calgary Scenic Car, and it operated in service at Heritage Park until being returned to Exporail in 1989. Heritage Park then built a second Calgary streetcar replica and numbered it 15. Streetcar service at Heritage Park was suspended following the 2006 season as major redevelopment of the site and an extensive new heritage replica building program was undertaken. Streetcar service is expected to be incorporated into this new plan. Once again visitors to the park will be able to experience a mode of transportation first introduced to Calgary 100 years ago.

Drawing by
Robert J. Sandusky

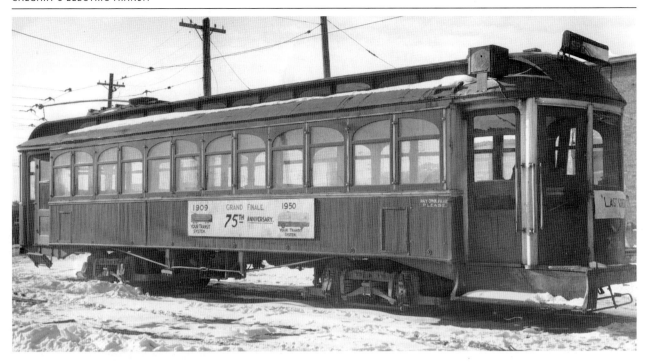

Above: Upon completion of the ceremonies surrounding the last trip, car 14 took its place at the end of the line of retired Calgary trams. Its trolley pole was lowered, and its lights were extinguished forever. (Anthony Clegg)

Below: Second 14 receiving finishing touches in the Heritage Park construction depot. The new tram, utilizing second-hand TTC trucks and the frame of the original Calgary Municipal Railway's 14, was placed in service during the summer of 1975. (
Bill Simpkins, Calgary Herald and Heritage Park)

Above: The Last Roundup. Calgary trams, their life's work done, await their fate in the yards behind the carbarn in January 1951. The sign on the left rear of the car is a message to automobile and truck traffic that might be following behind a car in service, warning: "KEEP BACK 20 FEET. DO NOT PASS CAR WHILE PASSENGERS ARE LOAD-ING OR UNLOADING". (Anthony Clegg)

Below: After the cessation of streetcar service in Calgary in December 1950, tram 14 was stored for some years in a yard beside the Calgary Brewing Company. The body is shown here devoid of its trucks and in somewhat dilapidated condition, September 25th1960. As explained in the text, the frame of the Ottawa-built tram was used in the construction of "Second 14" which at Heritage Park will bring back memories of the days when tramways were the objects of every town's desire. (Robert J. Sandusky)

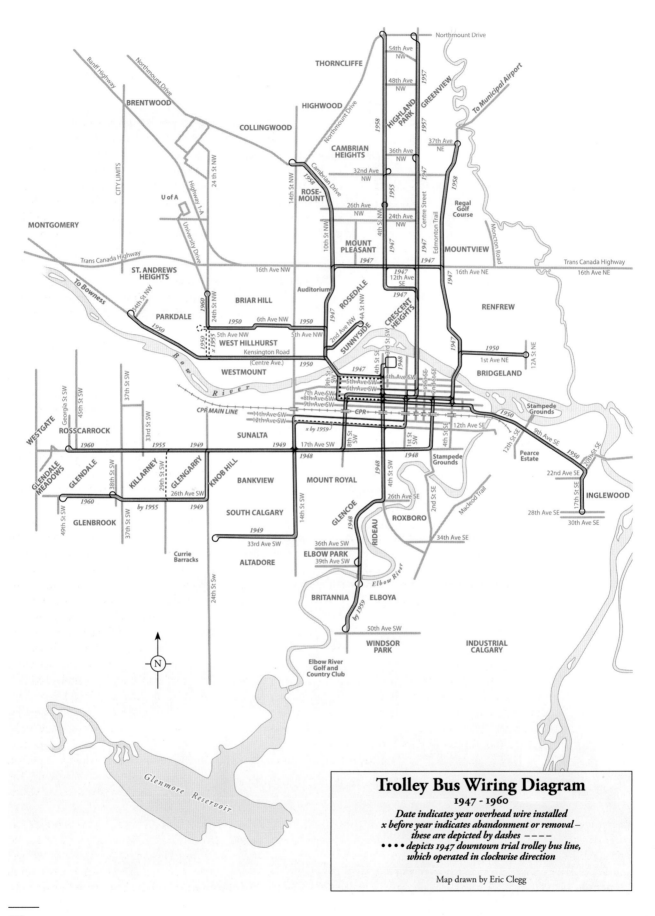

Trolley Bus Wiring Diagram

1947 - 1960

Date indicates year overhead wire installed
x before year indicates abandonment or removal –
these are depicted by dashes ————
•••• depicts 1947 downtown trial trolley bus line,
which operated in clockwise direction

Map drawn by Eric Clegg

CHAPTER NINE

Years of Change - Years of Growth

THE first intrusions into an all-rail transit system – the two Leyland motor buses purchased in 1932 (numbers 300 and 301) – stood alone for several years, and the streetcars continued to rule the system until the 1940s. The year 1941 saw the addition of a sixty-passenger (thirty seated, thirty standing) Leyland gasoline bus No. 302,[1] which was assigned to the Rosedale route, while the two others ran on the Mount Royal routes. Late in 1943, wartime demands brought about the purchase of five Ford-built gasoline buses, assigned to the Calgary system by G.S. Gray, the Canadian government's wartime federal Transit Controller.[2] During 1944, the continuing instability of the Sunnyside hill brought about finally the abandonment of rail service along 6th Avenue NW. The Calgary Municipal Railway contemplated the replacement of streetcars by buses at this location, but, in the face of instructions from the Western Regional Director, Transit Control, that the supply of buses was still restricted,[3] a start was made on rebuilding the rail line, but track was never restored to operating condition. With the return to peacetime conditions, Calgary, like many other cities, was faced with the choice of rehabilitating the trams or converting the system to one or more of the alternatives then available. These included gasoline or diesel motor buses, or electric trolley buses which were being promoted as the latest thing in municipal transit.

Such a difficult and important decision was not to be made without proper consultation, and several transit studies were undertaken in 1944 and 1945.

The first of these began in October 1944 when traffic experts from the Ford Motor Company were asked to make a survey.[4] (One wonders just how unbiased they could be.) In February 1945, W.H. Furlong, K.C., who was also the chairman and general manager of the Sandwich, Windsor & Amherstburg Railway Company, reported to the Calgary council on behalf of the Ford Motor Company.

Furlong's report recommended the purchase of a fleet of 99 twenty-seven passenger motor buses, presumably from Ford. He went on to compare the cost of trolley bus operation, estimated to be from 14.19 to 30.79 cents per mile. Mr. Furlong said he understood Edmonton's costs were about 24 cents per mile. The Ford motor buses, he claimed, could be operated for twenty cents a mile. He did not offer to explain the economics of a difference in capacity between the 27 passengers which the Ford bus held, and those of a 44-passenger trolley bus.[5]

Fortunately, cooler and presumably less biased heads prevailed. Norman D. Wilson of Toronto, an urban transportation expert who had recommended to the City of Edmonton a similar conversion from streetcars, was retained.

In June 1945, he presented his report, which proposed a three-stage plan mixing gasoline buses and trolley coaches, with the latter as the mainstay. Ten years earlier, Mr. Wilson had recommended to Calgary that it wait to see what the transit supply industry had to offer before phasing out the streetcar. Now, he said, the trolley coach had established itself as the modern streetcar. It was standardized, and had combined the flexibility of the automobile with the mechanical simplicity of the streetcar. It had minimum maintenance, high power and hill-climbing ability, was noiseless, odourless, and held 44 seated passengers plus thirty standees. It was five cents a mile cheaper to operate than a gasoline motor bus, and better at hill climbing than the diesel-hydraulic bus. Inexpensive electric power produced from hydro or gas-fired plants favoured the trolley coach. The disadvantage of overhead wires, he argued, was actually an advantage, as it stabilized routes, hence property values. The life of a trolley coach was at least fifteen years; that of the wire, twenty. In comparison, the Ford spokesman had estimated the life of the Ford bus to be ten years, even suggesting that it was a "throw-away" vehicle, to be discarded as newer designs came along. Obviously, while this would be good for Ford, it would be the contrary for the Calgary taxpayer.

Mr. Wilson went on to point out in a newspaper article, "Calgary was a difficult city to provide with public transit because of its topography. Street railway traffic had increased 100 to 120 per cent over the pre-war years and, he estimated, one-half of this increase would remain, given a reasonable measure of prosperity and an attractive and convenient transportation system." He then detailed the proposed phase-in of a modern transportation system for Calgary. First would be the conversion to trolley buses of the Elbow Park-Mount Pleasant and Tuxedo Park car line, followed by the Crescent Heights and Riverside lines.

Buses would operate on 17th Avenue sw from 1st Street sw to 14th Street sw, and there would be a shortened Belt Line route. One of the main changes in the Elbow Park route would be the use of 7th Avenue and 1st Street sw for Tuxedo Park buses. These would turn off Centre Street along 7th Avenue sw and then south on 1st Street to 17th Avenue sw. The Mount Pleasant branch would also use 7th Avenue and 1st Street sw to reach the south terminus. The Crescent Heights route would be converted in the next step, and finally, Riverside.

The second stage would include conversion of the Killarney, South Calgary, East and West Calgary, Sunalta and Sunnyside lines. The latter two would be linked via 1st Street sw. The Killarney route would remain unchanged, but South Calgary would eliminate its loop. This would be done by

Above: A trolley bus is coming along 4th Avenue sw, entering the Louise Bridge while a streetcar is coming off the bridge in 1947. This was the first trolley bus on the Crescent Heights line. Note the use of a common "hot" overhead wire. (Glenbow Archives NA-2891-28)

integrating a proposed 17th Avenue sw bus line which would run south on 17A Street to a loop at 25th or 26th Avenue sw. South Calgary buses would go directly south on 14th Street sw to 33rd Avenue, looping in the vicinity of 24th Street sw. The Riverside and Manchester lines would be linked. Ogden and Bowness would continue as streetcar lines.

The third stage would see the complete abandonment of streetcars. Trolley buses would replace them on the Burns Avenue and Manchester routes, with gasoline or diesel units on the Ogden and Bowness lines. Ultimately a trolley bus route was suggested for 4th Street W, Elgin Avenue, Premier Way, 10th Street, Council Way and 33rd Avenue to the RCMP barracks.[6]

During June 1945, Superintendent Charles Comba of the Calgary Municipal Railway lost no time in submitting his own report to Council. In it, he too assumed that rehabilitation of the existing street railway system in any form was not practical. The Mount Royal and Rosedale routes would remain as motor bus lines. The Dominion Transit Controller, Mr. Gray, had indicated that no new equipment would be available before 1946, and even then delivery would likely be unpredictable. As a result, Mr. Comba recommended a start should be made on those routes that were on level ground, and where track intersections were in the worst shape. Conversion of the Crescent Heights, Belt Line and Manchester-Riverside routes would follow. He proposed equipment for these routes consisting of thirty modern 44-passenger trolley coaches. These would use up all of the allotment that the city was likely to get from the Transit Controller for the next year.

Conversion of the Capitol Hill routes to buses would follow as soon as the Crescent Heights line was changed. The remaining routes would be converted in this order: South Calgary, Killarney, Sunnyside and Burns Avenue, depending on availability of equipment. East and West Calgary routes would be the last to be converted.

Total cost of the conversion plan was estimated at $811,508, of which $600,000 would be for the purchase of the trolley buses at $20,000 each. Removal of ties and rail would cost $20,525, and overhead trolley construction would be $190,983, including installation north on 1st Street sw to

7th Avenue and east to Centre Street. Light rail would be taken up, but the heavy steel embedded in concrete would be paved over. Seven intersections would also be taken up, making a total, including the light rail, of 110,250 feet.[7]

On Tuesday June 26th 1945, the members of the Elbow Park Residents Association were invited to a series of presentations from Council and others, in order to inform them prior to a vote on the form of transit they desired. Less than a hundred persons showed up. They were treated to talks on gasoline, diesel and trolley buses, and saw a film on trolley coach operation in the United States. City Commissioner V.A. Newhall represented the views of the Wilson report. Unbiased engineers, he said, have established the trolley coach as more economical to operate than the motor bus. Alderman McCullough, who owned Maclin Motors, a Ford dealership, argued for the gasoline bus, stating that more of those vehicles were in operation than trolley coaches "even though most of the transportation companies were electrical concerns."[8] He harkened to the fact that seventeen per cent of the city's prosperity was due to the oil industry, and then tried to compare the small capacity gasoline buses with the more expensive (but larger-capacity) trolley coaches. The savings, he added with a political flourish, would build a civic auditorium, swimming pools and many other projects.

The new diesel-hydraulic bus was then described by Mr. Mervyn Johnson as being clean, with no fumes outside or inside the bus. (One doubts that he had ever ridden one!) Safety features of the diesels were emphasized without mentioning that these were also available on the trolley buses. Moreover, the costs of diesels were claimed to be less. The last speaker, Mr. Peele, said it was peculiar that the reports presented by Mr. Wilson, the trolley bus manufacturers and Mr. Comba, were all similar in recommending a combination of trolleys, diesel and gasoline buses to best meet the city's needs. However, in defense of the trolley coaches, he stated that where they were used, passenger loads had increased due to the buses' popularity. In Edmonton, an 81 per cent increase had been recorded, that the city now had twenty such vehicles and had just ordered an additional ten. Edmonton hoped to have a complete trolley bus system by 1950. (How ironic that, in 2009, the year of this book's publication, the City of Edmonton has just abandoned all operation of trolley buses!)

Perhaps the comparison with the city to the north stung the assembly; at any rate, twenty members voted for the trolley buses, while fourteen said they would abide by whatever City Council would decide.[9]

On January 16th 1946, Council authorized the purchase of thirty Brill 43-passenger trolley coaches, ten Brill 36-passenger gasoline coaches, and ten GMC diesels. The total cost of the trolley buses was $519,000, with an additional $190,983 to be spent on overhead wires. On May 13th, in another report, Commissioner Newhall recommended that Council cancel the earlier order of the ten diesel-hydraulic GMC buses because of uncertain delivery dates and to avoid a probable price increase resulting from a recent automotive industry strike settlement.

The lines approved for conversion were Elbow Park-Tuxedo and Mount Pleasant routes, the Number 5 Belt Line, and the Number 4 Crescent Heights run.

Routes from the north were to travel through the city centre on 8th Avenue, and those from the south on 7th Avenue sw.[10] On May 27th 1946, Council instructed the commissioners to order thirty additional trolleys, thus enabling their production to be scheduled in groups of ten, as funds became available. This would give Calgary sixty trol-

ley coaches and ten gasoline buses by July. The ten diesels (presumably still on order) were still expected to be delivered whenever they became available. A few aldermen tried to delay the motion, with the result they were accused by the others of being prejudiced in favour of the gasoline bus and, therefore, trying to stall the orders.[11]

Finally, on August 8th 1946, a firm order for the additional thirty trolley coaches was made. *The Calgary Herald* quoted Commissioner Newhall: "This direction of council seems to be in accord with all the major cities of Canada which are adopting trolley coaches."[12]

By mid-October, five of the Brill gasoline buses had arrived. Superintendent C.V.F. Weir, who had replaced Charles Comba on the latter's retirement, was the first "passenger" on the motor buses. The vehicles were in the new Calgary Transit System colours – seafoam green and oyster white with gold trim and lettering – which were actually the colours in which the CanCar demonstrator bus had arrived. The interior was a combination of two tones of blue with a cream ceiling. The sixty trolley coaches were expected by December 1946, but there was no word on the delivery date of the ten GMC diesels.[13]

The Calgary Herald of October 17th quoted Commissioner Newhall saying he had received word from the Canadian Car-Brill plant in Fort William, Ontario, that the first dozen trolley buses would be shipped in early December. He advised that all necessary overhead wire and fittings would be delivered from the Ohio Brass Company to the city, by November. This would be sufficient to equip the Belt Line and Crescent Heights routes. "However," the newspaper article went on, "Calgary citizens will not have to wait until December to ride and inspect the new type trolley as an

Below: Conversion of streetcar to trolley bus lines on Centre Street and 16th Avenue N. (Glenbow Archives NA-2891-27)

Above: On 7th Avenue at 1st Street sw, a Calgary Transit crew is repairing power lines which fell to the ground when a transit system hydraulic truck inadvertently backed into a trolley wire and unknowingly carried it across to touch another live wire. Captured by a *Calgary Herald* photographer on April 20th 1948.
(Glenbow Archives NA-2864-1980b)

Below: On 7th Avenue near the intersection of 2nd Street se in June 1947, No. 408 passes a line crew installing the wire intersection for the buses to run along 2nd Street to the garage.
(Ohio Brass photo, Schwarzkopf collection)

exhibition pilot model will arrive here about Nov. 4 after being exhibited in Winnipeg.

"So that this exhibition unit can be put in operation, one mile of overhead will be installed shortly on a belt route on 8th Ave, W. from 4th St. to 9th St. W., north on 9th St. W. to 4th Ave., east on 4th Ave. to 4th St. W. and then south on 4th St. W. to 8th Ave. W."[14] This route was selected because the overhead could be installed permanently for connection with future routes, including the Crescent Heights line and the Belt Line. The demonstration coach would provide free rides around that belt run.

The article continued to describe the furious activity preceding Calgary's first trolley coach lines. Crescent Heights and the Belt Line were now the first candidates for conversion, as the roadway was suitable. The car tracks were to be left in place for the time being, and paved over the following year. Every available lineman was to be rushed into service to speed the work. The new overhead was to be strung from the old poles, and new poles would replace them as work proceeded. The existing positive power wire from the streetcar overhead could still be utilized by streetcars, so there would be no significant disruptions of service. Most of the major work was done at night so as to keep interruptions at a minimum.

Two of the Brill gasoline buses were placed in service on October 17th 1946, one each on the Rosedale and the Mount Royal routes. Three others were being "broken in" for possible use on the Sunalta run. This line, according to Superintendent Weir quoted in the *The Calgary Herald*, would be eventually converted to trackless trolleys, however, like many plans for Calgary's trolleys, this never materialized.[15]

The switch to motor buses improved the frequency from 24- and 30-minute car service to a straight 20-minute bus service.[16]

Finally the grand day arrived. The first Calgary trolley coach route went into operation Sunday afternoon June 1st 1947. The number 4 Crescent Heights line had the honour. It was a belt line, with service running both ways from 7th Avenue sw, north along 4th Street se, over the Langevin Bridge, up Fourth/Third Street ne, west on 16th Avenue, south on 10th Street nw, across the Louise Bridge, east on 4th Avenue sw, south on 4th Street sw, and east on 7th Avenue sw again. The trolley buses had to be parked on 7th Avenue between 3rd and 4th Street se at night as the connection with the Victoria Park car barns was not yet installed. (This was the route that had been chosen as the first trolley coach service because all the streets were paved.)

Public reaction to the service was positive, with both riders and civic officials remarking on the almost noiseless mode of electric transportation. Ridership increased noticeably, and Superintendent Weir was especially pleased with the trolley buses' handling of the 10th and 4th Street hills. Coincidentally, the ten GMC diesel-hydraulic buses arrived that same week, finally![17]

Conversion of the number 2 (Mount Pleasant) and number 3 (Tuxedo Park) routes was not to be completed until August as delivery of the fittings was delayed. By July

1947, streetcars were taken off the north portions of routes 2 and 3 to allow overhead construction and road improvements to start on the North Hill.[18] Motor buses were used in the meantime on the Centre Street portion of the two routes.[19] These interim motor buses may have been new GM diesels assigned primarily to the Manchester route, but also heavily involved in the streetcar-to-trolley bus interim services on several routes, along with the Fords and Brill C36s.

The Mount Pleasant route wasn't to be ready for trolley coach use until November 30th. This route, number 2, ran north on Centre Street from 6th Avenue sw to 12th Avenue nw, west to 4th Street nw, and north to the loop at 26th Avenue nw. The return journey retraced the line back to downtown, where it looped from Centre Street, west on 7th Avenue sw to 1st Street sw, north to 6th Avenue sw, east to Centre Street and north again.[20]

The Tuxedo Park number 3 run didn't open until Friday December 19th. A trial was operated on the previous day, and the quiet trolley coaches were declared fit to replace the motor buses. Coaches ran every fifteen minutes during the day and every 7½ minutes during peak hours.[21] Information is not clear on the original route, but it probably followed the streetcar line north on Centre Street and terminated in a loop at Centre Street and 36th Avenue. At the City Centre's end it probably followed the same loop as the number 2 Mount Pleasant trolley bus.

By the end of 1947, Calgary Transit System boasted that 42 per cent of its passengers, 2,250,000 per month, were now carried on rubber-tired vehicles. Nearly eighteen of the 82 miles of streetcar track had been torn up or covered over. There were 27 miles of motor bus routes and 24 miles of trolley bus lines. An Elbow Park route, which would link with the numbers 2 and 3 routes on the North Hill, was next in line for trolley bus conversion. It would be followed by the number 5 Belt Line, and then South Calgary and Killarney routes, which would link with the Belt Line. Twenty-four of the thirty trolley buses were in service, with ten more expected to be delivered in July of 1948. Another ten were to come later for the last two routes. The streetcars had not fared as well; eight were scrapped for parts to keep the remaining 74 alive for a few more years.[22]

By mid-June 1948, five of the second order of thirty trolley buses had been delivered, and the rest were to be in the city by the end of July.[23] On Sunday July 11th, the motor buses ceased operating on the Elbow Park section of the line. The trolley buses took over on this part of route 3, now linking Elbow Park with Tuxedo Park in direct service.[24]

The motor buses were now deployed on the Belt Line, whose conversion was to be more complicated since it involved stringing trolley coach overhead on sections still serviced by streetcars.[25]

The streetcar's days were numbered though. Saturday November 27th 1948 marked the last rail runs on the Belt Line, South Calgary and Killarney lines. The next day, testing was completed by noon. The trolley buses started operating in that afternoon, except for the southwest ends of the routes

Above: CTS 447, 441, 476 and 440, all T-44 CCF-Brill coaches, are in front of the CTS garage, clean and ready for another day's work. See photo page 127 showing newly-installed trolley bus washing system. (John M. Day)

Opposite below: A favourite spot for trolley bus photographers (see also photo on page 120). No. 405 is coming off the Louise Bridge onto 4th Avenue sw in June 1947. Notice the VEEDOL sign beside the pole near the gas station; also the motorcyclist – no helmet laws then. (Ohio Brass photo, Schwarzkopf collection)

from the 17th Avenue and 14th Street sw intersection. Here, they were met by gasoline and diesel buses until the route paving would be completed. The Belt Line operated on 7th Avenue S from 2nd Street se to 1st Street sw, south to 12th Avenue sw, west to 14th Street sw, south to 17th Avenue, east to 2nd Street se and north to 7th Avenue.

The downtown portion of the South Calgary and Killarney trolley routes ran on 7th Avenue sw from 1st Street sw to 8th Street sw, south to 12th Avenue sw, west to 14th Street sw, south to 17th Avenue sw, east to 1st Street sw and north to 7th Avenue sw.

These three routes operated on 7th Avenue S instead of 8th as the streetcars had done, and thus caused traffic congestion. But, the trolley buses ruled and motorists were asked to use 8th Avenue instead of 7th. It was intended to return the Crescent Heights trolley bus line to 8th Avenue sometime in the future.[26]

That August, *The Calgary Herald* wrote in glowing terms about the city's new Eau Claire transit garage, even though it was in reality two former aircraft hangers, hauled into the city from the old RCAF training school at De Winton, and placed back-to-back. The four trolley bus lanes could accommodate 32 buses and there was room for forty more outside. The latest in repair and maintenance facilities had been installed: bus washers, pits, a 24,000-pound hoist, as well as a battery room and carpentry shop. The 2nd Avenue and 2nd Street sw structure also housed a number of administrative functions for the growing Calgary Transit System.[27]

February 6th 1949 saw the South Calgary number 7 route extended to operate from 17th Avenue and 14th Street sw, along 14th Street sw to 33rd Avenue sw, and then west to the South Calgary terminal at 20th Street sw. In the fall of that year, R.H. Wray became Transit Superintendant succeeding C.V.F. Weir.

The first of the new order of trolley coaches had arrived by October 20th sporting some improvements over the previous ones. There were four additional vertical stanchions or handholds, and the earlier style sliding window sashes had been eliminated in favour of conventional lifting sashes.

The route signs were located behind double glazing which avoided the problem of them steaming up in winter, leaving the poor passengers wondering on what route the bus was travelling.

However, these new buses couldn't be used on the full Killarney number 6 route because bad weather had held up blacktopping, resulting in service on the southwest leg being delayed.[28] Finally, on the following Wednesday October 28th, full service began on the run. It extended from 14th Street sw along 17th Avenue sw, west to 29th Street sw, south to 26th Avenue sw, east along it to 24th Street sw, and then north to 17th Avenue. The buses were run alternately north and south around the loop, with one bus entering the loop at 24th Street and proceeding clockwise, the next bus continuing along 17th Avenue and going counter-clockwise around the loop. The paving was still not complete due to wet weather, but the trolley buses were placed in service anyway, and the paving waited until better weather.[29]

December 7th was the day streetcar service ended on route number 1. West Hillhurst residents, who had long used the trams as a meeting place and club room as they wended their way downtown, had now to contend with "somewhat garish, brightly-lit and speedy vehicles (that) would be far removed from the swing and sway, rattle and bang, and somewhat drafty club quarters of the past." These "garish" vehicles were, however, new Twin Coach gasoline buses, temporary replacements for the streetcars until the New Year, when the trolley would return, albeit with rubber tires and less "sway, rattle and bang."[30]

The number 1 trolley bus route was to run in East Calgary along the streetcar route to 10th Street NW and Kensington Road. From there, equal service was to be provided to 24th Street NW via both 5th Avenue NW and Kensington Road.[31]

Wire was to be strung along the Sunnyside and Bridgeland routes immediately, with trolley coaches slated for operation early in 1950. Bowness would be the next to get buses, with Ogden as the final route to change over. That was, however, optimistic planning; the Odgen car line's "interim" conversion to motor buses seemed to take forever[32] and trolley buses never did operate all the way to Bowness.

Trolley coaches were installed finally on route 1, West Calgary, on November 11th 1950, Remembrance Day. It had taken eleven months from the retirement date of the trams until their final replacement was put into service. In the northwest, the route was a loop, with two-way operation along Kensington Road, 24th Street NW, 5th and 6th avenues NW and 10th Street NW. That is, one coach would traverse that loop clockwise, and the next bus would travel it counter-clockwise. The route then followed the streetcar routing via 10th Street NW, 9th Street SW, 8th Avenue SW, deviating from the tram line through the city centre by continuing east on 8th/9th Avenue SE to a loop on 17th Street SE at 28th Avenue SE.[33]

The number 9 Riverside (Bridgeland)-Sunnyside route was converted to trolley coaches on March 25th 1950.[34] It ran from 12A Street NE along 1st Avenue NE to the Edmonton Trail. From there it went south on the Trail/4th Street to 8th Avenue SE, along it to 9th Street SW, over the Louise Bridge and along 10th Street NW to 2nd Avenue NW. It finished up in a loop on 2nd Avenue at 4A Street NW.

By the end of 1950, the trolley coach fleet had expanded with the arrival of four more buses costing $24,363.52 each, freight included.[35]

The latest in modern urban transport was not without its share of incidents, however. On July 20th 1950, a CTS trolley bus driver, no doubt trying to keep up with a tight schedule, was making good time up the 10th Street Hill when he noticed a flashing red light in his rear view mirror. A moment later, the ever-vigilant Calgary Police had pulled him over and charged him under the Alberta Vehicles and Highway Act of 1911 for exceeding the speed limit by going 42 MPH in the city. *The Calgary Herald* gleefully commented it as only fair "that bus-drivers are just as subject to the law as anybody else."

However the *The Calgary Herald*'s glee was short-lived. Six days later in an editorial, it revealed that the Act specifically excluded trolley buses and streetcars. The paper commented, "if a Rosedale bus (which is gasoline or oil-powered) and a Crescent Heights trolley are going up 10th Street N.W. together at 40 miles per hour, the police can prosecute the Rosedale driver for speeding but cannot touch the trolley bus driver. It is hard to see by what process of reasoning this sort of

thing can be justified." The paper went on to point out that in case of an accident, the onus would be on the injured to prove negligence of the trolley driver, rather than the driver having to prove that it wasn't his fault, as is required by law. It would appear however, apart from one case quoted in the editorial, that its consternation was somewhat exaggerated.[36]

At the end of 1952 the number of passengers carried annually on each trolley coach route was as follows: [37]

Route Number and Name	Passengers Annually
1: East & West Calgary	5,377,719
2: Mount Pleasant	1,530,525
3: Elbow Park-Tuxedo	5,107,443
4: Crescent Heights	4,360,711
5: Belt Line	2,004,630
6: Killarney	3,303,597
7: South Calgary	3,388,606
9: Riverside-Sunnyside	2,686,256

In 1953, the transit system had received an offer of sixty used 44-passenger ACF Brills, built in 1948, from John D. McGuigan Inc. Sunbeam Corporation of England had also inquired as to the possibility of supplying buses to Calgary, but the city seemed not to be swayed either by second-hand buses, or units not made in Canada. A quote had been received in May of that year on two 48-passenger model T48 Brill trolley coaches for a total cost of $53, 936. Superintendent Wray wrote to Commissioner J. Ivor Strong the following month, asking that these buses be ordered.[38]

On December 18th 1953, four T48A CCF Brill trolleys, fleet numbers 481-484, were shipped. Their cost was $27,158 each, freight included, an increase in price from the 1950 order. These buses were equipped with Grant fare boxes, double glazing on the standee windows to prevent frosting up, and a swing down driver's sun visor. The Grant boxes were a departure from the Cleveland type used previously. [39] These four trolleys arrived in the first week of the New Year, bringing the fleet to a total of 83 vehicles.[40] Roller curtains in the coaches showed the following destinations: [41]

Belt Line	Exhibition Grounds
Bowness	Garage
Bridgeland	Killarney - 17 Avenue
Sunnyside	Killarney - 26 Avenue
West Hillhurst	Manchester
Burns Avenue	Mount Pleasant
Capitol Hill	Mount Royal
City Centre	No Passengers
Crescent Heights	Ogden
East Calgary	(spare/blank)
Parkdale	Rosedale
(spare/blank)	South Calgary
Edmonton Trail	Special
Elbow	Sunalta
Tuxedo	(spare/blank)

Opposite: To accompany the *Calgary Herald* article on the "new" transit garages, the photographer caught No. 424 going through the automatic sprinklers wash on August 31st 1948. (Glenbow Archives NA-2864-1980a)

During 1954, construction on the 4th Street subway and the intersection at 8th Avenue and 4th Street sw meant that Elbow Park runs were re-routed on 4th Street sw, from 12th to 7th Avenue sw.[42]

A request was made to install two sets of trolley wire for northbound coaches on the Louise Bridge so as to eliminate delays from trolley buses turning west onto Kensington Road. This installation would separate Crescent Heights and Sunnyside buses going north on 10th Avenue NW from the 5th Avenue West Calgary buses. Apparently the suggestion was disregarded; instead schedules were adjusted.[43]

The week after the Calgary Stampede in July 1954, work started on an overpass at 8th Street and 9th Avenue sw. This overpass would carry 9th Avenue traffic over 8th Street and permit installation of a one-way street pattern. Four routes were affected by this construction: South Calgary service was rerouted to continue along 12th Avenue sw to 4th Street sw, north along it to 7th Avenue sw, and east to the city centre. Outgoing Killarney buses travelled from 7th Avenue sw, south on 4th Street sw to 12th Avenue sw, and then west on it. The Mount Royal buses which also used the subway were rerouted along 12th Avenue and 8th Street sw as the South Calgary trolley buses had been.[44] By October/November 1954, the one-way pattern was in full use, and the problems associated with Calgary's narrow streets, wide buses and heavy traffic were eased.

In April 1956, sidewalk construction and paving in the downtown area forced all transit routes using 7th Avenue between 1st Street and 4th Street sw, except the Killarney trolley bus route, to be re-routed via 8th Avenue sw. Construction continued from April 25th "around the clock" so as to minimize inconvenience to the public.[45]

The Tuxedo number 3 run was extended 1¼ miles into the Thorncliffe area on Tuesday September 3rd 1957. The terminal was moved from 36th Avenue NW at Centre Street to Northmount Drive at Centre. Trolley coaches operating in normal service carried the destination sign *THORNCLIFFE*. Rush hour trolley buses turned at the old Thirty-sixth Avenue loop and were signed *TUXEDO*.[46] The south terminus of the line was at Sifton Road (Fiftieth Avenue sw) in Elbow Park.

In February 1957, CTS purchased twenty 1948 ACF Brill trolley buses from the Baltimore Transit Company.[47] On Monday February 11th, five of them were unloaded with much publicity, and the balance followed quickly.[48]

The Calgary Herald of March 10th 1958 announced that the trolley bus system would be extended an additional five miles during the year at a cost of $117,000. Direct trolley coach service was to be extended to Highwood, Edmonton Trail, Mountain View, Cambrian Heights, Collingwood, Rosemount, the eastern part of Capital Hill, and Renfrew. The Mount Pleasant number 2 run was to be extended 1½

straight-through services into residential areas once covered by feeder motor buses" it reported. "CTS has today a total of 105 trolley coaches and 67 motor buses for a total of 182.3 round trip miles." Ridership had been maintained since 1947 even with the increase in automobile traffic. "In 1957, over 31-million passengers rode the CTS system – equal to the entire population of greater Calgary riding twice a week. Of this total, 22,877,596 persons rode trolley coaches as compared to 8,329,355 on motor buses.

"Heaviest travelled of the eight lines is the Thorncliffe line, [i.e. Number 3] carrying over 3.7-million white collar workers, shoppers, and students from the southern Station at 50th Ave. sw and Elbow Dr. northward into densely populated residential areas." The article went on to state that despite the congestion of narrow two-way streets, the trolley coaches maintained an average operating speed of 11.1 mph. By that time many of the coaches were eleven years old, having travelled about 400,000 miles. Nonetheless many more years of service was expected from these vehicles. Trolley bus operating expenses were 39.86 cents per mile, of which 3.42 cents was power, 1.73 cents overhead maintenance, and 5.82 cents equipment maintenance. This represented a saving of 5.23 cents per mile over motor buses. The article also commented that the CTS kept its wire well maintained, thereby keeping expenses down and minimizing damage from dewiring.

miles along 4th Street NW from the existing terminus at 32nd Avenue NW to Northmount Drive at a cost of $30,000.

Service in Crescent Heights was to be revamped also. Route number 4 was to be extended from 16th Avenue NE northward along the Edmonton Trail to a new terminal at the foot of a hill near 37th Avenue NE. "A complementary western terminal will be extended north on 10th Street NW to a new terminal at Cambrian Place and 14th Street NW."[49] That would convert the run from a belt line into a U-shaped one. These improvements were expected to cost $67,000.

A proposed extension of the number 4 route into Renfrew was contemplated, running off the northeast leg of the Crescent Heights service, eastward from Edmonton Trail on 8th Avenue NE to a terminal at 12th Street NE for a cost of $20,000.[50] This was never placed under wire, but was put into service eventually as motor bus route 17.

The first of these planned extensions, the Mount Pleasant expansion as outlined in the spring, went into service on Monday August 25th. Rush hour buses ran from downtown to the old terminus at 32nd Avenue and 4th Street NW.[51]

By the end of 1958, the extension of route number 4 into Crescent Heights, to the 37th Avenue and the Cambrian/14th Street terminals, was in effect. The following year was marked by a fare increase to seven tickets for $1.00. There was no increase for students or children.[52]

The March - April 1959 issue of Ohio Brass *"Traction News"* featured the Calgary trolley coach system. As a supplier of overhead switches and fittings, Ohio Brass had a bias in favour of the trolleys, but the article recorded faithfully their heyday in Calgary.

"Four miles of new overhead have been added to two lines of its 86.6 miles of round-trip trolley coach route, extending

Below: Transfer courtesy Edmonton Radial Railway Society Fonds Leslie Corness

CALGARY TRANSIT SYSTEM
12 N W E S
1 2 3 4 5 6 7 8
Ogden / Sunalta / Mt. Royal / Cap. Hill / Bankview — Bowness / Riverside / Rosedale / Manchester / Edm. Trail

SPECIAL	EMERGENCY
5 AM	0
6 AM	15
7 AM	30
8 AM	45
9 AM	0
10 AM	15
11 AM	30
12 NOON	45
1 PM	0
2 PM	15
3 PM	30
4 PM	45
5 PM	0
6 PM	15
7 PM	30
8 PM	45
9 PM	0
10 PM	15
11 PM	30
12 MIDN'T	45

A word about this is in order. CTS has been often accused of poor trolley wire maintenance. This in turn is shown as one of the reasons why the electric system was allowed to die. However, at least in the 1950s, maintenance seems to have been exemplary. Transit files record regular meetings of CTS staff responsible for overhead, where problems were aired and solutions put into effect. Trolley shoe wear was recorded and carefully monitored. Dewirements were investigated and wire tightened if that was the cause. Careful attention was paid to the trolley coach system during these boom days of postwar Calgary, when the automobile had not yet made its major attack on public transit. For a few more years at least, the trolley coach, powered by electricity, would remain supreme in Canada's oil capital.[53]

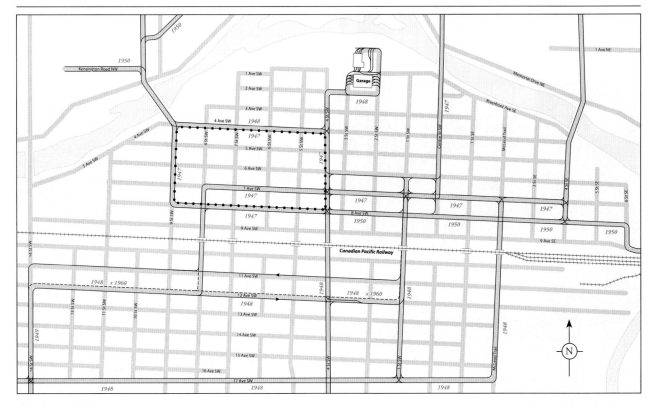

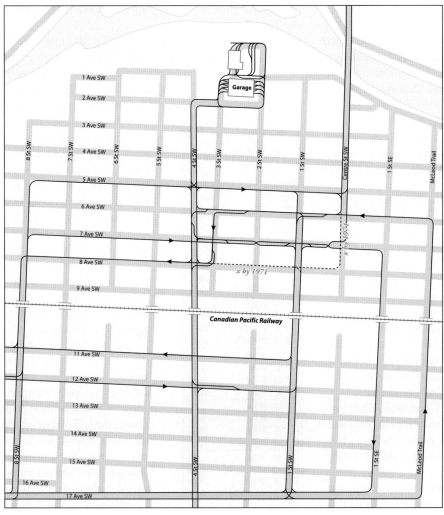

Downtown Overhead Wiring Diagrams
1947 to 1970s

Above: The above map shows the trolley bus wire arrangement in place in 1960. At that time, the only thoroughfares that had been converted to one-way operation (in the mid-1950s) were 11th and 12th avenues sw. This had necessitated stringing wire on 11th Avenue where there had been no trolley bus service previously, and resulted in the former north side wire on 12th Avenue being abandoned. The bold dots in the upper map show the clockwise direction and route of the original trial trolley bus installation.

Left: This map depicts trolley bus overhead in place in the early 1970s, by which time many routes had now been converted to diesel. It shows the major wiring changes which were required from 1961 onward, when all the major downtown streets became one-way.
Both maps by Eric Clegg

Opposite: An overload on the trolley bus electrical system caused a half-hour power failure, stranding buses at 7th Avenue and 2nd Street sw on a chilly January 25th 1957 day.
(Glenbow Archives NA-2864-1980d)

CHAPTER TEN

Growth and Sudden Death

DESPITE the boom years of the 1950s and the optimistic plans for trolley coach line expansions, by 1960 the first shots had been fired in the diesel/trolley bus war. In a letter sent to C.E. Patton of Wilkes-Barre Transit Corporation in March of that year, Superintendent Wray stated that City Council had decided to extend the diesel fleet. Consequently, there would be no additions to the 105 trolley coaches then in use, for the time being. However Wray had written to British United Traction Ltd. earlier in that year, asking for a comparative quote on six British-built trolleys buses.[1]

By 1958 the trolleys only covered 37.8 route miles one way. The reductions occurred because of rerouting, and in particular, discontinuing use of the wire on 16th Avenue N when route 4 (Crescent Heights) was restructured in 1958 to become the "Cambrian Heights-Edmonton Trail" route. During that year, the buses travelled a total of 3,069,738 miles. Only 6.04 passengers were carried per trolley coach mile, revenue was 72.80 cents per mile, while expenses were 57.82 cents. Despite route expansions in 1958, passenger riding in general was on the decline.[2]

With the creation of the University of Alberta's Calgary campus in September 1960, transit service was extended to serve its west-end campus. A temporary loop for the number 9 route was proposed to be located at University Drive and 24th Street NW.[3] Council agreed to the extension in August,[4] and by November poles were set on the north side of 14th Avenue NW and University Drive, south to the intersection of University Drive and 24th Street NW. The extension was slated for completion in 1961.[5] The then-current terminal (1960) of route 9 was at 7th Avenue and 5th Street NW via 10th Street and 2nd Avenue NW in Sunnyside. When the University extension was put into service in 1961, the Sunnyside leg went to the number 2 route. Formerly looping downtown, the number 2 route now came down Centre Street as before, through downtown along 7th Avenue sw to 4th Street sw, thence to 4th Avenue sw and across the Bow River, up 10th Street NW and along 2nd Avenue to the former number 9 terminus. The number 9 now branched west from 10th Street NW at 5th Avenue NW, jogged up to 6th Ave at 14th Street, back to 5th at 19th Street, and turned north at 24th Street to the aforementioned loop.

Another extension was planned for route 6 on 17th Avenue sw from Georgia Street west to Glenside Drive.[6] However, on this route, some late evening runs were replaced by gasoline buses, bringing some doubt as to whether trolley bus extensions would come about. On May 17th 1960, Belt Line (Route 5) runs 32 and 33, westbound on 7th Avenue s, were also operated with motor buses. June 7th marked the start of Belt Line runs in both directions. The conversion of 11th and 12th avenues s into one-way streets necessitated running the trolley coaches in both directions around the belt. Until August 10th, sewer construction interfered with the run between Mt. Pleasant and Sunnyside on route 2. August 30th saw motor buses replace trolley coaches on the Edmonton Trail/Cambrian Heights number 4 route, due to construction at 7th Avenue and 4th Street SE. By October 31st, route 2 trolley buses had resumed normal service,[7] as did the Edmonton Trail/Cambrian Heights trolley bus route.

Bureaucracy reared its head in February 1960. The Bay department store rented the CTS for an hour on a sale day to give the citizens "free rides" downtown. All was in readiness including full-page advertisements in the newspapers and promotional bags covering the fare box openings. The Alberta Department of Industry and Development then intervened, ruling that the free rides were the equivalent of "green stamps", thus contravening one of the government acts.

The newspapers were not very charitable towards the Department's attempt to "protect" the public from such promotions. Though CTS was even unhappier, it said nothing publicly.[8]

In 1960, the CTS vehicle fleet was made up as follows:[9]

Builder	Year(s)	Model	Type	No. of Units
Motor buses				
CanCar-Brill	1946	C-36	gasoline	6
CanCar-Brill	1947	TDH-3610	diesel	10
CanCar-Brill	1949	C-36 TC	diesel(orig.gas)	12
Twin Coach	1949	41-S	gas	16
Flxible (Twin)	1954	FT-2-40	diesel(orig.gas)	6
CanCar	1956-59	CD-52 TC	diesel	19
CanCar	1960	TD-51	diesel	10
Total:				79
Trolley Coaches				
CanCar-Brill	1947-50	T-44	electric	77
ACF-Brill	1948*	TC44	electric	20
CanCar-Brill	1950, 54	T-48A	electric	8
Total:				105

* acquired by CTS in 1959

Opposite, upper: No. 478, signed Thorncliffe, is "coming right at you" from the CPR railway-roadway underpass on 4th Street NW, August 25th 1969. (John M. Day)

Opposite, lower: On a nice June day in 1965, CCF Brill coach 412 is leaving the garage, ready to start the Bridgeland run. (Colin K. Hatcher)

Above: The Baltimore ACF Brills were quite distinctive. In June 1965, inbound trolley coach No. 493 is travelling north on 1st Street sw and turning on to 8th Avenue sw, sporting advertising for that "rival" city to the north's annual festival, Edmonton's "Klondike Days".
(Colin K. Hatcher)

The average operating costs, in cents per mile, were as follows : [10]

				Cost per	
Maintenance	Fuel	Depreciation	Operating	VehMi	seatMi
Diesel/Gasoline buses					
15.64	2.94	3.46	36.27	58.31	1.33
Trolley buses					
12.19	3.22	5.83	36.27	57.51	1.30

Even though their fuel or power and depreciation costs were higher, the trolley buses were still more economical than gasoline or diesel buses in terms of costs per vehicle mile or per seat mile.

A transit strike in mid-1961 hastened an imminent reorganization of the system. For some time, the politicians had been threatening a major shakeup of the transit system. The strike dragged on, but was finally settled by July. Reorganization followed and was completed by year-end.[11]

September of 1961 arrived and conversion of downtown thouroughfares into a system of one-way streets was in full swing. Diesels buses were used temporarily to replace trolley coaches on routes as needed. Trolley wire had been strung through the 1st Street subway as part of the new one-way street planning so buses could now go both ways on 1st Street sw.[12]

Calgary Transit officials' attention was drawn to the 4th Street sw underpass where the sidewalks on either side dipped under the railway tracks only low enough to accomodate the height of pedestrians, while the roadway was of course depressed further to provide the greater clearance needed for transit vehicles and trucks. The result was that trolley coach poles were on a level with a pedestrian's head as the buses passed through the underpass. The possibility of a dewired pole striking and perhaps killing a hapless pedestrian resulted in CTS erecting strong screening along the walkway that separated it from the depressed roadway.

In January 1961, the first of several cost comparisons between trolley and motor buses was published. It gave some hints as to the eventual fate of the trolley system. Total costs in cents per vehicle mile in the first nine months of 1960, as compared with 1958-59 were : [13]

	Motor bus	Trolley	Diff.
1960 Average	59.25	58.42	+0.83
1st nine months 1959 cost	61.55	57.36	+4.19
1958 cost	61.21	57.79	+3.42

The transit system was exempted from the previously imposed provincial fuel tax effective April 12th 1960, resulting in the immediate reduction of motor bus operating costs by two cents per mile. The trend, cited in the report, was toward lower operating costs for motor buses as compared to higher costs for trolley coaches. The newer motor buses were 52-passenger models, compared with 44 or 48 for the trolley coaches; in fact only eight of the 105 trolleys carried 48 passengers. Costs for the motor buses averaged out at 1.12 cents per seat mile, the trolleys at 1.30 cents. The purchase of electricity had also increased from a flat charge of 82 cents per kilowatt hour from the City's Electric Light Department to a peak load demand rate (from Calgary Power) at an

The framed area in the main map shows the downtown area as it existed before most thoroughfares were converted to one-way operation. The inset map (see larger version on page 128) shows the major changes needed to convert the overhead wiring to one-way street operation. By the 1970s compilation of data for the latter map, all routes to the northwest and those to the east had been converted to diesel buses (1965 through 1967). Trolley bus service continued to the northern, southern and southwestern extremities until final abandonment in 1974.

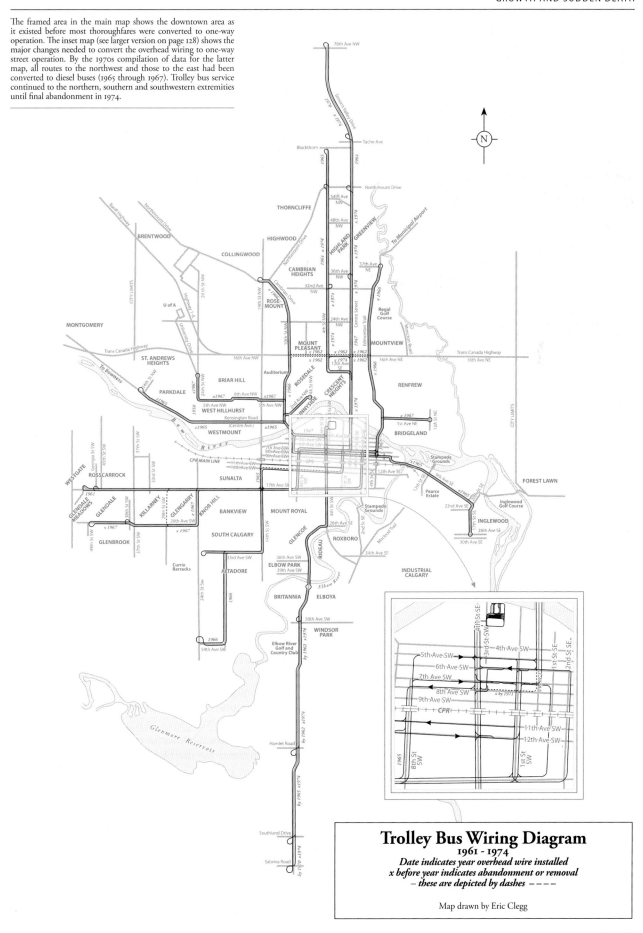

Trolley Bus Wiring Diagram
1961 - 1974
Date indicates year overhead wire installed
x before year indicates abandonment or removal
– these are depicted by dashes – – – –

Map drawn by Eric Clegg

Above: Even if you just missed it, you could tell what route it was. ACF Brill coach No. 501 pulls away along the one-way 8th Avenue sw toward 2nd Street sw. It is a nice early summer day in June 1965, so maybe you could grab some Chubby Chicken before the next bus arrives. (Colin K. Hatcher)

Opposite, lower: In the suburbs in the late 1960s, bus zones were very simply demarcated. Number 433 on the 2 – Mount Pleasant run waits in the loop at 4th St. NW and Blackthorne. (John M. Day)

estimated 60% higher. The effect was estimated to raise trolley bus costs by two cents a mile.

Motor buses were cited as being more flexible in that they were able to be short turned at peak hours, allowing them to do the work of two trolley coaches on heavily-travelled portions of routes. The motor buses did not need overhead infrastructure, and were able to pass stopped buses on the same route. Finally, the motor buses were presented as more attractive and modern, and when equipped with automatic transmissions, able to start as smoothly as any trolley coach. Finally, no new trolley buses were being produced in North America, the last Canadian Car-Brill production model having been delivered in 1954. Adding in the cost of the overhead to the trolley coaches put the vehicle cost of a trolley at $921.48 per seat, while the Canadian Car 52-passenger motor buses came in at $582.69. Whether the report's authors included the cost of all the motor buses, some of which were fully depreciated, worn out and held only 36 passengers, or how the costs of overhead were calculated (depreciation, maintenance and repair) is not clear, but the direction was evident, and the system's former enthusiasm for the trolley coach was now clearly on the wane.

It must be said in fairness to the report's authors that they recommended a blended bus fleet, with extensions to the trolley lines limited to the present main lines, but only after carefully studying economics and applicability of conversion to motor bus. The report concluded by recom-

mending more diesels be added to the fleet, but the basic transportation vehicle was still to be the trolley coach.[14]

On May 18th 1961 there was a request for resumption of the former routing of the Crescent Heights trolley bus line.[15] Then, in January 1962, it was proposed that the Crescent Heights route be withdrawn entirely.[16] Other service changes at that time resulted in the number 5 Belt Line being used in rush hours only, but additional service was added to the number 7 South Calgary route. Route numbers 1, 4 and 9 used diesels only during roadway construction in mid-June.

On October 15th 1961, Mr. Wray wrote to A.H. Nicholson, Engineering Department, asking that the extension of the number 9 Bridgeland route be completed by year-end. It was to continue from the existing terminal at 12th Street and 1st Avenue NE south on 12th Street NE, west on McDougall Road and south on 11A Street NE to the terminal. The route extension would serve homes for the aged and the Canadian National Institute for the Blind (CNIB). The loop was to be situated off a private road (11A Street) which, in turn was located off McDougall Road. However, in a January 1962 letter, Mr. Wray remarked that the approved extension may not be required until late 1962 or early 1963.[17] On January 16th 1963 service was inaugurated on the Bridgeland end of the number 9 route to the senior citizens' home.[18]

At the end of 1961, there were 115 miles of trolley bus routes, compared with 145 miles of motor bus routes. There were 72 miles of trolley wire, while 87.4 miles of street had motor bus service.[19]

The trolley routes left at the end of 1961 were: [20]

1: East Calgary -Parkdale
2: Mount Pleasant-Sunnyside
3: Thorncliffe-Elbow Drive
4: Cambrian Heights-Edmonton Trail
5: Belt Line
6: Killarney
7: South Calgary
9: Bridgeland-West Hillhurst
Crescent Heights
No number assigned to "Crescent Heights" route.

Other extensions considered included the west end of route 9 from the West Hillhurst terminal at 24th Street NW and University Drive, north along the latter and then west along 13th Avenue NW, crossing 29th Street and terminating on the grounds of the new Foothills Hospital site. It was estimated that this would not be required before 1963. However, that service was never instituted by trolley bus. It was also proposed to extend the Elbow Drive trolley route south on Elbow Drive, from its then-present end at Hamlet Road to a new terminal at Sackville Drive, possibly before the end of 1962; however, the need for this was to be reassessed later in the year. Finally, an extension of the Cambrian Heights route was also under review, timing and routing to be determined. [21]

Unused two-way wire on 16th Avenue NW from 10th Street NW to 4th Street NE, except for the eastbound portion from 4th Street NW to Centre, was to be removed when the street was widened. The commissioners concurred with this economy measure in December. This was the wire that became surplus when the route 4 went from a belt configuration to a "U" in 1958. [22]

Fares rose at end of 1962, effective December 15th. Adults rode for six tickets for $1.00; cash fare was 20 cents. Children's tickets were sixteen for $1.00; cash fare was 10 cents. Student's tickets were fifteen for $1.00; cash fare was 10 cents. At this time, the largest city in Canada (in area) had 245 miles of transit routes, but its trolley bus fleet was still held at 105 units. [23] Night routes changed in January 1963. Numbers 1 and 26 (East Calgary and Forest Lawn) were combined, presumably as a motor bus route. Number 3 was split into two routes: north (Thorncliffe) and south (Elbow Drive). Number 6-Killarney operated as a trolley route direct to the city centre from both the 17th and 26th Avenue termini. After 9:15 PM however, the Killarney – 17th Avenue portion operated as a feeder motor bus from 17th Avenue and Glenside Drive to 24th Street SW (Tecumseh), making direct connections with the 26th Avenue (number 6) trolley route. [24]

By December 1963, the number 1 and the south end of the number 3 routes were being served by diesels in the late evening. [25]

On October 16th 1964, Superintendent Wray wrote to D.B. Ball of Goodyear, advising that ten trolley buses were to be removed from service effective immediately. They were fleet numbers 485 to 489 and 495 to 499 inclusive. In response to a questionnaire, Mr. Wray stated that, while there was no formal plan to discontinue trolley buses, all new buses purchased since 1954 had been diesels. Trolley coaches were no longer manufactured in North America, and he repeated the argument that the fixed nature of their routes was now being cited as a disadvantage, as compared with the original assertion (of that being an advantage) when trolley buses were first introduced. He felt that modern diesels could handle peak loads better than a trolley coach could. Capacity of a diesel bus had now grown to 52 passengers, and they were felt to be able to operate on faster schedules than trolley coaches. However, he again stated that there was no formal abandonment plan for the trolleys.[26]

Trolley bus overhead wires were affected by several roadway improvements and reconstructions carried out during 1964. An unused loop on the number 6 route at 17th Avenue and 37th Street sw was removed when the street was widened. The intersection at 5th Avenue and 10th Street NW was improved, as was the Elboya traffic circle. The intersection of 19th Street and 5th/6th Avenue NW was rewired, as was that at 8th Avenue and 4th Street sw. Approved were an extension of the number 3 route on Centre Street north from Northmount Drive to Tache Avenue at a cost of $13,300, and one on the number 2 route from Northmount Drive to Blackthorne Road, at a cost of $8,656. The wire at the 15th Street and 9th Avenue se subway suffered constant damage from oversized truck loads and had to be repaired frequently. In December, the combination of a generator out-of-service at the Wabamun power plant, and the annual rate setting by Calgary Power, forced CTS to use ten diesels to reduce the peak electricity load for a few days.[27]

Trolley destination signs in 1964 are shown in the figure below:[28]

(spare)	Elbow Drive
Belt Line	Tuxedo
Bowness	Windsor Park
Bridgeland	Thorncliffe
West Hillhurst	Exhibition Grounds
University	Garage
(spare)	Killarney - 17 Ave.
Cambrian Heights	Killarney - 26 Avenue
Edmonton Trail	(spare)
Renfrew	Macleod Trail
City Centre	Mount Pleasant
Crescent Heights	Sunnyside South
East Calgary	Calgary Special
Parkdale	(spare)
(spare)	

In May of 1965, an American consultant, John Curtin of Philadelphia, was asked by CTS to evaluate the system and suggest its future direction. In his initial report, he recommended more through routes and improved service west of Centre Street. He also suggested an immediate change in the size of the bus complement - from 101 trolley buses and 87 diesels, to 85 trolley buses and 107 diesels. He recommended that the Mount Pleasant trolley bus route run directly to Killarney-17th Avenue (sw) instead of to Sunnyside, and that the Edmonton Trail run be converted from trolley coach to diesels and extended to 48th Avenue NE. The Sunnyside route would also be converted to diesel buses and connected with the Burns Avenue route.[29] The report was considered

Opposite, upper: Route 3, Elbow Drive via the Belcher Hospital, Holy Cross Hospital and points south – a good run to be on if you were ill during June of 1965. (Colin K. Hatcher)

Above: Number 460, one of only two trolley buses painted in the new two-tone blue scheme, is heading south on 20th Street sw, having just crossed 34th Avenue sw on its way to the loop at 54th Avenue sw and 24th St. sw (Crowchild Trail) on June 29th 1973. (Ted Wickson)

Below: On August 25th 1969, southbound T-44 coach number 427 comes out of the CPR underpass on the 7-South Calgary run between 9th and 10th avenues on 1st Street sw, carrying advertising for the then premier way to fly – Wardair. The clearance was only 12' 6". (John M. Day)

Above: Number 431 signed Killarney – 7th Avenue Route 2 on August 25th 1969. (John M. Day)

Below: In June 1965, ex-Baltimore Brill number 492 passes through the city centre, southbound on First Street sw approaching 8th Avenue sw, carrying Route 7 destinations. (Colin K. Hatcher)

by the CTS, but for the time being more modest changes were made.

Some of these changes took effect on September 6th 1965. The Bowness-Forest Lawn line, made up of parts of routes 1, 25 and 26, became a through diesel route all day. Route number 2 became Mount Pleasant-17th Avenue Killarney, as a result of linking the Mount Pleasant leg of the old route 2 to the 17th Avenue/Killarney leg of route 6. This remained as a trolley bus route operating on 17th Avenue sw, 8th Street sw, 7th and 8th Avenue sw in the downtown area, Centre Street, 12th Avenue NW and 4th Street NW. To make this connection, trolley wire was strung on approximately five blocks of 8th Street sw between 12th and 17th Avenues sw. The Sunnyside portion of route number 2 was converted to diesel at this time by incorporating it with the route 8 Burns Avenue motor bus route. This had already been the routing for late evening service.[30]

Changes to route number 3, Thorncliffe-Elbow Drive were scheduled for December. The Southwood area was again proposed to be connected by direct trolley route from Sackville Drive / Sabrina Road to the downtown area. This time 1⅜ miles of overhead and a new rectifier station were constructed. This was completed by the autumn of 1965, and service commenced immediately thereafter.[31]

Many transit properties experienced ridership decline in the 1950s and tried various means to attract the bus patron. The wait for a bus in Calgary's noted winter conditions was not a major attraction, so a novel way of keeping ridership up was tried − 1500-watt electric heaters were installed at some bus stops on route number 7. They were intended to make the wait for the trolley bus more bearable, however, the results must have been inconclusive, as they were eventually removed.[32] In 1965, a number of extensions were proposed for 1966 and 1967. Route number 4 Cambrian Heights-Edmonton Trail was a candidate for conversion to diesels when sufficient buses became available. An extension was then to be made along the east leg of the route to a new terminal in Greenview. The west leg of the route number 4 would be incorporated into the North Haven service. Route 6 Killarney/26th Avenue was to be altered slightly from the current route. It would run east on 26th Avenue from 24th Street sw to 17A Street, north on it and then east on 17th Avenue to the old route into city centre, and return. This change would give direct service to the 26th Avenue and Bankview areas which were densely populated with many apartments. This required 1.1 miles of new wire, but would eliminate a half mile of wire from the proposed expressway to be built along 24th Street sw from 26th to 17th Avenue sw.

South Calgary route 7, was to be extended into Altadore via 20th Street sw and 50th Avenue sw, to a new terminal at 54th Avenue and 24th Street sw, and would require new overhead to be strung. This extension was to provide downtown service to the residents of the area, and to the future Lincoln Park development. As a result, the Altadore feeder (route 18) could be shortened. Route 9 West

Hillhurst-Bridgeland was to remain as a trolley route for the time being, with no electric extensions. Feeder buses would connect it with Foothills Hospital, and Uxbridge and Utah Drives in University Heights. Eventually, the number 9 route would be converted to diesel buses and the feeders incorporated.[33] The east leg of route number 9 was to be extended south on 12th and 13th Streets NE to a local road paralleling Memorial Drive, west on a service road to 11th Street NE and north to the current route. However, the only extension of route number 9 put into effect was the one proposed in October 1961 for implementation in 1962 or 1963; service was finally extended from the Senior Citizen's home to the CNIB on July 1st 1965.[34]

The proposals were many, and seemed to imply a continuing commitment to the trolley bus, despite some conversions to motor buses. But this was not to be. Although Stampede week in June 1965 saw greater transit activity, with both motor and trolley buses making extra trips, the increased trolley bus activity was short-lived. Stampede events at the Grounds dictated buses coming from downtown looping westbound on 6th Avenue down 1st Street sw, along 17th Avenue to a temporary stop in the Stampede grounds and then returning along 2nd Street sw.[35]

But, on May 16th 1965, the number 4 Cambrian-Edmonton Trail route became victim to the diesel with the early delivery of new buses. The route number 1 East Calgary-Parkdale was changed over in July 1965 and number 2 Sunnyside district, in September.[36]

Anticipated dates for removal of the wires were: 1967 for the overhead on 1st Avenue NE, 5th Avenue-24th Street NW, and 24th Street sw, and 1968 for Kensington Road.[37]

Conversion of the number 9 trolley bus route to diesel was set for March of 1967; thereafter no further conversions were planned. In fact, Calgary Transit officials stated that the trolley buses were good for another ten years. Despite the conversions, costs were again calculated for an extension of the number 9 route into the University of Alberta, Calgary. However, once again, it never materialized.[38] Number 4 was permanently converted to diesel sooner than planned, on Monday May 6th 1966, because the new diesel buses were delivered earlier than promised. Trolley bus wire was subsequently removed from unused portions of the route, and some intersections rebuilt to simpler configurations to accommodate the remaining lines.[39] The trolley fleet stood at 99 coaches, despite the earlier plan to remove ten from the original 105. Of the 99, only 70 were required in regular service. Fourteen of the second-hand ACF Brill trolley buses were left; the remainder were of Canadian Car-Brill manufacture. Only eight were the larger T-48 models.[40]

At the end of April, the old portable substation that dated from the streetcar days blew its last fuse. The 1929 Brown Boveri mercury arc rectifier was still sitting in a rail car. It had survived the end of the streetcar era, located at Haddon Road in the Haysboro area. It was notorious for its tendency to fail at critical times and in the worst weather. None of the CTS electrical crews were sorry to see it go. However it didn't really die; while the rail car was scrapped, the rectifier parts were refurbished and housed in a new building.[41]

Route number 5 was converted to motor bus during 1968, though much of the route wire remained active for portions of the remaining lines. As previously announced, number 9 followed in 1967 and, despite the prior comment that no more conversions were planned, so did the number 6 Killarney 26th Avenue line.[42]

By 1970, only three trolley coach routes were left serving the primary transit arteries of the city. These were the numbers 2, 3 and 7. Nonetheless, trolley bus expansions continued. An extension of route number 3 Thorncliffe route for a half mile north, along Simons Valley Road to 78th Avenue NW, was planned for completion by late 1970.[43]

In keeping with its modernization, the name of the system was changed from "The Calgary Transit System" to "Calgary Transit" on July 7th 1970, and a two-tone blue colour scheme officially adopted.[44] Two of the trolley buses were repainted in the new colours; concurrently, twelve of the ex-Baltimore trolley buses were sold for scrap. Six more were stored as unavailable for revenue use, and two were re-painted in a candy cane striped pattern for use as portable passenger shelters. Despite these scrappings, the Thorncliffe extension opened into the Huntington Hills area to 78th Avenue NW on December 7th 1970. Destination signs continued to read Thorncliffe. The new trolley bus service was favourably received by the area residents.

At this point the following were the remaining route terminals:

3: Elbow Drive / Sackville Drive (Sabrina Road) in the south and Simons Valley Drive/78th Avenue NW in the North;

2: Glenside / 17th Avenue SW in the west, and 4th street NW/Blackthorne in the north;

7: Two south termini: 54th Avenue SW / Crowchild Trail (24th Street SW), and also at 33rd Avenue SW / Crowchild Trail; at the other end, a large loop going from 17th Avenue SW, north on 14th Street SW, then turning east on 12th Avenue SW, to 8th Street SW, north on it to 7th Avenue SW, east along it to 1st Street SW, and south to 17th Avenue SW where it turned west, proceeding back to 14th Street SW.

Responding to enquiries about the fate of the trolley bus network, Calgary Transit stated the routes 2, 3 and 7 would remain electrified, at least until the advent of rapid transit; after that time they would be under review.[45] The lack of spare parts, added to the high cost of those that *were* available, as well as the expense of maintaining such an operation were cited as reasons why many transit properties, including Calgary, were looking seriously at eliminating trolley buses. By mid-1971, the working fleet was reduced to 65 vehicles, with 20 in reserve.[46]

January 26th 1972 dawned as a clear, crisp day. For trolley bus aficionados, this day had special significance, for the long awaited candidate for salvation of the trolley bus had arrived in Calgary. Built by Western Flyer

Opposite, lower: Number 479, signed for Elbow Drive Route 3 on August 25th 1969, is followed by its nemesis – a GMD diesel bus. (John M. Day)

Above: Numbers 429 and 477 head the line-up of trolley buses waiting to go into service on August 24th 1969 at the bus garage. (John M. Day)

Company in Winnipeg, and on loan from the Toronto Transit Commission, TTC number 9213 was intended as the modern trolley coach for transit companies to replace their aging Brills. At last, there was a trolley bus manufactured in Canada, with all of the latest features, and with readily available spares and parts. The next day the demonstrator bus was operated on the number 3 Elbow Drive-Thorncliffe route. It was subsequently used on several other routes until February 29th, when it left for a demonstration in Hamilton, Ontario. A letter to *Trolley Coach News* magazine from Calgary Transit said, "the trolley coach functioned well during this demonstration. The Calgary Transit is now preparing a report comparing the operating costs of modern trolley coaches with the new diesel buses. The operating costs of these new units are very similar. At this time the City of Calgary has made no final decision with respect to the policy to be followed for the replacement of our present trolley equipment which will likely occur within the next five-year period."[47] By the end of the year, that report was in draft form, but had not been released. Curiously, the Number 5 Belt Line still operated two trolleys in one direction only during rush hours.[48] Finally, late in 1973, the report was presented to City Council. Considering the success of the demonstrator, the Council, in a startling move, voted to phase out trolley buses over the next three years. The reasons given were that all the overhead, feeder wires and power sup-

plies would have to be replaced at an estimated cost of $800,000. "Improved maintenance costs of the modern diesel bus lets it compete much more favourably with trolley coaches than the diesel buses of ten and twenty years ago." said a letter to *Trolley Coach News*. It continued, "At the end of 1973 the… cost-per-vehicle mile for diesel fuel was less than 50% of the powered cost-per-mile for trolley coaches."[49]

The final nail was driven into the trolley coach's coffin on April 26th 1974. Construction work on the Centre Street bridge put all trolley bus operation north of the bridge in suspension.[50] The old span poles on the bridge were removed and replaced with widely-spaced lamp standards, obviously not designed for trolley coach overhead. These changes placed the north ends of the number 2 Mount Pleasant and number 3 Thorncliffe routes under diesel power at last.[51] Route 7 (South Calgary) remained electric as did the south parts of the number 3 (Elbow Drive) and number 2 (Killarney/17th Avenue).[52] This left three routes to the south and west of the centre running, utilizing 34 scheduled coaches out of a fleet of 39. Service remained at this level until the end. Twenty coaches were sold to Edmonton for parts, while ten went to Vancouver and sixteen were retained as spares.[53]

Trolley coach service ended abruptly, almost without public announcement. While the remaining routes had been scheduled for abandonment in July after the Stampede,

Above: In June 1965, trolley bus 498 showed both Route 4 and also additional destinations on the front – "Riley Pk., Tech Institute, and Northmount." Another of the ACF Baltimore Brill trolley coaches. (Colin K. Hatcher)

Below: An Ohio Brass advertisement extolling the safety virtues of the modern trolley bus – from *Canadian Transportation*, probably in the late 1930s. Similar advertisement ran throughout the 1940s to convince North American properties to adopt the trolley bus and use Ohio Brass overhead and special work. (Schwarzkopf collection)

Apply the *Safety Factor* OF TROLLEY COACHES TO YOUR INVESTMENT THINKING

The Trolley Coach Will Help Prevent Accidents on Your Property

The management of every successful mass transportation system knows the importance of safety in operating transit vehicles. Every possible precaution is taken to safeguard passengers, motorists and pedestrians.

ments and the loss of valuable time. Since so much importance is attached to the prevention of accidents, it is only natural that vehicle choice should merit serious consideration. For instance, the trolley coach has a long record of safe operation, and has materially reduced the percentage of accidents on many representative properties.

Drivers are instructed to exercise care at all times.

Equipment is frequently inspected and kept in good repair.

Transportation men know that even a slight injury can cause serious legal entangle-

In the first place it is safe because it is so easy to operate. Acceleration is controlled with one simple pedal. To increase or decrease speed of the trolley coach the driver has only to make a single movement with his foot.

And when fast schedules are to be maintained, the smooth flow of electric power literally floats the coach through traffic.

The standee, or the passenger making his way to a seat, need have no fear of a mishap caused by the irregular stages of ordinary acceleration.

Electric braking is another important safety feature. Again there is a marked smoothness, but now it is evidenced in checking momentum. As the coach glides to an easy stop, passengers can safely walk the length of the car, or to the center exit, without fear of being thrown off balance. There are no sudden, jerky stops so common with some

transportation units. The combination of electric braking and rubber tires helps prevent skidding on slippery or icy streets.

An aid in avoiding traffic hazards, as well as maintaining fast schedules, is the maneuverability of the trolley coach. It can operate over the full width of a 30-foot street to avoid careless pedestrians, stalled traffic or trucks parked across the right of way.

Since it can pull up to the curb to load and discharge passengers, it eliminates the danger of crossing from curb to loading zone.

There are many reasons why the public likes to ride trolley coaches, one of the most important is that they are safe. This is a factor well worth considering when making plans for the future enlargement and modernization of your transit system.

Canadian Ohio Brass
COMPANY, LTD. Niagara Falls, Canada

OHIO BRASS COMPANY   MANSFIELD, OHIO, U.S.A.

KEEP BUYING WAR BONDS

a threatened strike (with overhead line crews setting up pickets which bus operators would honour) forced Calgary Transit to move more swiftly. Seventeen CanCar diesel buses in storage were pressed into service together with the 82 General Motors modern diesels that had arrived earlier than expected. This gave the system sufficient capacity to end trolley bus service permanently

In the early morning hours of March 8th 1975, electric passenger transit service came to an end in Calgary. Coach 446 carried W. Kuyt, Director of Transportation, R.H. Wray, the Director of Operations, and Messrs. L. Armour, D. Miller and S. Foffenroth to the barns, where at 12:20 AM revenue service ended.

Some form of official last run was felt to be in order, so coaches 422 and 465 were selected for the honour. Number 422 was repainted inside and out, and on May 8th 1975, the overhead was energized for the last time. At 6:34 AM, trolley bus 465 left the garage with Ted Kendricks, badge number 1, at the wheel. Five trips were made along route number 3 Elbow Drive. All passengers boarding the coach were given a souvenir folder and a free trip. After three trips, number 465 had to have its trolley shoes changed – one last kick at the system that had let it down. It arrived back at the garage at 1:20 PM, then at 1:50, coach 422 rolled out into the sun in its gleaming new paint with "last run" banners on its sides. Ted Kendricks was again at the wheel, as the coach left for downtown carrying officials and invited guests. As a backup, coach 465 followed at a discreet distance, piloted by instructor Milt Anderson.

They proceeded to 6th Avenue and 2nd Street sw where they met a charter diesel bus carrying officials and guests from City Hall. At 2:10 PM, both coaches departed for downtown with 422 leading. At Windsor Place and Elbow Drive, 422 pulled over and 465 ran quickly to Sabrina Road loop so the photographers could catch the arrival of 422 pulling into the loop for the last time. Both coaches then left the loop and returned to 6th Avenue and 2nd Street sw. Number 465 then left for the garage as the speeches began.

B.H. Cornish, Commissioner of Transportation and Planning presided over the ceremony. Alderman Virnetta Anderson spoke on behalf of City Council, and then with help from Operator Kendricks and Chief Supervisor of Personnel Services, H. Parsons, pulled down the trolley poles. The officials then adjourned for refreshments, and the poles were raised for the final trip to the garage. On board were H.L. Simons, Supervisor of Maintenance (at the wheel); L.J. Penny, Night Maintenance Supervisor; Don McDermid, Passenger Services Representative; and the chronicler of the event, trolley bus fan Chris Radkey. At 4th Street and 2nd Avenue sw, a stop was made for Mr. Penny and Mr. Simon to photograph each other at the wheel. Then Mr. Penny drove the bus down 2nd Avenue sw to the garage. At 4:17 PM the poles were lowered forever. An era of fast, silent, electric transportation in Calgary had completely ended.[54]

Above: This ad that ran in *Canadian Transportation* probably during the late 1930s and throughout the 1940s shows a smaller version of the ACF coaches that Calgary bought second hand, coincidentally from the company shown here – Baltimore Transit. (Schwarzkopf collection)

Twenty-eight non-operational coaches were sold to Vancouver for $500 each; 25 additional coaches in working order, at $1,000 each, went also to the west coast, shipped by Canadian Pacific Railway in September of that year. Spare parts, as well as usable overhead (including a great deal of the special work), was sold to Edmonton. One coach, number 432 was sold to a private buyer.[55]

Rumours of renewed trolley bus activity surfaced from time to time, but were just that – rumours. Eventually the wires came down and the trolley coach, like its forerunner, the streetcar, became only a memory. However, electric transit aficionados in Calgary had only a short period of mourning, for plans were already underway for the "C Train" system, operating a modern version of the streetcar: a light rail vehicle. Soon the residents of Canada's oil capital would once again hear the singing of a trolley on overhead wire on a frosty western morning, as they had for most of that city's life.

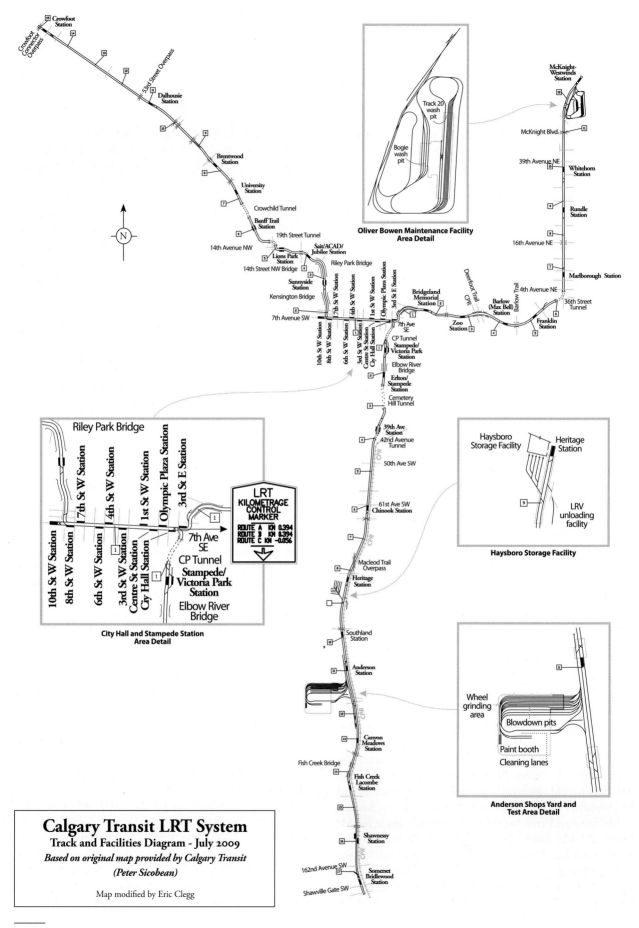

Oliver Bowen Maintenance Facility Area Detail

Track 20 wash pit

Bogie wash pit

McKnight-Westwinds Station

McKnight Blvd.

39th Avenue NE

Whitehorn Station

16th Avenue NE

Rundle Station

Marlborough Station

4th Avenue NE

36th Street Tunnel

Crowfoot Station

Crowfoot Connector Overpass

53rd Street Overpass

Dalhousie Station

Brentwood Station

University Station

Crowchild Tunnel

Banff Trail Station

19th Street Tunnel

14th Avenue NW

Sait/ACAD/Jubilee Station

Lions Park Station

Riley Park Bridge

14th Street NW Bridge

Sunnyside Station

Kensington Bridge

7th Avenue SW

10th St W Station
8th St W Station
6th St W Station
3rd St W Station
4th St W Station
1st St W Station
Centre St Station
City Hall Station
Olympic Plaza Station
3rd St E Station
7th Ave SE

Bridgeland Memorial Station

Deerfoot Trail CPR

Barlow (Max Bell) Station

Barlow Trail

Zoo Station

Franklin Station

CP Tunnel

Stampede/Victoria Park Station

Elbow River Bridge

Erlton/Stampede Station

Cemetery Hill Tunnel

39th Ave Station

42nd Avenue Tunnel

50th Ave SW

61st Ave SW Chinook Station

Macleod Trail Overpass

Heritage Station

Southland Station

Anderson Station

Canyon Meadows Station

Fish Creek Bridge

Fish Creek Lacombe Station

Shawnessy Station

162nd Avenue SW

Somerset Bridlewood Station

Shawville Gate SW

Riley Park Bridge

7th St W Station
4th St W Station
1st St W Station
Olympic Plaza Station
3rd St E Station

10th St W Station
8th St W Station
6th St W Station
3rd St W Station
Centre St Station
City Hall Station

7th Ave SE

CP Tunnel

Stampede/Victoria Park Station

Elbow River Bridge

LRT KILOMETRAGE CONTROL MARKER

ROUTE A   KM 0.394
ROUTE B   KM 0.394
ROUTE C   KM -0.056

City Hall and Stampede Station Area Detail

Haysboro Storage Facility

Heritage Station

LRV unloading facility

Haysboro Storage Facility

Anderson Shops Yard and Test Area Detail

Wheel grinding area

Blowdown pits

Paint booth

Cleaning lanes

Calgary Transit LRT System
Track and Facilities Diagram - July 2009
Based on original map provided by Calgary Transit
(Peter Sicobean)

Map modified by Eric Clegg

CHAPTER ELEVEN

The C-Train Concept

At 1:00 PM on Monday, May 25th 1981, electric rail transit returned to Calgary after a thirty-year absence. Calgary Transit's new 12.5 km (7.8 miles) light rail transit (LRT) line was officially opened. Operating as the "C-Train", the line accesses south central Calgary on a private right-of-way from the downtown area, effectively reducing commuter traffic congestion on roadways leading into the downtown area and reducing travel time for commuters going to and from work. Calgary's abandoned streetcar tracks formerly crossed the city on 8th Avenue s. The new LRT line serves the downtown area with surface tracks on 7th Avenue s, sharing the roadway with transit buses, police and other emergency vehicles. In 1981, the twelve-block east-west LRT street operation from the western terminal between 9th and 8th streets sw to 3rd Street se was unique in North America. However, the concept of LRT street-running common to many European cities has since been employed on other North American LRT systems operating in San Diego and Sacramento, California, Buffalo, New York and Portland, Oregon. In Calgary, street running helped to acclimatize the public to the sensitive idea of having LRT become an integral part of the environment in a residential community. The opening of the northwest leg, Calgary Transit's third C-Train route, in September 1987 introduced surface LRT to residential areas, once again setting a North American LRT precedent.

Calgary's transportation needs changed dramatically after the old streetcars were retired in 1950. The population grew from 127,057 in 1950 to 650,618 in 1980, resulting in a considerable expansion of settlement well beyond the city's 1950 boundaries. Calgary's 2009 population is over one million and the three current LRT lines reach into areas that were sparsely settled even in 1980. Following the demise of the streetcar, the private automobile became the chief means of transportation within the growing metropolis, a transition so rapid that the volume of traffic soon became too large for the streets and avenues leading to, and within, the city core. Efforts to maximize efficiency included a network of one-way streets and the construction of multi-storey parkades, but these measures proved to be ineffectual. These circumstances led to a series of transportation studies which ultimately resulted in LRT being put forward as a viable public transit alternative.

The first rail transit option considered by Calgary was the Simpson & Curtain Ltd. proposal of 1966. Their study resulted in a recommendation calling for a 32 km (20 mile) grade-separated heavy rail rapid transit system. City Council approved two of the recommended high-priority corridors; right-of-way protection and land acquisition began immediately.[1] One of these corridors was located along the Macleod Trail adjacent to Canadian Pacific Railway's Macleod Subdivision leading to Lethbridge. The proposed new rail line would travel through an area formerly served by the Manchester streetcar line, abandoned in June 1947. The second corridor extended from the downtown area northwest toward the University. However, slower population growth, lower population density, changes in roadway construction plans and rapidly-escalating construction costs all combined to make the several hundred-million dollar rapid transit proposal of 1966 an unsuitable alternative for Calgary.[2]

In the meantime, continued traffic congestion and high downtown parking fees created renewed interest in public transportation. In 1972, Calgary Transit introduced its "Blue Arrow" express bus system to help cope with this demand. Ridership on the buses did begin to increase in proportion to the number of high-rise buildings completed in the downtown core. In 1973, another report entitled *A Balanced Transportation Concept for the City of Calgary* recommended a more modest road construction program than that proposed in previous studies, in addition to a number of transit improvements. It was at this time that an extended express bus system, additional bus shelter installations and an expanded traffic control system giving priority treatment to buses were all introduced.[3]

In 1975, two additional studies were completed. *The Transportation Improvement and Priority Study*, and *Light Rail Transit for Calgary,* described the need for rapid transit in the south corridor between city centre and the Manchester district, as well as the need to carry out transit and roadway improvements. The recommendations in these reports were approved by City Council. However, financial support from the Province of Alberta was withheld, pending a further independent review of these studies, to verify the propriety and costs of light rail transit in the south corridor.[4] This review considered various options: bus lanes along the main corridor (Macleod Trail); a "bus way" or reserved bus right-of-way separate from the street; and finally, light rail transit. Although the capital cost of the light rail transit alternative was the highest, the long-term operating cost was significantly lower. The "bus way" was considered impractical, not only for its operating costs, but also because the downtown area would be unable to accommodate the large number of buses required to serve it. The bus lane alternative was deemed to have too much impact on automobile traffic as well as contributing to downtown congestion.[5] On May 25th 1977, the results of that review, which endorsed light rail transit, were presented to City

Above: An LRV car is about to be switched into the Anderson Shops yard. The round warning bell below and to the right of the headlight, the four-step anticlimber, and the running lights adjacent to the destination signs, differentiate the Calgary LRVs from the Edmonton LRVs. (Calgary Transit)

Below: Inside the three-track maintenance area at Anderson Shops, the work of assembling LRV cars progresses. In the foreground, electric motors are mounted on trucks while assembly takes place in the background. Mobile cranes carry out the work which the yet-to-be-installed overhead crane would normally perform. (Calgary Transit)

Council, which accepted the LRT alternative at that same meeting.[6] By endorsing the LRT alternative, the City of Calgary chose to implement a light rail transit concept which drew on the highly successful streetcar technology developed during the first half of the twentieth century. Significant advances had been made in the electrical, mechanical and aesthetic appearances over the original technology. The application of the technology and its relationship to the surrounding environment is another significant improvement. Following the May 25th 1977 approval of the LRT concept, steps were immediately taken toward finalizing plans and preparing all of the necessary contracts.

Construction Begins

The contract for the light rail vehicles (LRVs) was the first let. However, plans for the shop where the LRVs were to be assembled and finished received early attention. Both were required for the south leg, but the shop would also support a more extensive LRT network. In July 1977, City Council awarded a contract for 27 LRVs to Siemens Duewag of Dusseldorf, West Germany valued at $25,751,671. The price for each LRV was $953,765.[7] The city opted for award procurement on the basis of a negotiated price rather than inviting tenders. The award was partly based on the excellent ten-year performance record of the similar U2 LRVs in Frankfurt, West Germany.[8] The letting of the $6.4 million contract for Calgary Transit's Anderson Road shop complex soon followed. In addition to providing space to assemble the LRVs, it would ultimately house efficient complete maintenance and storage facilities for up to 54 LRVs and light maintenance and storage facilities for 115 buses. As work on these two projects progressed, contracts were let over the following three years for the construction of the right-of-way, tunnels, bridges, underpasses, track, the 7th Avenue s transit mall, stations, electric power substations and the overhead electric catenary system.

The Rolling Stock

Calgary's first light rail vehicle components arrived in January 1980; it was completely assembled by April of that year. The last unit of the initial order of 27 LRVs arrived in September 1980, and it was completed by January 1981. The LRVs arrived as body shells from Duewag (Waggonfabrik uerdingen AG), Werk Dusseldorf, West Germany. Trucks from the same manufacturer, and electrical equipment from Siemens, arrived with each corresponding LRV shipment. These components were assembled in the Calgary shop. All of this equipment came to Alberta via the Port of Vancouver, where it was transferred to Canadian Pacific Railway flat cars for the balance of the trip to Calgary. A connection from the Canadian Pacific Railway Macleod Subdivision permitted delivery of the LRVs directly into the Anderson Shops rail yard. Assembly of the LRVs included interior finishing plus installation of all electrical and mechanical

components. When completed, the Canadian content of the finished LRVs totalled 42%.[9]

Underframe, side frame and roof frame components are welded together. The equipment boxes, cable and air ducts are welded to the underframe. The sidewall sheets are in turn welded to the side frame. Car ends are fabricated from reinforced fiberglass and fastened to the car body members. This design permits easy removal and replacement in the event of collision damage. The articulation is patterned after Duewag's own widely-proven design. The articulation and its bellows are covered by reinforced fiberglass parts which blend into the interior décor of the car. Passengers can pass safely across the articulation platform from one section of the car to the other. A durable rubber covering laid on the plywood floor minimizes accidental slipping.[10]

The seats are arranged transversely in facing pairs, parlour style, along each side of the car body. The foam back and seat pads are covered with an attractive brushed nylon fabric, while the frames are supported from the ceiling at the outer or aisle sides by the stanchion poles. All windows are of safety glass and held in place by rubber profiles. The frameless upper sash on each of the side windows opens inward. Additional summer ventilation is available with outside air drawn through roof top ventilators.[11] The air in the passenger compartment is changed about thirty times per hour. In the summer, air drawn through the vents in the side skirting is used to cool the under-floor resistance grids. These grids generate heat constantly as the LRV stops and starts. In winter, the outside air continues to cool resistance grids but, after passing over the grids, the resultant warm air is forced into the passenger compartment to provide heat.[12]

An operator's cab, completely enclosed with door access through the passenger compartment, is located at both ends of each articulated unit. At the left of the operator's position is the master controller. This determines acceleration and braking of the car or train. As an operating safety precaution, the operator must keep a foot pedal depressed continually, or alternatively, press and hold a thumb button on the instrument panel. Should the operator release the selected safety feature either through incapacitation or inadvertence while the unit is in motion, the braking system will bring the unit to an immediate stop. This safety appliance is called Automatic Train Stop (ATS).[13] Passenger safety is further assured by the fact that a unit cannot move until all doors are properly closed. Any object breaking a photoelectric cell beam across a doorway will prevent an open door from closing prematurely. Pressure-sensitive door edges closing on a passenger or an object will cause a closing door to retract immediately. When all doors are safely closed and locked, a single stroke bell sounds in the cab to signify to the operator that the train may proceed.

The panel in front of the operator has several buttons controlling auxiliary functions on the unit. These include selecting the side of the car on which to open the doors, activating or deactivating the interior and exterior passenger-operated door-opening buttons, operating the windshield

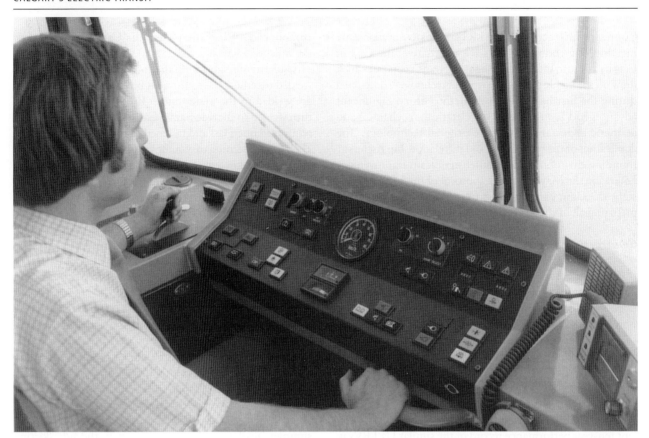

Above: Ernst Thiele, Maintenance Engineer, sits at the control panel of an LRV. His left hand is on the throttle/brake lever, while his right hand clasps the handle where the thumb button for the automatic train stop switch is located. The radio to the right allows the operator to communicate with Calgary Transit's central control.
(Colin K. Hatcher)

wipers, raising or lowering the pantograph and several other functions related to the automatic signalling system. A microphone mounted in the cab enables the operator to speak to the passengers on the train, or to people outside the unit, via speakers mounted on the car roof.

The master controller provides a very sophisticated means of running and braking single or coupled LRVs. Moving the controller handle forward sets the semi-automatic electronic SIMATIC unit into running mode, while pulling the handle back orders it to activate the braking system. The SIMATIC unit features jerk-limitation in acceleration or deceleration, controls the current delivered to the traction motors, and responds to wheel spinning or slipping, holding it to a minimum. The unit monitors the cam-controller position in the motor-driven controller which governs the series/parallel starting of the traction motors. The controller has twenty driving steps, including two field-weakening steps, which change motor speeds. It also governs rheostatic braking in seventeen steps. In the event of power loss, the SIMATIC unit, which draws its power from a 24-volt battery, automatically brings the train to a stop.[14]

The braking system relies primarily on the rheostat resistances. Once speed is reduced to five km per hour by the rheostatic braking system, the SIMATIC unit activates the mechanical spring brake, bringing the car to a full stop. Because of the line's street running and the steep grades, the Calgary LRVs have a mechanical spring brake installed on all three trucks as an added safety precaution. If the operator pulls the master controller handle all the way back, an emergency brake application is immediately activated. The electromagnetic track brakes located between the wheels on both sides of all trucks grasp the rails with a powerful magnetic force. The track brake works in conjunction with the signal system. It is also activated under certain conditions relative to the function of the Automatic Train Control System. Power for the track brake comes from the 24-volt direct current battery bank.[15]

Finally, a motor-generator set with a 600-volt direct current motor generates 230 volts alternating current for all the auxiliary electrical equipment on the car, such as lighting and ventilation fans.[16]

Calgary Transit officially refers to its 27 first generation LRVs as RTC 1 (Rail Transit Car). They are assigned fleet numbers 2001 through 2027 inclusive.

Anderson Shops

Anderson Shops, built during 1979, became one of the first operational facilities on the system, and it received the first LRV in January 1980.

The shops are located east of the Macleod Trail at Anderson Road. The LRT portion of this building was laid out with nine storage tracks, three repair or maintenance tracks, and one entry track. Most of the LRV assembly work

Above: On April 24th 1981, few cars were finished in C-Train stripes. These two cars stand outside the maintenance shops on tracks 10 and 11 at the east side of the Anderson Shops building. The partially dismantled track in the foreground is the lead to the CPR Macleod Subdivision. (Colin K. Hatcher)

Below: The Cline Shuttle Wagon stands above the pit on track 10 in the maintenance shops. Note the standard railway coupler and air brake hose. An LRV Scharfenberg mechanical and Fabeg electric coupler is on the front. (Colin K. Hatcher)

Above: The track leading into Anderson Shops has been completed in this April 24th 1981 view taken from the pedestrian overpass at Anderson station. The CPR Macleod subdivision track is on the left. (Colin K. Hatcher)

Below: Cut and cover tunnel work begins on the south approach to Cemetery Hill. (Calgary Transit)

was carried out in the three-track self-contained section within the building which became the LRV maintenance section once operations began. There is plenty of room between the tracks in this area to allow extensive mechanical, electrical and body work to be carried out on the LRVs.

The shops are designed so that LRVs returning from passenger service enter the east side of the building at door 16, close to the south end of the building. Immediately after entry into the building, a three-car train can be accommodated at a vacuum stand. Here, the interior is given a thorough cleaning, and the sand boxes are refilled. Once these tasks have been completed, the train moves slowly through the wash rack. It then negotiates a sharp, ninety-degree curve and heads north along the back wall of the building where it approaches the first turnouts in the ladder track leading into tracks 12, 11, and 10. These three tracks pass through the maintenance shop. LRVs not requiring maintenance continue straight along the back wall until they reach another series of turnouts leading into one of the nine storage tracks numbered 9 through 1. These tracks run parallel to the shop tracks. Having been cleaned, turned and stored in that sequence within the building, the LRVs are then ready for their next assignment. As a single LRV or full train is required for service, it can simply be run off the storage track, through the ladder tracks outside the front of the building, to the line at Anderson station. When Anderson Shops first went into service as an operational base for the south leg of the LRT system, only storage tracks 9 through 5 were installed.[17] Subsequent to the opening of the south leg, as additional cars were received to support service on the proposed extensions, it was necessary to install tracks 4 through 1 inclusive in the covered storage space already provided within the building. These lanes or tracks were powered in mid-1984. Almost all tracks in the building are made up of girder-groove streetcar rails set in concrete.

All of the maintenance facilities, with the exception of the wheel grinding and wheel-press apparatus (which is located on track 9), are housed in a well-lit and heated shop area within the main building. Overhead doors just off the ladder tracks 10, 11 and 12 allow the shop to be entirely closed off from the storage area. These run-through shop tracks exit directly to a paved apron area outside the front (east) side of the building. An eight-tonne overhead crane used for transferring truck assemblies, wheels and axles, motors and other LRV parts spans tracks 11 and 12. In order to allow the crane to perform effectively, this portion of these tracks is free of overhead wire. Each of the tracks in the shops includes an inspection pit. The rails are supported on steel pedestals set at intervals along the length of the pits. The usual open area between the rails also extends about one metre (one yard approximately) on the outer sides of the rails. These extensions are covered by a grated steel deck, enabling technicians to have a full view of the underside of the LRV from all angles.[18]

Switching chores around Anderson Shops are carried out by a diesel powered road-rail vehicle called a "Cline Shuttle

Wagon". It has four highway truck tires which power the unit whether it is running on or off the rails. Two hydraulically-raised four-wheeled bogies, one set ahead of the front tires and the second set behind the rear tires, guide the unit along the railway tracks. The front can be fitted with a standard transit coupler, a snow blower or a rotary snow broom. A standard railway coupler with air brake hose is fixed to the rear. A "cherry picker" type crane is mounted on the deck behind the cab. A City of Calgary Electric System distribution truck fitted with retractable flanged wheels enables workmen to perform overhead maintenance as required.[19]

The South Leg – Right-of-Way

Contracts for major structures for the various sections of the right-of-way were let during 1979. The first of these, awarded on January 5th of that year, was for a three-span, four-lane bridge carrying Southland Drive over the LRT and Canadian Pacific Railway right-of-way west of the Macleod Trail. That project was scheduled for completion in June of the same year.[20]

Three tunnels were constructed on the south leg. The cut and cover method was used in all three cases, as opposed to boring a passage into the ground or through a hillside and removing the spoil from the bore as it progressed. The Cemetery Hill tunnel under the Macleod Trail, between 34th and 24th Avenues SE, is the longest of the three. Here several coffins had to be exhumed and reburied in another area of the cemetery before tunnel construction began. The tunnel was excavated or opened from the top and the floor poured. A collapsible form was then assembled for the pouring of the walls and ceiling. After the concrete had set, the form was collapsed and moved forward, to be used on the next section. As each section of the tunnel was completed, it was back-filled and covered over again. The tunnel itself is a double box, 700 m (2,296 feet) long. A much shorter tunnel south of Cemetery Hill at 42nd Avenue SE takes the LRT right-of-way under the Canadian Pacific Railway service track. Another short tunnel north of Cemetery Hill takes the LRT underground just south of 12th Avenue SE. After passing under the Canadian Pacific Railway mainline and 9th Avenue SE, it rises steeply to surface level again at 8th Avenue SE before turning sharply into the 7th Avenue S transit mall.[21]

On January 12th 1979, the contract for the Elbow River bridges just east of Macleod Trail near 26th Avenue was awarded. The 124 m (407 feet) long bridges carry the double track line across the Elbow River. During construction, one of these spans accidently fell, raising some concern about the project being completed on schedule. There was plenty of lead time, however, and the ensuing bridge construction was completed without delaying the opening of the line. In May 1979, a contract was awarded to take Glenmore Trail and Fairmont Drive over the LRT and Canadian Pacific Railway lines.[22]

Above: Streets intersecting with 7th Avenue s were closed for brief periods to enable contractors to get access to the utility lines below. Work at 1st Street SE is well underway in this scene. (Calgary Transit)

Below: In July 1979, 7th Avenue s was closed to traffic from 2nd Street SE to 9th Street SW to enable work to begin on renewing, relocating and mapping underground utilities. That work is illustrated in this scene on 7th Avenue SE between City Hall on the left and the Calgary Public Library building on the right. (Calgary Transit)

Top left: Note the track construction from the tunnel leading up the grade to the 25th Avenue SE crossing and Erlton station.
(Colin K. Hatcher)

Top right: Once the excavation work for relocating underground services had been completed along 7th Avenue s, the concrete base for the final surfacing was laid. Girder groove rail is being set in place in this scene looking east from 2nd Street sw to 1st Street sw.
(Calgary Transit)

Tracklaying began at the south end of the line. As the three tunnel contracts and the 7th Avenue s paving base neared completion, tracklaying continued north into the downtown area. For most of the distance south of 7th Avenue s, 50 kg/m (approximately 110 lbs/yard) welded T rail was set down on Conforce Costain concrete ties and fastened with Pandrol clips. The ties were tamped into a solid layer of high grade ballast. The tunnel track is secured to individual concrete pads on the tunnel floor, with Pandrol clips, spaced about the same distance apart as ballasted ties. Grooved rail in the paved streets weighs 60 kg/m (approximately 130 lbs/yard).[23] All special girder-grooved rail is set in pavement at Anderson shop and on 7th Avenue s. All turnouts along the line and the special ladder track at Anderson shop were fabricated at the Krupp steel works in West Germany. While most street railway systems formerly employed single-moving-point turnouts, those on Calgary's LRT lines have double points because of the generally higher operating speeds. Due to the large percentage of pavement-set grooved rail on the system, the wheels of the LRVs are profiled after streetcar wheels, with very shallow flanges.

The 7th Avenue Transit Mall

In July 1979, immediately following the close of that season's well known Calgary Stampede, 7th Avenue sw between 2nd Street sw and 9th Street sw was closed to traffic as workmen began to prepare it for the LRT tracks.[24] On July 16th 1979, Calgary Transit rerouted ten bus routes from most of 7th Avenue s due to the closure. This was the first phase of the lengthy closure of this busy thoroughfare in the downtown core. Excavation began to complete the extensive task of relocating all of the utility lines from under the centre of the roadway to either side, below the sidewalks. Portions of the avenue remained open for local traffic as construction permitted. Every effort was made to keep the cross streets open, so most of the intersection work took place on weekends to minimize traffic disruptions. A periodic newsletter called *On Track* was introduced by the City of Calgary Transportation Department, Light Rail Transit Division, to keep residents and business people informed of the construction progress. As the utilities work was completed, the sections were backfilled and work moved on. The second stage involved closing 7th Avenue s from 2nd Street sw to 3rd Street SE so that similar utilities relocation work could be completed. That work was carried out from November 1979 to November 1980.

Track laying began in the spring of 1980. First, a solid gravel base was laid over the backfilled excavation work. A concrete base was then poured, followed by an asphalt-like substance called mastic, which reduces noise and vibration and insulates the flow of electricity. The rail was then laid upon the mastic, with gauge bars set between and bolted to

the rails to hold them to the proper 1435mm (4'8 ½") gauge. Standard railway ties were not used in the 7th Avenue SE/SW paved section. Concrete was then poured around the rails to a level even with the top of the rails to provide a smooth surface. Concrete was also poured for the bus lanes along both sides of the avenue.[25] As track-laying progressed, special promotions along 7th Avenue S were held. These promotions, called "Hard Hat Days", were sponsored by the Downtown Businessmen's Association. A monthly eight-page flyer offered many bargains to downtown shoppers for the period from June to December 1980. In this way, citizens were attracted back to 7th Avenue S after the construction disruptions which had begun a year earlier, and they could see the track-laying progress.

The contract for the construction of the downtown stations along 7th Avenue S was awarded in September 1980.[26] These platforms are simple pre-cast concrete structures which were assembled off-site and then transported to their respective locations along the curb lane of the avenue immediately

parallel to the sidewalk. Like the suburban stations, each accommodates a three-car train. About two-thirds of the platform is protected by a roof. Eight steel poles along the centre of the platform, each with four arms radiating out umbrella-style, support the outer roof beams which in turn support the total roof structure. The centre portion of the roof is constructed with two separate peaks of tempered glass panes. These enhance the downtown stations by giving them the same brightness as their suburban counterparts. A shelter located under the roof provides seating for waiting passengers. The open platform also has a glass-panelled shelter and lamp standards of the same design as the suburban stations. Access is from the sidewalk. There is a five-step stairway at each end, as well as five narrower stairways parallel to the platform and the sidewalk. A long ramp also connects the sidewalk and platform about midway along the latter. Hand rails fitted with tempered glass panels border the sidewalk edge of the platforms. These "couplets" of platforms are staggered, one on each side of an intersection. As

Opposite: On May 21st 1985, car 2048 leads an Anderson-bound train east along 7th Avenue sw past the Court House and the westbound 4th Street sw station. (Ted Wickson)

Above: A City of Calgary Electric System truck, equipped with rail bogies to enable it to aid in servicing the overhead line along the LRT right-of-way, stands between Southland and Anderson stations on April 24th 1981. (Colin K. Hatcher)

a result each "directional" platform bears its own distinct location name. The platforms are staggered in this manner to allow buses to operate along 7th Avenue s.

Finally, the overhead power supply for the LRVs was installed.

Electric Power

The overhead power system carries 600 volts direct current. Along 7th Avenue s, a single contact wire is suspended over each track from span wires which are supported, in turn, by steel poles lining each side of the street. Upon leaving 7th Avenue se southbound, the overhead line becomes standard catenary with an upper messenger wire supporting a lower contact wire. The pantograph on top of each car has two carbon bars which collect current from the overhead. The catenary wire is staggered 300 mm (12 inches) to either side of centre for the full length of the system, to make maximum use of the carbon collector bars on the panto-

graph and to prevent excessive wear in the centre portion of the collector bar. The City of Calgary Electric System installed the overhead line using one of its trucks adapted for rail-borne use. Power substations located at regular intervals feed direct current power into the line to ensure an even distribution of power to the system.

Transit Stations

In August 1979, contracts were let for the three major suburban stations: Heritage, Southland and Anderson, the southern terminal. Work began on Erlton and Stampede stations in March 1980, while work at Chinook began in May 1980. All of these stations were designed to admit passengers via passages over the transit tracks to island-type loading platforms between the double tracks. Platforms stretch 80 m (262 feet) from the foot of the stairways, enough to accommodate a three-car train. They are capable of being extended a full 105 m (345 feet) in order to handle five-car trains.[7]

Above: A southbound three-car C-Train departs Stampede (Victoria Park/Stampede) station in 1985. Note the extra track and platform to facilitate extra C-Train services during Stampede and Pengrave Saddledome events. The northbound lanes of the Macleod Trail pass along the far side of the C-Train. In streetcar days it was 2nd Street SE and streetcars passed by the building in the background, Fire Hall No. 2, on their way to and from the carbarns. The tower of that building appears in some of the streetcar photographs.
(Colin K. Hatcher)

The general concept of design and passenger handling at the four southernmost stations (Anderson, Southland, Heritage and Chinook) provides for about two-thirds of the platform length being under cover, protected by an aesthetically-pleasing tempered glass roof, supported by sidewalls with large glass panels which also enclose the tracks. This design produces a very bright, open atmosphere, while offering some protection against cold winds and wet weather. On the open section of each platform, there is a small transparent shelter to offer protection against the elements.

The 39th Avenue station, initially known as the 42nd Avenue station, stands in austere contrast to those just described. It consists simply of two high-level concrete platforms on the outside of the tracks, accessed by a few steps up from street level off 39th Avenue SE.

Erlton station possesses the same general design features as the four southern stations. It is located at 24th Avenue SE, just north of Cemetery Hill, and it serves an area across the Elbow River from the Calgary Exhibition and Stampede Grounds. Architecturally, however, it is characterized by two distinctive "chuck wagon"-style arched roofs over the island platform at track level, with a second, narrower parallel arch roof over the passageway above the north track. The end walls of the latter arched roof section are floor-to-ceiling panelled glass, affording an excellent view of the Calgary skyline to the north, and of Cemetery Hill to the south. The platform roof stretches south for only one car length, leaving the rest of the platform open.

Since the platform roof does not extend out over the tracks, there are no side walls enclosing the tracks to protect the platform. The "chuck wagon" roof design is particularly appropriate at Erlton as the chuck wagon races are a widely-known and popular feature of the annual Calgary Exhibition and Stampede.

The Stampede station located at 17th Avenue SE is also unique. It is designed to handle large crowds attending events at the Stampede Grounds and at the Calgary Pengrowth Saddledome, home of the Calgary Flames Hockey Club. In contrast to other suburban stations, the Stampede station has a wide loading platform, with stairway access leading to the centre of the platform rather than to one end. The platform is completely covered and trimmed with canvas awnings stretched over a curved steel frame around the outer edge of the roof. There is no sidewall protection for the platform. Another unique feature, due to the line's very close proximity to the Macleod Trail at this point, is an overhead walkway across that thoroughfare. This gives pedestrians from the neighbourhood west of the Macleod Trail safe access to the station. A holding siding long enough to store two three-car trains and connected at both ends to the northbound track is located at Stampede station.

C-Trains travel along a very heavy traffic corridor and – as they were designed to ease automobile congestion along the Macleod Trail and decrease travel time into the downtown area – the four stations at the extreme south end of the line have large "Park 'n' Ride" parking lots. Each parking stall is equipped with an electrical outlet so that passengers leaving their cars at the station all day can keep their engine blocks warm for more reliable starting during the severely-cold winter months. In 2009 The City of Calgary gradually initiated a parking fee program to cover the cost of maintenance and security at each of its LRT parking lots. The 39th Avenue station also has a small parking lot. Drop-off areas for passengers from automobiles (called "Kiss 'n' Ride") are also located at Chinook, Heritage, Southland and Anderson stations. Feeder buses bring passengers to all of the stations between Erlton and Anderson stations from nearby residential areas. This provides a convenient transfer to the C-Train for a fast trip into the downtown area or to a Stampede Grounds or Pengrowth Saddledome event. The Stampede station is restricted to pedestrian access and con-

Above: Passengers wait to board an arriving northbound C-Train led by LRV 2023 at Southland station on August 28th 1981. (Ted Wickson)

Below: A two-car C-Train led by LRV 2012 awaits departure from Anderson station. Note the tracks of the CPR Macleod subdivision left of the 2012 and the bus in the transfer station. (Colin K. Hatcher)

Above: Two distinctive roof arches characterize the Erlton station at 24th Street se. The arches depict the profile of a chuckwagon to promote a "Calgary Stampede" theme. The date is September 3rd 1981. Today the station is called Erlton/Stampede station.
(Colin K. Hatcher)

necting bus service from the major crosstown routes. The proximity of this station to downtown precludes the need for passenger drop-off or parking areas; however, as the system developed, Stampede Grounds management offered paid parking service to commuters. As the system extended further south to Fish Creek-Lacombe station in 2001 and Somerset-Bridlewood in 2004, LRT parking lots were established at all of the new stations on these extensions.

Fare Collection

Planning for the public service features of the LRT system – such as station design, fare collection, information and marketing strategies, passenger convenience and schedules – began early in the development process. Station design and access in the suburban and in the downtown transit mall settings has already been discussed. Passenger access to all of the stations is easy and unimpeded, reflecting the "proof-of-payment" or "non-barrier" fare system. Passengers simply walk through the station directly to platform level and board the trains at will. Each passenger, however, must carry valid proof that his or her fare has been paid whenever travelling outside of the 7th Avenue s fare-free corridor (this fare-free corridor is described later).[28] Failure to present, upon request, such proof-of-payment to a protective services

officer of the City of Calgary while riding on a C-Train will result in a fine being levied.

Several fare options are available. Regular transit riders had been accustomed to carrying what was once known as a monthly "Zipcard" (prepaid fare card) to present to the operator upon boarding a Calgary Transit bus. It was also valid proof of payment on the C-Train. Calgary Transit now markets this prepaid fare option as a Monthly Pass. Other pass-type proofs of payment include a student pass available through schools, or a senior citizen's pass available through the City of Calgary Information Centre. Passes for the Canadian National Institute for the Blind (CNIB), war amputees and CT employees are accepted as well. In addition, police officers and Canada Post mail carriers travel free when they are in uniform. A valid bus transfer, issued upon payment of cash fare on a CT bus, is also proof of payment. Passengers transferring from buses to C-Trains are required to carry their transfers throughout the whole C-Train trip. Passengers who do not carry any of the above fare checks can purchase a single-trip ticket from ticket vending machines (TVM) located at C-Train stations and platforms, or from the LRT station concessions. When C-Train service was initiated, a ten-trip multi-ride ticket was issued which had to be validated at a TVM. This ticket was replaced in January 1983 by the Calgary Transit ticket book, which offers ten

Above: In this 1985 view a northbound C-Train leaves Stampede station (now called Victoria Park/Stampede Station) and prepares to enter the tunnel under the CPR right-of-way in downtown Calgary. The stub track stores extra LRVs during Stampede and Pengrowth Saddledome events. (Colin K. Hatcher)

Below: LRV 2012 leads a southbound two-car train at the austere 42nd Avenue station on August 28th 1981. (Ted Wickson)

rides for the price of nine. The tickets in this book can be validated at a TVM for use on the C-Train, or to transfer from the C-Train to a bus. Passengers can use a validated ticket to transfer from the C-Train to a bus to complete a continuous trip for a period of ninety minutes after the ticket is validated.

Calgary Transit introduced a fare-free zone permitting the C-Train to be ridden at any time between any stations along the 7th Avenue s corridor. All passengers however, must be prepared to produce valid proof of payment upon demand once the train has departed from the corridor. For this reason, all downtown stations have fare dispensing and validating machines identical to those found in the suburban stations.

Schedules and Operations

The frequency of service first offered on the south leg became the general pattern for the expanded LRT system. C-Trains operate seven days a week. Weekday (Monday through Friday) service begins at 5:20 AM with the last train returning to the garage after 1:00 AM the following morning. Peak frequency is every five to six minutes with three cars running; off-peak it is every ten minutes with two cars. Saturday service is every ten to fifteen minutes with one car running. Initially, travelling time from one end of the south leg to the other (8th Street sw to Anderson station) was twenty to twenty-five minutes. In 1985, after service on the line was extended to 10th Street sw, the travel time varied from twenty-two to twenty-six minutes, depending on the time of day.

The design capacity of each car can accommodate 64 people and an additional 97 standing, for a total of 161 passengers. Crush capacity of each car is 260. Therefore, with twelve trains running (three cars each) per hour, the line is capable of moving 5796 per hour at design, and 9360 passengers per hour at crush capacity.

The first public schedules for the initial C-Train route identified the service as the "Blue Line", carrying on a tradition established by the original Calgary streetcars whose routes in the early years were all identified by colour designations. This practice never became a tradition for the C-Train, as the new service soon became identified as route 201.

C-Train traffic is directed by standard railway automatic block signals (ABS). The three colour aspects (red, yellow and green) each instruct the operator in accordance with the standard set of written operating instructions to stop, proceed with caution or proceed at normal service speed. When the line first opened, block signals generally controlled C-Train traffic outside the downtown corridor while traffic signals controlled train movements along the downtown 7th Avenue s corridor. The block signal system as initially installed also controlled and protected movements through the automatic track switches (interlocking) which directed C-Train traffic in and out of Anderson station. Initially, train movements into the 8th Street sw station

Above: Fare dispensing machines were installed at all LRT stations. The "Blue Line" route designation to identify the original LRT line was later dropped and the route became known as route 201. (Ted Wickson)

were controlled by a supervisor located at the 7th Street sw station. A fully automatic interlocked system was later installed at the 8th Street sw crossover on 7th Avenue sw. The signal system of necessity became more sophisticated as the LRT system expanded and traffic from additional lines began to operate along the common downtown 7th Avenue s corridor. Due to the high water table in the area, the signal system is also able to warn C-Train operators of the presence of water in the tunnels.

Along the original south leg corridor, the C-Train crossed the following seven roads at grade where C-Train passage continues to have priority over road traffic:

25th Avenue SE, east of Macleod Trail.

36th Avenue SE and Burnsland Road SE.

39th Avenue SE and Burnsland Road SE.

50th Avenue SE two blocks east of Macleod Trail within the CPR right-of-way.

58th Avenue SE two blocks east of Macleod Trail within the CPR right-of-way.

61st Avenue SE two blocks east of Macleod Trail within the CPR right-of-way.

Above: On August 28th 1981 a westbound C-Train passes the Court House at the intersection of 5th Street sw. (Ted Wickson)

Heritage Drive se two blocks east of Macleod Trail within the CPR right of way.

Each of these crossings is protected by railway crossing signals, bells and barriers which are activated by an approaching C-Train. Upon leaving a station where a grade crossing exists, a trackside signal advises the C-Train operator when the barriers are completely lowered, thus indicating that the C-Train can safely proceed through the crossing. At Erlton station, the LRT line and the intersection of the Macleod Trail and 25th Avenue se are in close proximity. The traffic signals at this intersection are therefore interlinked with the LRT line. An approaching C-Train will not only lower the barriers to protect the 25th Avenue se crossing, but will also affect the cycle of the traffic signals at the intersection to prevent left-hand turns from the Macleod Trail onto 25th Avenue se. The amber signal warns oncoming traffic not to enter the intersection to make a left hand turn and warns traffic already in the intersection to quickly clear it. The tunnel south of 39th Avenue station takes the LRT right-of-way under a CPR spur line which serves a number of light industries along the west side of the LRT tracks. Once

the LRT emerges from this tunnel south of 42nd Avenue se, it actually shares the right-of-way the rest of the way south to Anderson station with the CPR Macleod subdivision. The CPR line runs immediately east of the LRT line. Although the C-Train operates on its own tracks, completely independent of the CPR tracks, certain railway operating rules do apply to C-Trains as they traverse this common right-of-way. In the event of a level crossing accident; for example, railway flagging rules apply to C-Train operators. The CPR line must be flagged for 2850 m (9,350 feet) in both directions and CPR officials must be notified.

In the downtown area along 7th Avenue s, the trains are directed by traffic signals specially mounted for bus and C-Train use. There is a special "amber flash" countdown sequence incorporated in the signal timing. Automobile traffic crossing 7th Avenue s is controlled by traffic signals synchronized, of course, with the signals controlling transit traffic along 7th Avenue s. The C-Train does enjoy a "measure of progression" on a "green wave" along 7th Avenue. If a C-Train hits the window upon leaving a downtown station, then it will be able to proceed through to the next station.

The C-Train shares 7th Avenue s with several Calgary Transit bus routes but, apart from automobile traffic crossing at intersections, the avenue is closed to all other traffic except police and emergency vehicles.

Opening Day

As opening day drew near, considerable detailed cleanup tasks remained to be completed. A month before the official opening, most of the cars had yet to be given their final exterior striping. Crews worked at the stations on last minute tasks, while sweepers plied back and forth along 7th Avenue s, cleaning out the rail grooves. Fare dispensing and validating machines had yet to be installed at all of the stations. While the construction people were busily finishing their work, the marketing and public relations staff began to unveil their plans to familiarize potential riders with this new transit operation.

By mid-May 1981, the City of Calgary's Transportation Department arranged to host a four-day "open house" – from Thursday May 14th to Sunday May 17th – at several C-Train stations. On Thursday and Friday May 14th and 15th, Calgarians were invited to visit the stations at 2nd Street SE (now called City Hall), 1st Street SW and 4th Street SW, where they could board and inspect a C-Train parked at each of these stations. The Anderson station, with a train available for inspection, was open to the public on Saturday and Sunday, May 16th and 17th, from noon until 4:00 PM. Interpretive material was developed to assist the public in making use of the new system. The Public Information Department and the Transportation Department of the City of Calgary produced a letter-sized booklet entitled *C-Train Arriving 1:00 PM, Monday May 25th, 1981*. It described all of the public service features of the new LRT operation, such as fare system, how to board and disembark, parking, feeder bus service, C-Train safety features, and some benefits of the C-Train. It was delivered to every household in Calgary prior to the opening of the system. Other materials such as the Easy Fare Option leaflet, the Blue Line schedule leaflet, individual feeder bus route schedules and newspaper features all helped to orient Calgarians to this new form of public transportation.

Finally, on Monday morning May 25th 1981, the C-Train's official opening took place at the 2nd Street SE station beside City Hall. One of the key speakers was Henry Kroeger, Transportation Minister for the Province of Alberta. The provincial government contributed a total of $73.1 million to the C-Train project, while the City of Calgary spent $94.2 million. Total cost of the 12.5 km (7.8 mile) south corridor light rail transit project amounted to $167.3 million. After a number of other speeches, Mayor Ralph Klein took his place at the controls of car 2005 and slowly drove the three-car train through a banner across the tracks. A Calgary Transit operator then took over the controls and two train loads of officials travelled to the south end of the line at Anderson station. After a brief tour, they headed

north again to the 42nd Avenue SE station (now 39th Avenue station) where they detrained for an official function at an adjacent hotel.

An enthusiastic general public, enticed by curiosity and free rides, crowded aboard the C-Trains for their first rides at 1:00 PM on the same day. For one week, the trains offered free riding to passengers along the full length of the line. This one-week "shakedown" operation afforded passengers the opportunity to familiarize themselves with the system. It also enabled Calgary Transit to isolate and work out any operational problems before the initiation of the feeder bus services on June 1st 1981. The crowded cars indicated that the C-Train was an "instant hit" with Calgarians. Three-car trains glided quietly along 7th Avenue s in the downtown area, stopping at each station along the way. At 7th Street sw, after detraining passengers, they paused to wait for the signal to proceed into the crossover onto the eastbound track and across 8th Street sw into the west-end terminal station.

For several days during that week, the turnouts were operated manually to switch the trains from one track to the other. Towards the end of the week, the remote control switching unit went into service, operated by a supervisor positioned at the 7th Street sw station. While most of the minor operating problems normally accompanying the opening of such a system were being worked out successfully, a major accident occurred at the 7th Street sw station just before 3:00 PM on Saturday May 26th. As a westbound train waited in the station at 7th Avenue sw, an eastbound train began its journey from the 8th Street sw station. It appears that the track switch tripped a split second before the third car in the eastbound train passed over it. That car lurched into the crossover, dragging the second car off the rails, and collided head-on with the stopped train. Several passengers were slightly injured. The accident closed the system for the rest of the day, but service resumed the following day.[29]

Revenue Operation Begins

On Monday June 1st 1981, revenue service began. At the same time, a widely-publicized realignment of Calgary Transit bus routes in the southwestern area of the city provided an extensive feeder bus network, bringing commuters from the outlying southern suburbs into the C-Train stations. The feeder bus network replaced all DART (Dial-A-Ride-Transit) buses, three Blue Arrow South routes and five express bus routes. The three Blue Arrow South routes had been introduced in 1972 as a successful interim strategy to encourage transit use by residents of new developments on either side of the Macleod Trail se and thus reduce automobile congestion along that thoroughfare. The initiation of LRT service along this corridor made them redundant. The new feeder bus service substantially swelled the crowds of people arriving to use the C-Train. With five damaged cars out of service, most runs could only be furnished with

two car sets. Train schedules were hampered by a change in switching procedures at the downtown terminal station, where operators understandably negotiated the crossover from the westbound to the eastbound track very gingerly. Unexpectedly high ridership, reduced car availability and delayed operations all combined to tax the system to the absolute limit, particularly during the morning and evening peak hour periods. By mid-June, however, four of the five damaged cars were back in service, and the anticipated train capacity and frequency of operation could then be restored. Unlike the Frankfurt cars, Calgary U2 LRV cars are "cabled" together at the articulation in the centre to allow quick separation of the two sections and rapid reassembly of one section with one from another articulated pair. This permitted the rapid re-introduction of one LRV car made up from sections undamaged in the accident and a second one a short time later from sections suffering minor damage only. Anderson shop craftsmen had the remaining two damaged cars back in service by early 1982.

In July 1981, another mishap occurred at the same City Centre crossover switch. A small stone, scattered on the pavement from a nearby construction project, lodged in the switch point, preventing it from closing completely. This resulted in a very minor derailment. For a brief period following this incident and while the interlocked switching and signaling system was being evaluated to prevent further mishaps, the track switch at 7th Avenue sw and 8th Street sw was operated manually by a switch tender. A bus shelter with a door was erected near the switch to provide shelter for the switch tender, particularly during cold weather.

Above: LRV 2001 approaches 1st Street SE station. The straight striping across the front of 2001 was unique to that vehicle and was later replaced by the "V" stripe. The Anglican Cathedral Church of the Redeemer is at the left of the photograph. Note the bus at a stop on 7th Avenue SE. (Ted Wickson)

Arriving
1:00 p.m., Monday
May 25th, 1981

THE CITY OF CALGARY
PUBLIC INFORMATION DEPARTMENT
TRANSPORTATION DEPARTMENT

Calgarians quickly and enthusiastically accepted the new C-Train. In the early weeks of operation, the system handled 28,000 riders daily. After six months of operation, the average daily passenger count on the C-Train had risen to 35,000. During the Calgary Exhibition and Stampede week early in July 1981, the C-Train was taxed to the limit as it carried between 80,000 and 85,000 riders each day. Local Calgary C-Train riders have become accustomed to the operating procedures. Although some visitors to Calgary find the fare arrangements a little perplexing, many downtown workers take advantage of the 7th Avenue s free riding privileges during their lunchtime breaks. The unique staccato clang of the C-Train's bell, warning that it is about to depart from a station, has become a familiar sound to regular users. Before Calgary Transit installed facilities on the cars for announcing the station stops via audio-tapes, operators announced the stops over the public address system, sometimes pointing out sights along the way and sharing the occasional joke with passengers. Calgarians crowded onto the C-Train especially at peak hours. In order to ease the crowding, Calgary Transit ordered three additional cars to service the south line shortly after it was opened. They were delivered during 1982. Identical to the first group or generation of U2 cars on the Calgary system, they are designated second generation RTC 2 and bear fleet numbers 2028 through 2030 inclusive.

Three-car trains were operated at peak hours and for special events on the Calgary Exhibition and Stampede Grounds. Two-car trains were common in regular mid-day, evening and Saturday service. On Sundays service was often provided by single LRVs.

Opposite, top: A switch tender aligns the track switch on 7th Avenue sw at 8th Street sw. The C-Train has just proceeded into 8th Street sw station at the west end of the line from the westbound track on 7th Avenue sw. The train will shortly depart for its eastbound trip along 7th Avenue sw and the track switch has just been manually set to allow that movement. (Colin K. Hatcher)

Opposite, bottom: On August 28th 1981 an Anderson-bound C-Train glides past the Royal Canadian Legion (Alberta No.1 Branch) Building at 116-7th Avenue SE. The wording in relief in the parapet reads "1914 GREAT WAR VETERANS' CLUB 1919". The building stands today as an historical resource and is still the home of Legion activities. The York Hotel has fallen to the wrecker's ball. The Regis Hotel building is still standing. (Ted Wickson)

Below: On September 3rd 1985 a peak hour three-car train westbound on 7th Avenue SE passes Centre Street station where passengers await the next eastbound train's arrival.
(Colin K. Hatcher)

Above: On August 28th 1981, shortly after the system opened, a north-bound three-car peak-hour C-Train makes its way onto the 7th Avenue SE transit mall from its private right-of-way alignment between 3rd and 4th Streets SE. Behind the train is the ramp leading into the tunnel under the CPR tracks. Compare this photograph with the one on page 172. (Ted Wickson)

Below: Passengers enjoy the trip to the Stampede on July 5th 1991. (Robert J. Sandusky)

Above: On August 3rd 1985, C-Train interface with pedestrian and auto traffic is evident as LRV 2001 negotiates its two-car train through the curve from the at-grade side of the road right-of-way along the east side of 4th Street SE into the 7th Avenue SE transit way.
(Colin K. Hatcher)

Below: A northbound C-Train led by LRV 2023 pulls up to a stop at Erlton station on August 28th 1981.
(Ted Wickson)

Above: A Whitehorn-bound C-Train on the northeast line led by LRV 2018 crosses the Bow River on August 3rd 1985. The bridge, built exclusively for LRT traffic, is located immediately east of the old Langevin or 4th Street SE bridge. (Colin K. Hatcher)

Below: The Calgary downtown urbanscape of 1985 dominates the horizon as LRV 2024, on a Whitehorn-bound two-car train, approaches Zoo station on the Memorial Drive median. (Colin K. Hatcher)

CHAPTER TWELVE

LRT Network Expansion

THE success of the south LRT, coupled with Calgary's well-defined transportation policy, bodes well for additional LRT extensions. While the City of Calgary was anxious to begin work on extending LRT, the Government of Alberta continued to take the same cautious view toward cost sharing LRT extensions as it had toward the original concept.

Studies suggested extending the south line from Anderson station some 6.3 km (4.2 miles) to 162nd Avenue sw, and building a new line off 7th Avenue sw from 9th Street sw to run northwest into the University of Calgary area. The economic recession of the mid-1980s hampered immediate development of these plans, particularly in the south where anticipated population growth had fallen well short of projections. Since the northwest line would pass through established business and residential areas, intense community opposition was generated toward some sections of the proposed route. As a result, final decisions on the placement of the LRT right-of-way through these areas were delayed.

In the meantime and while the south leg was still under construction, Calgary City Council adopted the Calgary General Municipal Plan on March 12th 1979. While the general concept of the south leg and the proposed northwest leg was congruent with the concepts and guiding principles of this plan, the extension of the LRT into northeast Calgary was greatly influenced by the policies described in this plan. The two key principles were:

"a recognition of the relationship between the use of land and the transportation facilities needed to serve it; and the concept of maintaining a balance between different modes of transportation, allowing each to do the job best suited to it."

The proposed northeast extension was designed to encourage development of land along its route for commercial purposes, and to improve access from the northeast residential areas into the downtown core. Its proposed right-of-way did not pass through established areas, therefore securing the right-of-way met with little opposition.

On Thursday May 20th 1982, almost a year after officially opening Calgary's first LRT line, Mayor Ralph Klein turned the first sod to commence construction of the second LRT project in Calgary, the northeast line.

The Northeast Leg – Right-of-Way

Most of the 9.8 km (6 mile) northeast LRT line is built at grade in the centre median of Memorial Drive, an east-west roadway, and 36th Street NE, a north-south roadway. It terminates at 39th Avenue NE, on the edge of the settled part of the city, at Whitehorn station. A ramp and concrete bridge takes the tracks westward, up over Memorial Drive, crossing the Bow River beside the old 4th Street SE bridge, then down to grade level again, east of the sidewalk along 4th Street SE. It turns west into the centre of 7TH Avenue SE, joining the original line at 3rd Street SE.

Plans call for the northeast line ultimately to go underground on 4TH Street SE immediately south of 7th Avenue SE, then curve west and north under the new civic development project in the City Hall area, with an underground station near the Macleod Trail. The line would surface again to connect at grade with the 7th Avenue S line from the south, immediately east of 1st Street SE.

The northeast line differs in some respects from the original south line. The new line's east-west axis is placed in the median of Memorial Drive while its north-south axis is in the median of 36th Street NE. It interfaces closely with significant volumes of automobile traffic along most of its route. Traffic signals, particularly along 36th Street NE, are computerized and operate to favour safe through-passage of the C-Trains. A *Calgary Herald* special section in the Saturday, April 27th 1985 issue describes how this all works.

"As a C-Train approaches an intersection, the traffic signal is automatically adjusted to give vehicular traffic a red light and allow passage of the C-Train through a green signal.

If, for example, north-south traffic on 36th Street NE has a green signal, an approaching C-train will prolong the green long enough to permit the train to pass.

If east-west traffic on the avenues has a green, the approaching train will cause the traffic signals to enter the amber-red cycle to give C-Train and north-south traffic a green signal.

The computer will then compensate for any lost 'green time' during the next signal cycle."

Vehicles are warned to clear the intersection when the amber signal is displayed and other motorists are warned not to enter. All of the crossings along the 36th Street NE LRT corridor are protected by railway crossing gates. These gates are designed to prevent left turns from 36th Street NE

Above: A striking interior-exterior view greets passengers going to platform level at Bridgeland/Memorial station. (Colin K. Hatcher)

and east-west movements on the avenues. Similar facilities are installed at the 28th Street NE and Deerfoot Trail intersection on Memorial Drive. Similar to standard railway crossing protection devices, the crossing gates are equipped with flashing red lights and bells which are activated as the C-Train approaches.

The Stations – Northeast Line

Stations on the northeast line are accessible to those unable to use stairs or escalators. All but two of the northeast line stations have spiral ramps leading to overhead walkways spanning roadways and LRT tracks. An elevator under closed circuit surveillance is available to take disabled passengers from the walkway to platform level. Access to the elevators and their associated approach areas are all under surveillance and operated by remote control. The passenger simply requests access through a telephone speaker. Security personnel, after surveying the situation, then grant or deny access, depending on need, thus preventing abuse of, and reducing vandalism to, the elevator system. The Zoo and Barlow/Max Bell stations do not have elevators as access is available through underground tunnels and wide ramps leading to platform level.[1]

A standard architectural design characterizes the northeast line stations. Architects Ross Hayes and Neil Robinson of the IBI Group had a budget of $16.25 million for building

of the LRT stations, power substations and hardware located in the communication, electronic and signal rooms in the station service areas. Six of the eight stations are above grade. They were designed as narrow structures to fit between the tracks. Their high roof line extends straight out over the escalators leading down to platform level rather than following the slope of the stairway. A floor to ceiling glass end wall offers passengers the brightness of a spectacular skyscape before they step out onto the platform ahead. Glass sidewalls follow a stepped pattern dictated by the slope of the stairway. This liberal use of glass lets in plenty of natural light. With this design, the architects have successfully enhanced the clear blue skyscape with its light, crisp and changing cloud pattern. They have also captured the brightness of Calgary through emphasizing the skyscape, since the landscape is often drab. The stations on Memorial Drive feature green as their dominant colour, to reflect the parkway character of the area. The 36th Street NE stations use burgundy as their primary colour. The Zoo and Barlow/Max Bell stations are below grade, yet natural light streams down into their high ceiling foyers through glass atrium-like roofs. The Zoo station has an imaginative three-dimensional life-size display of pre-historic animals in its foyer. This display is partially lit by natural light from the high ceiling. In keeping with the animal theme, animal murals are etched into the concrete walls of the evenly lit passageways leading from the parking lot into the foyer, and from the foyer out to the Zoo entrance. On a very gentle grade, these passageways lead down into the foyer directly under the LRT right-of-way. Since these two stations are below grade, there are no overhead walkways spanning the LRT tracks or the roadway access at the station locations.[2]

Passenger access and warmth in winter were major considerations regarding station design on this line too. Passengers can reach the stations on the northeast line via automobile, feeder bus or on foot. The four outermost stations, Franklin, Marlborough, Rundle and Whitehorn, have parking lots offering among them a total of 2000 spaces free of charge. Most of these spaces are equipped with electrical outlets for automobile block heaters, similar to those found at some of the south line stations. Automobile drivers are permitted to drop-off passengers in the bus bays at Marlborough station and continue on their ways. Bus service operates into several stations. Barlow/Max Bell is served by two routes, Franklin by one route, Marlborough by eight routes, Rundle by three routes and Whitehorn by seven routes and one community shuttle bus. All stations have pedestrian access and presently this is the only access to Bridgeland/Memorial and Zoo stations. Unlike the south line stations, platforms on the northeast line stations are completely open except for the substantial heated shelters positioned along the centre of each platform. Passengers can also wait inside the station during inclement weather, proceeding to the platform as their train approaches. Signs over the doors leading onto the boarding platforms direct passengers to one side to board trains destined for the City

Centre, and to the other side for trains heading to the north-east. In an improvement over the south line stations, the northeast stations have separate escalators to take passengers to and from platform level.

The northeast line features an additional downtown station of the same design as the other downtown stations. It is located between 3rd and 4th streets SE, serving primarily as a disembarking point for inbound passengers only. This station will close when the proposed extension of the line south along 4th Street SE, leading into a tunnel under City Hall complex, is built. Plans call for the 3rd Street SE station to be replaced by a new surface station to be erected at 4th Street SE between 6th and 7th avenues SE. It will serve inbound and outbound passengers.

Downtown Transit Mall Extended

In preparation for the linking of the northeast line to the south line at 7th Avenue SE and 3rd Street SE, C-Train traffic on the south line had to be cut short for a number of evenings at the end of June 1984. Double track turnouts at this intersection, a double crossover west of the intersection, and new signals to govern C-Train movements through the intersection, were installed at this time. At the same time, track at the west end of 7th Avenue SW was extended another two blocks to terminate at 10th Street SW. A station platform was constructed in the centre of the avenue. Passenger access is from the west end only via ramps or steps. The platform is wider at the west end, narrowing considerably toward the

Below: Outbound LRV 2017 pauses at Bridgeland/Memorial station on May 21st 1985. (Ted Wickson)

east end as the tracks on either side converge toward the centre of the Avenue. This station was originally intended to be a narrow catwalk for operators only, allowing them to walk from the control cab at one end of the train to the cab at the other end of the train when the train reversed direction. It was subsequently converted for public use, however, it does not have any shelter. The station is temporary, pending eventual extension of the LRT westward. West of 9th Street sw, 7th Avenue sw is accessible to C-Trains only because of the island terminal station. Immediately east of the 10th Street sw terminal is a double crossover which directs an arriving westbound train into one or the other side of the terminal station, or directs a departing train onto the eastbound track after it leaves the terminal. East of 9th Street sw, a double track turnout has been installed to give the proposed northwest LRT line access to the 7th Avenue s transit mall.

Below: LRV 2058 leads a two-car train as it pauses at the Bridgeland/Memorial station, the first outbound station on the northeast line, on August 3rd 1985. The church on the hill, St. Matthew's Lutheran Church, was originally a Moravian church serving the Bridgeland community populated largely by German people who had emigrated from Russia in the early decades of the Twentieth Century. The Riverside or Bridgeland streetcar line operated along First Avenue NE about one block beyond the church. (Colin K. Hatcher)

Additional LRVs and the Haysboro Siding Storage Facility

The 53 new Light Rail Vehicles (LRVs) ordered to service the northeast and northwest extensions, and delivered between April 1983 and November 1984, brought the total roster of LRVs to 83 units. These LRVs are identical to the original units. They are described as RTC 3 and RTC 4, and numbered 2031 through 2083 inclusive. Even after the mid-1984 completion of the four additional storage tracks in the empty space at Anderson Shops, lanes 1 through 4, there was not sufficient space to store all 83 LRVs. The Northeast LRT Functional Study described plans to acquire land for an additional LRV storage facility north of McKnight Boulevard north of the Whitehorn terminal station. Additional storage space was required long before the northeast line was opened, as the new LRV shells were arriving during 1982-1983 at a regular rate, to be assembled at Anderson Shops. In fact, Anderson Shops also assembled five of twenty new LRVs destined for Edmonton Transit. Both the Calgary and Edmonton systems placed car orders at the same time to obtain the most favourable unit price for both properties. At the time, Edmonton Transit's small Cromdale Shops did not have the space to complete the assembly of all twenty LRVs, and its new D.L. MacDonald Shops had not yet opened. The Edmonton LRVs had to be set up on "shop dollies" because the flanges on the Edmonton units are too

Above: At the afternoon peak period, passengers disembark from a Whitehorn-bound train while a downtown-bound train departs. (Ted Wickson)

deep to sit on the girder groove rail in Calgary's Anderson Shops. Calgary Transit also carried out extensive rebuilding of a heavily accident-damaged Edmonton LRV (1012) during 1982. This work was being done even while assembly work on the joint order of cars for Edmonton and Calgary was being carried out.[3]

Calgary's Anderson Shops are capable of accomodating only sixty of the 83 LRVs. Haysboro storage facility, a five-track yard and storage building located south of Heritage station, was opened in 1983. It has accommodation for thirty LRVs under cover and thirty LRVs in the yard. The latter has been designed so that the building can be extended in the future to double its present storage capacity. The switches in the yard were initially thrown by hand, but by 1988 the yard switches had become fully automated. For safety reasons, the operation of the cars in the yard is completely independent of mainline operation. Some incoming trains are assigned and dispatched by a duty dispatcher at Haysboro. Operators for these trains report directly to Haysboro. There are no train movements out of Haysboro in the afternoon. At the end of the day, as LRVs come out of peak hour and regular service, they are all sent to Anderson Shops to be washed and cleaned. Maintenance personnel then return the assigned LRVs to that facility. There is a platform along the main line at the Haysboro switch. This enables the operator of a northbound dispatched train to walk from one end of the train to the other, after moving it southbound out of the yard onto the northbound mainline track.[4]

Northeast LRT Opens

The official opening of the northeast LRT line took place on Saturday April 27th 1985 at 11:00 AM, at the downtown station near City Hall, presided over by Mayor Ralph Klein who had been Calgary's mayor when the south line opened in 1981. The Mayor moved a C-Train through a red ribbon stretched across the tracks, and Alberta's Minister of Transportation Marvin Moore presented a $51 million cheque to Calgary's Transportation Commissioner Bill Kuyt. This cheque represented Calgary's share of provincial transportation grants for 1985. A portion of this sum was earmarked for construction of the northwest LRT. The official party was then taken to the end of the new line at Whitehorn station. On the return trip, the party disembarked at Zoo station to attend a reception marking the occasion at the Calgary Zoo. Following the official opening, citizens had the opportunity to ride free from 1 PM to 5 PM on Saturday and 9 AM to 5 PM on Sunday. The first train in revenue service on the line left Whitehorn station at exactly 5:49 AM on Monday April 29th 1985.[5]

The new service replaced six bus routes, including Blue Arrow buses east of the downtown area. Several feeder routes in the northeast area were adjusted to serve the new stations. Peak hour service (Monday – Friday 6 to 9 AM and 3 to 6 PM) on the northeast line operated every six minutes. Ten-minute service was available mid-day Monday through Friday and all day Saturday. Fifteen-minute service was offered evenings and Sundays. Coincident with the opening of the new line, C-Trains from both lines began using the new 10th Street SW terminal on 7th Avenue SW. Another new feature of the new northeast LRT was the introduction of half-hourly bus service between the Calgary International Airport and the Whitehorn station. This service operated daily approximately between the hours of 6 AM and 8:30 AM and between 12 noon and midnight.[6]

The northeast C-Train route is known as route 202 Whitehorn. Northeast C-Trains are signed Whitehorn when running in both directions. Similarly route 201 C-Trains on the south line are signed Anderson regardless of the direction of travel. The LRVs also carried card signs in the upper side sash indicating their respective destinations.

The extension of the C-Train tracks along 7th Avenue S, and the introduction of two routes along this downtown corridor, initiated some changes in operations. First, the signal system became more sophisticated. Using a system called "Vee Tag", developed by the Dutch company, Philips,

Above: An inbound C-Train from Whitehorn on the northeast line waits at 3rd Street SE station while an inbound train from Anderson on the south line enters the 7th Avenue S transit mall. The date is May 21st 1985. (Ted Wickson)

operators on the C-Trains dial in a pre-set code on a device built into the control panel as part of their preparation for departure from a terminal station. This procedure activates the vehicle identification system for that train. As the train progresses along its route, information from this vehicle identification system is transmitted to loops set at line side. On the basis of this information, track switches or turnouts are automatically set as the train approaches them. For example, as a route 201 Anderson-bound train approaches the City Hall station, the track switches are automatically set to allow the train to turn south toward Anderson. Should a route 202 Whitehorn train be following, as soon as the route 201 train is safely through the interlocking, the switches are set to allow the route 202 train to travel straight through the intersection. Station platforms along the downtown corridor are all equipped with digital signs indicating the destination of the next approaching train. The vehicle identification system activates the destination message on these signs. Other messages about service delays or alternate services available in the event of delays can be transmitted to these signs from a computer centre located at the Victoria Park bus garage.

Secondly, as a result of the westward extension of the tracks along 7th Avenue SW, the 7th Street SW station had to be moved 25 metres west, locating it closer to the intersection of 8th Street SW. The original location of this station was dictated by the presence of the crossover switch directing westbound C-Trains to the eastbound track in preparation for their return trip. Since the station's location hindered access to the Nova Building, the City agreed to relocate the station once C-Train service was extended west along 7th Avenue SW and the crossover switch was no longer required. This relocation took place on a Sunday July 21st 1985. For that day, C-Trains terminated at 3rd Street SE. Shuttle buses provided the service along 7th Avenue.

The opening of the northeast LRT has resulted in some interesting train movements. Calgary Transit has tradition-

ally provided special services to many sporting, cultural and Stampede events. For each Calgary Flames hockey game, a special C-Train operates from Whitehorn station directly to the Stampede station on the south line near Calgary's Olympic Saddledome (now Pengrowth Saddledome). This special train returns directly to Whitehorn station fifteen minutes after the game ends. Such a move from the northeast to the south line and vice-versa requires the train to enter City Hall station. Here, the operator must change ends so that the train can continue its southbound journey. Frequency of service on both LRT routes is increased for the duration of the Calgary Stampede. However, passengers from the northeast must disembark at the 1st Street SE station, then walk back half a block and across the avenue to the City Hall station, where they transfer to the south line train to Stampede station. Passengers bound for the northeast returning from the Stampede also disembark at the 1st Street SE station and board a northeast line train at City Hall station.

Whitehorn station has sufficient track beyond the station building to allow extra cars from the morning peak hour service to be stored there all day. During peak hours, all trains operate with three-LRV consists. As the morning peak service concludes, each northeast line train remaining in service for the duration of the day drops one LRV from its consist at Whitehorn station. These extra LRVs remain at Whitehorn station until they are required for the afternoon peak service. At that time, one LRV is added to each regular service train. At the close of the evening peak service, one LRV is once again dropped from each regular service train continuing in service for the evening. Once all of the extra LRVs have been taken off, they are coupled together and

Above: LRV 2041 has led its train across the Deerfoot Trail and begins its climb up out of the Bow River and Nose Creek valleys. In the photograph the train is heading in a southeasterly direction but will swing to a northerly direction to line up with 36th Street NE. (Ted Wickson)

Below: LRV 2048 on Anderson route 201 and 2065 on Whitehorn route 202 pause at the end of the line for both routes at 10th Street SW on May 21st 1985. They await their respective signals to proceed east along the 7th Avenue transit mall. Following the opening of the northwest LRT, only route 202 trains used this station. (Ted Wickson)

operated directly to Anderson shop as a single five-LRV out-of-service train. As the system was extended and new LRVs entered service, it became common practice to store cars at the northeast and later the northwest terminals all night.

Passenger ridership on the northeast line initially fell short of expectations. Pre-construction estimates indicated that the line would attract 30,000 to 35,000 riders per day. Initial reports recorded some 22,000 riders per day, while October 1985 statistics indicated an increase to some 23,000 riders per day. These figures do show that the new LRT line did indeed outperform the former Blue Arrow express bus network into the northeast area, which carried 18,000 riders per day. The local press carried out some random trip time comparisons with taxi, private automobile and public transit modes, including LRT, immediately after the northeast line was opened. While trip times on the public transit mode were slightly longer by only a few minutes, the direct cost of the trip to the user definitely fell in favour of the public

Below: LRV 2034 departs Lions Park station on the northwest line on its way to University on May 31st 1989. The sheltered side platforms are accessed from either end at grade level.
(Colin K. Hatcher)

transit mode. A decade after its opening, the weekday ridership on the northeast line had risen to 58,900.

The northeast line was built for the sum of $218 million, considerably under the original estimate of $289 million. With the northeast line operational, attention turned to the third LRT project in Calgary, the northwest line.

The Northwest LRT Line

Plans for urban rail transit service into northwest Calgary date back to the 1966 Simpson & Curtin consultants' report. The line then proposed to serve established business and residential areas on its way to the University of Calgary area. The modern LRT proposal would serve the same geographic population. The largely populated area beyond the University remains to be served by LRT. Therefore, before the line was even opened, priority was given to extending the line beyond the University of Calgary terminal station. Since the proposed line did go through some established neighbourhoods, considerable opposition surrounding concerns about aesthetics and property values were generated toward the alignment proposed by Calgary City Council. The most vociferous opposition arose concerning the placement of tracks along 9A Street NW in the Hillhurst-Sunnyside area. This would be on the river flats, tucked between the north bank of the Bow River and the bottom of the steep escarpment, overlooking the river valley and defining the edge of the river valley. Several different alternative alignments through this area were considered. Some of these alternatives were along 14th Street NW, 10th Street NW, 9A Street NW and 9th Street NW. So intense was the opposition that the City of Calgary turned its attention from building the northwest LRT line as its intended priority to favour commencement of construction on the northeast LRT line. Other portions of the northwest proposed LRT alignment also met with opposition. Residents of Houndsfield Heights and Briar Hill opposed the 14th Avenue NW alignment, favouring instead a routing along the north side of the North Hill Shopping Mall. Residents along Banff Trail also opposed the proposed alignment through that area. The communities organized themselves, putting pressure on the provincial government (which provided funding for the project) and to the City to change the alignment. The issue went on to court. In the end, the City stood firm and built the northwest line as planned. The City did make two major concessions. Residents living in homes in the corridor from the alley west of 9A Street NW to a line 150 feet east of the LRT line could sell their properties to the City at current market value. This offer was available to residents who owned these properties at the time the arrangement was made and it was to expire January 1st 1989. The second concession was an agreement by the City to build extensive berms and to landscape the right-of-way so that it blended effectively into the surrounding community. Some $3 million was set aside specifically for this purpose.

Above: LRV 2072 leads its train into a station on the northeast line. At this point 36th Street NE is flanked by shopping malls. The date is May 21st 1985. (Ted Wickson)

Right-of-Way

Construction for the right-of-way was consistent with the standards adopted for the other two lines. A well-ballasted roadbed supports the concrete ties and 50 kg/m (110 lbs/yard) welded T-Rails are fixed to each of these ties with a pair of Pandrol clips. The bridges and tunnels have concrete floors. When these floors were poured, raised pedestals – precisely placed to follow the line of the rails – were an integral part of the floor casting. These pedestals are longer than the width of a concrete tie. Once the concrete had set and track laying was about to begin, two sturdy rubber pads were laid out on each pedestal. The rail was mounted on these pads. Two Pandrol clips at each pad (four per pedestal) hold the rails firmly in place. These pedestals are spaced about the same distance apart as the concrete ties found on the ballasted sections. The rubber pads reduce noise and vibration as a train passes. The turnouts on 7th Avenue sw, as well as the rails extending across the sidewalk and around the curve into 9th Street sw, are set in concrete. They were installed when 7th Avenue sw track was extended in preparation for the opening of the northeast line. Once around the curve, the rail is laid on concrete ties on a ballasted roadbed. The LRT double track alignment follows the east sidewalk of 9th Street sw. The area on either side of the track, extending along 9th Street sw toward the Bow River, is a plaza finished in interlocking bricks. 6th, 5th and 4th avenues sw are crossed at grade, before the tracks reach the approach to the Bow River bridge. As in the other two lines, rails for the level crossings were laid long before track laying began. Movement

of the C-Train across these avenues is governed by traffic lights. There are no barriers.

The line crosses the Bow River on an arched concrete bridge. Below the track deck is a combined bicycle way and pedestrian walkway. The LRT bridge is east of the Louise Bridge, which once carried the streetcar tracks into west and northwest Calgary. It takes the tracks over Memorial Drive before returning them to grade level on their own private right-of-way along the east side of 9A Street NW. Between 3rd and 4th avenues NW, it passes through Sunnyside station, named for the surrounding residential area. Upon leaving Sunnyside station, it continues at grade along 9A Street NW, then it begins a steep climb up out of the Bow River valley, crosses 10th Street NW, continues its climb to crest in the Southern Alberta Institute of Technology (SAIT) grounds. Here it enters the SAIT/ACA/Jubilee station which serves SAIT, the Alberta College of Art and the Southern Alberta Jubilee Auditorium. The line travelling up the grade is protected from above by terraced and planted concrete retaining walls. Attractive terracing is featured below the line.

Turning west after leaving the SAIT/ACA/Jubilee station, the line crosses over 14th Street NW and follows along the south side of 14th Avenue NW. It travels through a green area, where it borders closely on the Houndsfield Heights and Briar Hill neighbourhoods, until it reaches the Lions Park station, located just east of 19th Street NW. The line then turns very sharply north across 14th Avenue NW to parallel 19th Street NW and begins a descent into a tunnel under 19th Street NW and 16th Avenue NW (the Trans Canada Highway). The line rises from the tunnel along the north side of 16th Avenue NW, having negotiated a second sharp curve in the tunnel. From this point, the line takes an easier curve at grade to head north along the Banff Trail and into the Banff Trail station. Here, the line is flanked on the west by the Motel Village development and McMahon Stadium, and on the east by single-dwelling homes. However, the line is slightly lower than the homes in this area. Trees and landscaping separate the right-of-way from the homes. North of the Banff Trail station, the line enters another tunnel passing under 24th Avenue NW and the southbound lanes of the Crowchild Trail. It emerges in the median of Crowchild Trail, where the terminal, University station, is located. Crossover tracks are installed at strategic locations along the line, some with facing points and some with trailing points. An interlocked scissors crossover is located immediately south of University station. The line is fully protected by automatic block signals.

The Stations – Northwest Line

The architectural style used in four of the five stations on the northwest line bears a strong resemblance to styles once commonly found in railway depots. The most prominent features exhibiting these designs are the roof lines. The application of those styles is not only attractive and nostalgic, but very practical too. For example, roofs protect the side loading platforms from wet weather at three of the stations. In the fourth instance, the roof lines of the high

profile University station building are strongly suggestive of architecture from the grand era of railway stations.

Three of the five stations are low-profile walk-on stations, similar in design to the 7th Avenue S stations. They are located at grade, permitting pedestrians to access them directly from the street via four or five steps or ramps. All of the northwest stations are accessible to wheelchairs. The first of these stations is Sunnyside. It is located on 9A Street NW, between 3rd and 4th avenues NW. A pedestrian crossing is located at the south end of the station, while a level crossing and pedestrian access is available at the north end. Flashing signal lights and bells protect the pedestrian crossing at 3rd Avenue NW, while barriers, lights and bells protect the level crossing for automobile and pedestrian traffic. The predominant feature of the building is its light stained wood finish, but its two hip roofs, one extending part way along each side platform, evoke a railway station image. Steel pillars support the roofs. The area over the tracks is open. As one looks at Sunnyside station from across 9A Street NW, it appears similar to a restored building or a modest new mall containing a number of small shops or boutiques. The higher profile roof at one end suggests a small community general storefront. It is very "trendy". Lions Park is the second walk-on station. It serves the residential areas of

Below: LRV 2074, operating in Saturday service on August 3rd 1985 as a single unit, takes the turn off the 7th Avenue SE Transit Way onto 3rd Street SE as it heads south toward its terminus at Anderson station. LRV 2067 signed Whitehorn heads west into the city centre. (Colin K. Hatcher)

Above: LRV 2022, in a flurry of snow, leads its train across the Bow River towards Sunnyside station on it own bridge near the location of the old Louise Bridge. The date is December 26th 1996. (Robert J. Sandusky)

Below: LRV 2047 trails a two-car train down the grade to Sunnyside and the Bow River crossing. Note the terraced and planted concrete retaining walls. (Colin K. Hatcher)

Above: The design of centre-median and centre-platform stations is well illustrated in this view of Bridgeland/Memorial station on the northeast line. This was typical of stations on this line and on the outer section of the northwest line. Note the pedestrian approach bridges over the roadway and the spiral ramp approaches to the pedestrian bridge on the right side of the photograph. The passenger platform stretches out between the tracks from the far end of the building. While most of the station buildings on the northeast line are similar in architectural design those on the northwest line, each have distinct architectural characteristics. The C-Train led by LRV 2067 is eastbound along Memorial Drive toward Whitehorn in this August 3rd 1985 view. (Colin K. Hatcher)

Below: An inbound C-Train from Whitehorn trailed by LRV 2048 on February 2nd 1994 has just crossed 4th Street SE as it turns into 8th Avenue SE. The junction with the south line is immediately ahead of the train. The City Hall Building is to the left. (Robert J. Sandusky)

Above: LRV 2031 leaves Lions Park station south and eastbound on May 21st 1997 after a surprise May snowfall. (Robert J. Sandusky)

Houndsfield Heights and Briar Hill. Across 14th Avenue NW from the station is the Louise Riley Community Library, and nearby is the North Hill Shopping Centre. The north side of the station facing the library calls to mind the image of a series of one storey red brick store fronts along a downtown street. The residential side looks like condominium housing, with light blue siding covering a series of bay-window sets extending the length of the platform. On the platform side, these bays each contain seating for passengers awaiting the train's arrival. A flat roof extends over both platforms, supported by a series of curved overhead beams fixed securely to the wall at their bases, and supporting the roof overhang. These curved beams are modelled after railway station construction. Once again the tracks are open. Brick is prominent in the construction of Lions Park station. Banff Trail station is the third of this series. It is built in a very shallow trench across the street from single family homes. Since this station serves McMahon Stadium as well as the Banff Trail residential area, pedestrians crossing the tracks at 23rd Avenue NW pull open a spring-loaded gate. This gate is meant to discourage them from accidently running out in front of an approaching C-Train, particularly when traffic to and from the stadium is heavy. An approaching C-Train will activate warning lights and bells at this crossing. The platform roofs are hip-style supported by a single

row of steel pillars along the centre line, once again hinting of railway style architecture. Both side-loading platforms are partially covered.

The University station and the SAIT/ACA/Jubilee station are both centre-loading platform stations. The University station in the median of Crowchild Trail and Exshaw Road has a high hip roof line which gives a railway station appearance. The many small window panes and prominent high arch central window, accented by a gable on the roof immediately above it, give the station the appearance of a distinctive country club. The upper storey of the station is finished in light blue aluminum siding, accented by the many small white window frames. It has a blue aluminum roof. The platform extends along both sides of the station building. A roof overhang from the first storey level protects the platform. Red brick siding is used at platform level in the first storey. A small rectangular shelter of the same design, with blue and white colouring similar to the station, sits at the north end of the platform. The second storey of the station contains services such as ticket vending machines, ticket validating machines, concessions and transit information maps. Passengers enter the station via the second storey from a walkway extending over the Crowchild Trail on the University of Calgary side and from the Banff Trail residential area on the other. The station is similar to the

Above: LRV 2060 is southbound at Sunnyside station on August 5th 1988. (Robert J. Sandusky)

Stampede station in passenger access and platform design. The SAIT/ACA/Jubilee station has pedestrian access via steps at the north end and via an overhead walkway at the south end. The overhead walkway goes directly into the Alberta College of Art building on one side and the SAIT campus centre building on the other. The stairways and walkways are glass-enclosed, the main platform is open but covered with a flat roof, and the north-end entrance is glass enclosed. While the station is attractive with all of its glass, its architectural form blends in with the square form found in the surrounding buildings. The line and its structures do blend well into the surrounding communities, enhanced by artful, well-placed landscaping.

The northwest LRT line is designed to minimize the division of communities. As a supplement to the pedestrian walkways across the tracks at station and at level crossings, a pedestrian and bicycle underpass has been built at the

Below: The east face of University station as a terminal station with a C-Train waiting to depart southbound. (Colin K. Hatcher)

north end of 9A Street NW where the line begins its steep climb up the Bow Valley escarpment. Overhead walkways, with stair and spiral ramp access, have been built over the tracks east of Lions Park station, to allow pedestrian access between Houndsfield Heights and the North Hill Shopping Centre. A similar overpass crosses 16th Avenue NW and the LRT right-of-way east of Banff Trail. There are two grade crossings for automobiles in the Sunnyside area, three in the SAIT campus area and one at the Lions Park station, making a total of six fully-protected grade crossings on the 5.6 km (3.4 mile) northwest extension.

Service on the northwest line is provided by trains from the south line initially signed "University". Southbound trains leaving the University are signed "Anderson". The line carries a good balance of traffic as it moves students from the downtown area into the SAIT and University of Calgary areas in the morning peak period, while trips into the downtown area carry residential commuters going to work. The reverse is true during the afternoon peak period. Initially, the line primarily drew pedestrian traffic, Kiss'n'Ride traffic, and feeder bus traffic because when the line opened Park'n'Ride facilities were available only at the Banff Trail station. Service began on Monday September 7th 1987, some three months earlier than anticipated.

All of Calgary Transit vehicles, including the light rail transit line, successfully played their part as the City of Calgary proudly hosted the XV Olympic Winter Games from February 13th to 28th 1988. The opening of the Northwest LRT provided access to venues in the McMahon Stadium from Banff Trail station, and to those at the University of Calgary from University station. The LRT provided service to other Winter Games venues such as Olympic Square along 7th Avenue SE and the Olympic Saddledome and the Stampede Corral from Stampede station on the south line. Calgary Transit had a roster of 83 U2 LRVs available to handle the traffic for this event.

Following this major event, immediate LRT expansion was limited to one 1 km extension from University to Brentwood station. That extension opened on August 31st 1990. Brentwood station is a large, high building with plenty of glass. The main portion of the station has a towering roof-line which looks like a prairie grain elevator. Its access elevator follows a similar design, but on a smaller scale. The economic slowdown and the reduction in urban funding grants from the Province of Alberta prevented further LRT expansions for a decade.

Above: LRV 2034 emerges from SAIT/ACA/Jubilee station. The view is looking across Sait Way on August 5th 1988. (Robert J. Sandusky)

Below: LRV 2047 trails a C-Train crossing 14th Avenue NW and entering Lions Park station. The community interface with LRT is evident here as pedestrian access is easy and roadway crossings are safe but not divisive. (Colin K. Hatcher)

CHAPTER THIRTEEN

Extensions, Operations and Recognition

URING the 1990s, Calgary Transit participated in two significant demonstration opportunities. Two additional U2 AC (alternating current) LRVs 3001 and 3002 arrived in Calgary in 1990, following demonstrations on Edmonton's LRT system. The cars had been shipped to Edmonton in April 1988 from the builders in Dusseldorf, Germany.[1] The car bodies and trucks were built by Duewag while Siemens provided all of the electrical components. The Government of Alberta initiated this demonstration and owned the cars. Calgary Transit purchased the cars in 1992 and renumbered them 2101 and 2102.

The second opportunity involved the temporary extension of rail service south of Anderson LRT terminal station in 1996. This was the Commuter Rail Demonstration Project involving Calgary Transit, Siemens Electric of Dusseldorf, Germany and Canadian Pacific Railway (then operating as CP Rail). Siemens provided a diesel-powered car. CP Rail provided the use of its Macleod Subdivision track from Anderson LRT station to 162nd Avenue sw. CP Rail engine service personnel operated the car. Calgary Transit co-ordinated the project and handled the marketing and passenger services aspects. A Calgary Transit representative was on hand while the car was operating to ensure passengers safely boarded and disembarked from the car. The car used was a RegioSprinter, a diesel-driven three-section articulated unit developed by Siemens for use on European regional rail lines. Its concept is similar to that of a suburban or interurban electric car, but its diesel engines give it the flexibility to operate on rail lines without requiring electric power overhead lines. It is about the same length as Calgary's U2 LRVs, but slightly wider. It was powered by two MAN diesel engines, one mounted at each end of the unit. The unit could seat 64 passengers and accommodate an additional hundred as standees. A substantial but temporary

platform built along the CP Rail right-of-way at the north end of Anderson LRT station allowed passenger access to and from the car. A similar platform was constructed along the CP Rail tracks at 162nd Avenue sw. In order to prevent fouling during the passage of wider CP Rail equipment, these platforms were hinged on the side closest to the track so that they could be folded back to clear the right-of-way when the RegioSprinter was not operating. The service operated Monday through Friday between 6 AM and 9 AM, and between 3:30 and 6:30 PM. Eight round trips were made during each of the morning and afternoon periods. A one-way six-kilometre journey took eight minutes to complete.[2] Since all southbound passengers riding the RegioSprinter came directly out of the "fare-paid" zone at Anderson station, and inbound passengers passed into the same zone, same station, there were no fare collection facilities either on the car or at the 162nd Avenue sw station platform. Reports indicated that an average of 558 people were carried per day, with a peak high of 937 being carried on May 2nd, during the five month demonstration between April 12th and August 9th 1996.[3] The rail service concluded at the close of the demonstration period but work did commence on the extension of the LRT line south of Anderson station soon after. This demonstration project shared many similarities with the current O Train operation in Ottawa. That service, initiated in 2001, also utilized a diesel-powered unit on an operational Canadian Pacific Railway line.

A unique innovation took place when Calgary Transit announced its Ride the Wind initiative. The partnership with ENMAX and Vision Quest Windelectric Inc. proposed that all of the trains could operate with wind-generated energy. Calgary Transit buys the power generated by windmills near Pincher Creek in southern Alberta which are owned by Vision Quest Windelectric Inc. That power is sent into the power grid. The program was launched on Wednesday September 5th 2001 at Stampede LRT station.[4] That innovation drew a 2001 Pollution Prevention Award from the Canadian Council of Ministries of the Environment and the Sustainable Community Award for leadership in renewable energy from the Federation of Canadian Municipalities. Calgary Transit has continued to win awards for "leadership and renewable energy" with its Ride the Wind program.[5]

Calgary's CTrain operation received national recognition when Canada Post issued a 49-cent postage stamp on March 30th 2004 to mark the 50th anniversary of the opening of Canada's first subway. That was the Toronto Transit

Opposite, upper: Shortly after Brentwood station opened, single unit LRV 2034 operating on a Remembrance Day (November 11th 1990) holiday schedule waits at the station. The view looks east across the Crowchild Trail. (Robert J. Sandusky)

Opposite, lower: Alternating current (AC) LRV 3001 is ready to go into service on September 14th 1991 from the stub track at Anderson station. The view looks north toward the city centre. (Robert J. Sandusky)

Above: The Fish Creek-Lacombe station was at the end of the south line in this view on October 9th 2003. Compare the area development since 1996 as shown in the Regio-Sprinter photograph. (Robert J. Sandusky)

Opposite, upper: The Regio-Sprinter travels south just south of Fish Creek on April 12th 1996. (Robert J. Sandusky)

Opposite, lower: The Regio-Sprinter approaches on the CPR Macleod subdivision as passengers wait on the temporary platform beside the Anderson LRV station. The temporary gate is closed as the LRV prepares to depart for Brentwood. (Robert J. Sandusky)

Commission's Yonge Street subway in Toronto. Three other Canadian urban rail systems were portrayed in this urban transit issue: the Société de transport de Montréal "Métro"; Trans Link, the Vancouver "Sky Train" Millenium Line; and the Calgary Transit Light Rail Transit "CTtrain" – the latter by now officially without its hyphen. A block of eight stamps included two stamps illustrating each of the four systems. Each represented a different form of urban rail transportation. Calgary's contribution represented the flexibility of light rail transit which could operate on the streets, through neighbourhood private rights-of-way and underground. Each of the four systems featured a stamp depicting a train boarding passengers, and one with a train in motion. Station names of each respective system appear in very small print on each stamp. The Calgary CTrain illustrated is one of the SD 160 units in the then-current blue and white livery.[6]

The building of LRT extensions resumed early in the new millennium. On October 9th 2001, LRT service was extended 3.4 km south over a new line along the CPR right-of-way and through a new station at Canyon Meadows to Fish Creek-Lacombe station. While the city celebrated the opening, residents in the Canyon Meadows area expressed displeasure at the station located in that area, and at the intrusion of the line passing close to residential properties in their community.[7] Another 3 km extension to 162nd Avenue sw at Somerset-Bridlewood station, with a station mid-way at Shawnessy, opened on June 28th 2004. Both of these extensions continue to follow the right-of-way of Canadian Pacific Railway's Macleod subdivision. The new stations on this extension are individually designed and as a result very distinctive architecturally. The Fish Creek-Lacombe station, with its overhanging roof and supports, appears to follow the lines of a railway station. The tower in the centre gives it a modern touch, reflecting a style seen in many small shopping complexes. It stands near the site of the former CPR station at Midnapore. The Shawnessy station is a visually outstanding piece of work. Its precast concrete thin-shelled roof, featuring a series of half spheres, gives it a very light, simple and natural appearance. Its platforms are on the outside of the track rather than between them, and the platforms are staggered; that is, they are not directly opposite each other. The area is devoid of the overhead passageways found at many of the other stations. Somerset-Bridlewood station, set between the tracks, is basically a platform featuring a wavy roof with a hump in the centre that resembles the back of a dinosaur. There is a glass-enclosed waiting area in the centre of the structure. Once again, passenger access is from ground level, so there are no overhead access structures at this station. Following a pattern initiated with the build-

Above: Under the shadow of Calgary's new City Hall, LRV 2025 leads its train off 4th Street SE up onto the bridge over the Bow River. Behind the train at ground level is an LRT storage spur track leading from 4th Street SE at 7th Avenue SE. The northeast line had recently opened for service in this May 21st 1985 view.
(Ted Wickson)

Opposite, upper: Dalhousie station, with a train of SD 160 model LRVs, easing off the crossover to the south platform. Shopping centre and parking lot access is to the right. The date is October 7th 2004. (Robert J. Sandusky)

Opposite, lower: Northbound train of new SD 160 model LRVs is crossing Shawnee Gate. The Fish Creek LRT bridge and the CPR bridge are just ahead of the CTrain (its name by now non-hyphenated). The date is October 9th 2003. (Robert J. Sandusky)

ing of the Northeast LRT line, all subsequently constructed stations are wheelchair accessible. The system is not totally wheelchair accessible, as the original south line stations were not built to accommodate wheelchair passengers. However, ramps have been constructed at the end of the platforms at each of these stations leading from the adjacent roadway crossing, thus permitting wheelchair access. With a view to eventually increasing passenger-carrying capacity, the station platforms on the more recently completed extensions were built to accommodate four-car trains.

In the northwest, a 3 km extension opened to Dalhousie on December 15th 2003. Dalhousie station is described by its architects as a forest in the middle of Crowchild Trail. Its platform is protected by a roof the steel members of which are like branches of a tree diffusing the sunlight as it comes through the glass. The use of screens and reflective

blue glass on the south face helps to deflect the sun's hot summer rays. In announcing the opening of this extension, Calgary Transit officials noted that CTrain ridership had grown 93% since 1995.[8] The high station structure at the end of the platform houses elevator and stairway access from the overhead pedestrian passageways over the busy Crowchild Trail. Its height and roof overhang match the style of an early CPR prairie station. On December 17th 2007, a 2.8 km extension of the northeast line, bringing the track to the McKnight-Westwinds station, went into service. This $243 million extension was officially opened by Premier Ed Stelmach and Calgary Mayor Dave Branconnier on Saturday December 15th 2007. The provincial government contributed $187 million while $15 million came from federal funding.[9]

Along with the anticipated extension of the system, steps were necessarily taken to increase the size of LRV fleet. An order for thirty-two cars was placed with Siemens, fifteen to be delivered in 2000 and 2001.[10] This order introduced the new SD 160 Light Rail Vehicle to Calgary Transit. These are alternating current vehicles drawing direct current (DC) from the overhead line, then converting it on board, delivering the electricity to the motors as alternating current (AC). The most easily-observed features new to passengers are the units' sliding plug doors, the two doorways with ramps, and the seating arrangement. The ramps tilt out from the doorway floor once the doors are fully opened and retract immediately prior to the doors being closed. Seats at the articulation between the centre doors are longitudinal while seats in the sections on either side of the articulation all face toward the operating end of the car; therefore passengers in one end of the car ride facing forward while passengers at the trailing end of the car ride facing backwards.[11] These cars were assigned fleet numbers from 2201 to 2215. By the close of the year 2003 another fifteen cars were delivered – fleet numbers 2216 to 2230. Cars 2231 and 2232 arrived in early 2004.[12] The livery on all of these cars (2201 to 2232) matched that on the original U2 cars.

On July 18th 2007, Calgary Transit officially accepted the first fifteen of an additional forty new CTrain cars. In the streetcar, trolley coach and early motor bus era, new equipment usually went into service with little public notice, as the municipality funded the purchase either from the sale of bonds or debentures, or through the passing of the required municipal money bylaws. Since these new LRT cars were purchased using federal, provincial and municipal funds, they were delivered in the presence of Ms. Diane Ablonczy, Parliamentary Secretary to the Minister of Finance and Member of Parliament for Calgary - Nose Hill; Minister Greg Melchin, Minister of Seniors and Community Supports and Member of the Legislative Assembly for Calgary North West; and Mayor Dave Branconnier. The three levels of government – federal, provincial and municipal – invested $158 million in the project. The City of Calgary committed $24 million of the $140 million it will receive over a five year period from the federal Gas Tax Fund to this project. The provincial government contributed $133.5 million.[13] These new cars raised the capacity of the CTrain system by more than thirty per cent, thus allowing CTrain frequency to increase to every three minutes (from a former every five minutes) during peak periods. In fact, between the hours of 7:20 and 8:00 AM on a typical week-day morning, route 201 train headways are occasionally as close as two minutes passing the 7th Avenue and 7th Street sw station. When route 202 trains are factored in, a train is scheduled to pass this point every two minutes between these times with a few exceptions, when it becomes a maximum of a three-minute headway.[14] The new LRT cars are decalled in an attractive new colour scheme featuring a sweeping, flowing red wave pattern along the lower body and white on the upper body.

A 2.2 km extension of the northwest alignment beyond Dalhousie station to Crowfoot opened on Saturday June 13th 2009 and went into service on Monday June 15th 2009. Funding for this $220 million project which included enhancements to the Crowchild Trail and the development of two new interchanges once again came from the Federal Gas Tax Fund, the Government of Alberta and the City of Calgary.[15]

The system now has 47.1 km of track accessed by 27 major stations plus eleven side-loading platforms in the downtown area. It has a fleet of 82 U2 DC LRVs, 2 U2 AC LRVs and 72 SD 160 LRVs. Many of the stations along the 7th Avenue transit mall have been renewed. Some of the original stations have been taken out of service and replaced with aesthetically pleasing open platforms under high lofty ceilings, often at new locations. Calgary Transit has used the

LRT technology in a variety of ways to effectively provide accessible, safe and reliable public transportation service to various areas of the city along three major corridors.

The future for LRT in Calgary is promising. The Oliver Bowen LRV storage facility on the northeast segment is being developed. Plans have been drafted for a new leg to run directly west from the 7th Avenue sw terminal station. Long range plans call for extensive development of LRT and other forms of public transportation. Included among them is the possibility of an underground operation in the downtown area to supplement the current 7th Avenue SE/sw surface corridor as it is nearing its capacity to handle LRT traffic. This demonstrated commitment to ongoing improvement and expansion confirms that electrified public transportation will continue to have a strong future well into its second century in Canada's oil capital.

Above and below: Jim Scott rode the first Crowfoot train. His ticket is illustrated above with older tickets. He also picked up a copy of Calgary Transit's "Crowfoot Rider's Guide" illustrated in part below.

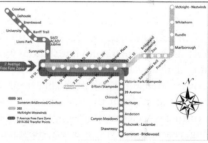

Opposite above: On February 16th 2006 a train of SD 160 LRVs proceeds west along 7th Avenue sw, having departed from the new station at 1st Street sw. Note the old station at Centre Street behind the train. (Robert J. Sandusky)

Opposite below: A view of the new Crowfoot station, the fourth LRT station to be located in the centre of the Crowchild Trail. It features very distinctive, clean, sweeping lines with touches of artwork. (Ticket above and photo right courtesy Jim Scott)

ROUTE MARKERS:

(1) Known as the Red Line.
(2) Known as the White Line.
(3) Known as the Blue Line.

(1) (2) (3) In 1909, cars carrying the Red, White and Blue coloured markers also carried the respective lettering EAST-WEST, NORTH-SOUTH, BELT LINE. No other identification was carried on the cars until 1912 when the signboards, described in *Note A*, were applied.

(4) The star with the blue border was applied to the TUXEDO PARK cars on November 11th 1920 (see *Note 5*). These cars operated from Tuxedo Park to downtown only and return.

(5) The star with the blue border was originally applied to the MANCHESTER cars and stayed with this route when it was extended to Tuxedo Park in 1915.

(6) The star with the green border is thought to have been applied to the MANCHESTER-RIVERSIDE cars in March 1934 when these cars were routed to Riverside from Manchester via 2nd Street SE, 17th Avenue SE, 1st Street SW, 8th Avenue, 4th Street SE, 1st Avenue NE and return.

(7) Effective November 11th 1920, the MANCHESTER cars began to run under the relatively new white and yellow skyward pointed arrow (See Note 12). At this time MANCHESTER cars began to operate north on Centre Street to 20th Avenue NW, west to 4th Street NW, south to 12th Avenue NW and east to Centre Street, whence they returned to the downtown area and then on to Manchester. This sign was in use on these cars until March 1924. Then, as far as it can be determined, it became a sign used for rush hours only, because the 12th Avenue NW and 4th Street NW line was used during peak periods only.

(8) The red cross with the white border could have been introduced in April 1915 when Riverside did not require the same frequency of service as the south end of the white line. Alternate White Line cars ran through to Riverside and the General Hospital, so it seems likely that these White Line cars might have been identified with the red cross marker. During the late teens, Riverside had service which did not go through to any other section of the city. The cross marker was used on these cars.

(9) The green diamond was used on cars routed to the Sunalta area.

(10) The red, white and blue rectangle was carried by BOWNESS cars when service was introduced to Bowness loop on March 1st 1913.

(11) The red rectangle with white lettering was in general use on Bowness cars in the late teens. One could surmise that cars running directly from downtown to Bowness carried the three-coloured rectangle while the BOWNESS transfer car meeting the Red Line car at Richmond Road and 14th Street NW carried the red sign with the lettering.

(12) The white and yellow skyward pointed arrow marker was first used on November 19th 1919. This was the opening of the Centre Street line from Sunnyside cut-off north to 20th Avenue NW, west to 4th Street NW, south to 12th Avenue NW and east to Centre Street to downtown where it looped to return to the Centre Street North area again. (Also see *Note 7*).

Note A
During the early 1912 period, certain Calgary Municipal lines also carried signboards lettered with details of the routes followed and bearing the colours used to designate the lines, Red, Blue, Red and White, etc. Lettering on the signboards, which first appeared on March 3rd 1912, varied in colour according to the colour of the board; red and blue signboards had white lettering while white signboards featured black lettering. Signboards were applied to cars travelling on routes other than those mentioned, but the information on them is not known. Photographs reveal that cars assigned to the White and the Bowness lines carried similar signs in the appropriate colours. On these signboards, the car's destination was indicated by a moveable arrow, which was altered by the motorman at each terminal.

Note B
Hunter type roller signs were applied to 24 cars during 1912 and another fifty cars during 1913. The roller signs were placed on the roof of the front platform and on each side of the clerestory windows towards the rear of the car. Original linens in these signs featured coloured discs illustrating the route colour beside the respective name. This practice was gradually terminated during the 1920s as it did not lend itself to route changes. (When Red Line cars began operating from West Calgary to Burns Avenue, eastbound cars carried BURNS AVENUE on the destination roller. But the linen also showed the red and blue disc beside the name, and it was confusing to have an otherwise Red Line car identified with the red and blue disc beside the Burns Avenue name.) Some variations appeared on these roller signs, such as ELBOW PK for ELBOW PARK, S CALGARY in lieu of SOUTH CALGARY, BURNS AVE. instead of BURNS AVENUE.

Note C
The name RIVERSIDE did not appear on the original linen roller signs. It was applied during the teens after route changes called for a service between Riverside and downtown. Citizens of the area objected to the use of the name "Riverside", so BRIDGELAND appeared on some of the cars.

Note D
As far as can be determined, indications for CAPITOL HILL, GRAND TRUNK, and SARCEE were never applied to the linens.

Note E
Although not route designations, these names were applied to most linens, sometimes with some variations, e.g. PRIVATE, TO CITY etc.

Note F
The route numbers assigned during the period 1928-1936 have not all been verified. It has been suggested that the numbers assigned during this period were even numbers only.

COLOURED MARKERS (1909 - 1936)	ROLLER SIGNS (1912 - 1936)	ROUTE NUMBERS	
		1928-36	1936-50
(Note A)		*(Note F)*	
■	EAST CALGARY ●	10	1
	WEST CALGARY ●	10	1
⌂	ELBOW PARK ○	12	2, 3
☆	MOUNT PLEASANT		2
	TUXEDO PARK		3
◧	CRESCENT HEIGHTS ○ ●	14	4
⌂	BELT LINE ●		5
⇨	KILLARNEY ○ ●		6
◖	SOUTH CALGARY ○ ●		7
◐	SUNNYSIDE ● ●		8
	BURNS AVENUE ● ●		8
☆ ☆ ⇧	MANCHESTER ● ○		9
✚	RIVERSIDE *(Note C)*		9
	BRIDGELAND *(Note C)*		
OGDEN LINE ⊙	OGDEN		0
✚ ▮▮ BOWNESS	BOWNESS PARK ● ○ ●		B
TO BOWNESS PARK			
◇	SUNALTA		S
⇧			
	(CAPITOL HILL) *(Note D)*		C
	(GRAND TRUNK) *(Note D)*		A
	PRIVATE CAR CAR BARNS *(Note E)* CITY		

Above: Car 43 on route 8 headed for Burns Avenue has just crossed the Elbow River bridge at 12th Avenue SE and is starting up the grade toward 8th Street SE. The track becomes a single to cross the bridge but breaks out into a double-track line just ahead of the car.
The date is July 22nd 1950.
(J.J. Buckley photo, Colin Hatcher collection)

Below: Car 19, one of the trams received in trade from Saskatoon in 1919, is operating on route 8 Burns Avenue. The track to the right leads into 9th Avenue SE and in this March 18th 1950 view is still being used by the Bowness and Ogden cars as part of their round-the-block loop in downtown Calgary.
(Robert W. Gibson photograph, Robert Halperin collection)

Above: It is a cold Saturday March 18th 1950 as cars 32 and 83 approach the carbarns on 2nd Street SE from their early afternoon run in from Ogden. At this time most non-operating railway employees worked a five-and-one-half day week. The afternoon sky is clear but it is cold as smoke drifts from the smoke jacks on both cars.
(Both photos: Robert W. Gibson, Robert Halperin collection)

Below: Car 42, operating as a regular car on the Ogden line, makes a left-hand turn from 8th Avenue SE onto 2nd Street SE. It will proceed south for one block and then turn right onto 9th Avenue SE, run west one block to Centre Street, turn right and go north to 8th Avenue S, then be prepared to run back east toward Ogden.
Date of the photograph is March 18th 1950.

Above: Car 45 travels along 12th Avenue SE, having just crossed 2nd Street SE. Although headed for downtown, it is signed for Burns Avenue and carries a route 8 indicator. After the abandonment of the Manchester portion of route 9 in 1947, the Sunnyside link to route 8 was transferred to Route 9 and those cars ran through from Riverside to Sunnyside. As a result, the route 8 cars began to permanently short-turn back to Burns Avenue via a downtown loop following 12th Avenue SE/SW, 1st Street SW, 8th Avenue SW/SE, 2nd Street SE and back to 12th Avenue SE. The cars were always signed Burns Avenue. This view shows a clean-looking long car which has folding steps and a modern life guard and fender. The date is July 22nd 1950.
(J.J. Buckley photo, Colin Hatcher collection)

Below: Car 55 pauses on the outer end or west end of the Bowness line on March 18th 1950. The car is a long Preston-built one carrying a large interurban headlight. Generally speaking long cars (46'6") were assigned to route 1 East Calgary-West Calgary, route 2 Elbow Park-Mount Pleasant, route 3 Elbow Park-Tuxedo Park, route 8 Burns Avenue-Sunnyside, route 9 Manchester-Riverside, route B Bowness and route O Ogden.
(Robert W. Gibson photograph, Robert Halperin collection)

Above: Car 45 travels south on 2nd Street SE at 12th Avenue SE. It is about to make a left hand turn onto 12th Avenue SE to continue its route 8 trip to the Burns Avenue terminal. The date is July 22nd 1950. Route 8 and route O to Ogden are the only two remaining streetcar lines at this time. There are many changes to the downtown urban building profile since this photograph was taken.
(J.J. Buckley photo, CRHA Fonds Bailey)

Below: Long car 50 is an Ogden regular car evidenced by its large head-light. It is the afternoon of March 18th 1950 and half-hourly service is being provided on the line. The car has just made the turn off the bridge over the Bow River as it makes its way out to Ogden.
(Robert W. Gibson photograph, Robert Halperin collection)

Above: On March 18th 1950 car 58 climbs the grade on 2nd Street SE from the CPR main line underpass. The car running on route 8 Burns Avenue is approaching 10th Avenue SE. On the right of the photograph are the CPR freight sheds. Beyond is the Imperial Hotel. The tower is that of City Hall up on the corner of 7th Avenue SE. (Robert W. Gibson photo, Robert Halperin collection)

Below: Coach 447 is southbound on Elbow Drive near Britannia Drive as the bus nears the crest of the hill coming up from the Elbow River crossing on June 21st 1973. Elbow Drive then dips back down just past this point. (Ted Wickson)

Above: A trio of trolley coaches at bus barns in July 1974.
(G.M. Sebree photo, Krambles-Peterson Archive)

Below: Coach 441 on route 3 at 4th Street sw and 17th Avenue sw. The
TD Bank facade had vibrant colours back in 1969.
(Steven Scalzo collection)

Above: In June 1964, coach 413 is northbound on 4th Street NW, turning into Blackthorn. Thorneycroft curves off directly in front of the camera. Glen Anderson shot this west across 4th Street NW. The bus will loop back clockwise and cross over the northbound wire to access its southbound run on 4th Street NW.
(G.M. Anderson photo, Krambles-Peterson Archive)

Below: Bus 494 is eastbound on 7th SW Avenue, running toward 3rd Street SW. That is the 4th Street SW intersection behind the bus. Fisher's Music is at 332-7th Avenue SW, and Safaris Restaurant is at 330-7th Avenue SW in this April 1964 image.
(G.M. Anderson photo, Krambles-Peterson Archive)

Above: Number 448 is on route 3 at 3rd Avenue sw and 4th Street sw in September of 1969. That icon of Canadian retailing, Eaton's in the background, had a strong presence in downtown Calgary. (Steven Scalzo collection)

Below: It's a busy afternoon in June of 1973 as coach 423 navigates the tangle of overhead at 14th street sw and 17th Avenue sw. (Ted Wickson)

Above: Coach 483 heads South on the Centre Street Bridge on route 3 bound for Elbow Drive and Hamlet Road. Winter casts long shadows on a crisp January day in 1960. (Robert J. Sandusky)

Below: The TTC demonstrator trolley coach 9213 signed for route 3 Elbow Park, in the North loop, 1971. (Robert Loat photo, collection of Peter Cox)

Above: Bus 460 sports the new two-toned blue scheme June 29th 1973 at 20th Street sw at 34th Avenue sw. Note that 20th Street makes a slight jog at that point as evidenced by the overhead. (Ted Wickson)

Below: Coach 473 on route 3 at 6th Avenue sw and 2nd Street sw looks a little worse for the wear on September 30th 1969. (Steven Scalzo collection)

Opposite above: LRV 2235 bound for Somerset leans into the curve coming out of SAIT/ACA/Jubilee station. The train is on its way down into the scenic Bow River valley on this December 2008 day. (Ted Wickson)

Opposite below: A train of SD160 LRVs led by 2209, with its front window shade drawn against the afternoon sun, stands at Dalhousie station on Crowchild Trail on October 7th 2004. At the time, Dalhousie was the terminal station on the northwest LRT. The 52nd Street overpass is in the background. Tracks were extended beyond the station platform to accommodate off-peak and overnight storage of LRVs. Crowchild Trail at this point is built on the alignment of the old highway 1A to Banff. (Robert J. Sandusky)

Right: The Calgary Tower, the City Hall complex and a "plus-15" pedway over 7th Avenue SE frame a departing C-Train led by LRV 2022 as it departs the 2nd Street SE station on September 4th 1981 on its way to Anderson station. At the time Calgary's LRT system was 12.5 kilometres long. One of the early new high-rise office towers is under construction in the background. (Ted Wickson)

Below: LRV 2036 signed for Somerset trails a three-car LRV train running north from Dalhousie station on June 15th 2009. Note the intriguing roof over the station platform as described in the text. (Jim Scott)

Above: An eastbound C-Train is framed by downtown high-rise buildings in this January 7th 1988 night scene. The train is stopped at the 3rd Street SW station in front of the Devonian Gardens (TD Square). (Robert J. Sandusky)

Below: On New Year's Day 1993, Brentwood-bound LRV 2050 climbs the grade at 10th Street NW to the SAIT/ACA/Jubilee station. The city skyline in the background contrasts with the parkland in the foreground. (Robert J. Sandusky)

Above: LRV 2011 swings into the Bow River valley at 10th Street NW on its southbound journey on January 19th 1992. The Southern Alberta Jubilee Auditorium forms a backdrop. The day is cold and still as the hoar frost still clings to the trees.
(Robert J. Sandusky)

Below: U2 LRV 2082 and SD 160 2242 head respective lines of LRV trains stored for the night at Dalhousie station on February 13th 2009. Such overnight storage of units allows trains to begin their scheduled runs from the outer ends of the line. As the LRV roster increased in size, end-of-line storage also helped to reduce overnight storage needs at Anderson and Haysboro. The phased opening of the new Oliver Bowen Maintenance Facility in the northeast made on-line storage in the northeast redundant. (Robert J. Sandusky)

Above: On May 21st 1985 an outbound Whitehorn train in the foreground trailed by LRV 2076 continues east along the extended 7th Avenue SE transit mall. Pedestrians proceed across a cross-walk as a C-Train from the south waits for its clear signal to enter 7th Avenue SE and continue westbound into the City Centre to terminate at 10th Street SW and 7th Avenue SW. (Ted Wickson)

Below: In the early morning light of Monday June 15th 2009, a southbound CTrain with LRV 2271 trailing departs from Dalhousie station. Here the northwest LRT is in the centre of the Crowchild Trail. Inbound automobile traffic is increasing as the time of the morning peak traffic period approaches. (Jim Scott)

APPENDIX 1: BIBLIOGRAPHY

Angus, F.F. "The Class 80 Cars of St. John, NB." *Canadian Rail* 202 (1968).

Anonymous. "Recent Developments at Calgary." *Electric Railway Journal* 57, No. 20 (May 14, 1921).

Anonymous. "Shawnessy LRT Station, Calgary, Alberta." http://www.lafargenorthamerica.com/wps/portal/ lna products/datasheet? (accessed August 20, 2009).

Anonymous. "Why Calgary Makes Money on a Four-Cent Fare." *Electric Railway Journal* 52, No. 13 (December 28, 1918).

Bailey, William and Douglas Parker. *Streetcar Builders of Canada*. Montreal: Canadian Railroad Historical Association, 2002

Bain, Donald M. *Calgary Transit Then & Now.* Calgary: Kishorn Publications, 1994.

Bain, Donald M. "Calgary Transit's CTrain and the Dalhousie Extension." *The Trip Sheet* 14, No. 2 (April 2004).

Bain, Donald M. "Western Canada's Newest Commuter Rail Service." *Branchline* 35, No. 6 (June 1996).

Binns, Richard M. *Montreal's Electric Streetcars*. Montreal: Railfare Enterprises Limited, 1973.

Canada Post. *Canada's Stamp Details* XIII, No. 1 (January - March 2004).

Canadian Car & Foundry Co. Limited. "Steel-Frame One-Man Motor Cars Built Complete for Calgary Municipal Railway 1928." *Bulletin* No. P. 30 (December 1928).

Canadian Railway and Marine World. Toronto: Acton Burrows, Ltd., August 1912 - December 1936.

Canadian Transportation. Toronto: Acton Burrows, Ltd., January 1937 - January 1948.

City of Calgary Planning and Building Department. *The Mission District, A Heritage Walking Tour.* Calgary, undated c1990.

Cox, Peter. "CMR Calgary Municipal Railway." *The Steam Chest* 66, No. 7 (September 1963).

Davies, Russell. "Calgary's West LRT Alignment Approved." *Branchline* 48, No. 3 (March 2009).

Dorman, Robert. *A Statutory History of Steam and Electric Railways of Canada, 1836 – 1936.* Ottawa: The Queen's Printer, 1938.

Fraser, W.B. *Calgary.* Toronto: Holt Rinehart and Wilson of Canada Limited, 1967.

Halperin, Robert. *Canadian Trolleys in Color, Vol. 2 Western Canada.* Scotch Plains, NY: Morning Sun Books Inc., 2008.

Hatcher, Colin K. *Stampede City Streetcars.* Montreal: Railfare Enterprises Limited, 1975.

Hemstock, J.D (City of Calgary Transportation Dept). "Siemens-DuWag Light Rail Vehicle for Calgary." A Paper prepared for the 1979 APTA Rapid Transit Conference, Montreal (June 1979).

Historic Sandon web site. "Canadian Car & Foundry Brill Trolleys." (July 10, 2006), http://www.sandonbc.com/ brilltrolleys.html (accessed Feb. 2008).

Hitt, Rodney. *Electric Railway Dictionary.* Navato: Newton K. Gregg, 1972.

Holcomb, Bruce, Edwin Mitchell, and Foster M. Palmer. "Front Entrance Doors in Dash Characterize Calgary Trolleys." *Electric Railroaders Association* 12, No. 4 (April 1950).

Hubbell, John and Dave Colquhoun (Calgary Transit). "Light Rail Transit in Calgary: The First 25 Years." A Paper presented to the 2006 Joint International Light Rail Conference, St. Louis, MO (April 2006).

Kuyt, W.C. and J.D. Hemstock (City of Calgary Transportation Department). "Calgary's Light Rail Transit System." A Paper prepared for presentation at the Second National Conference on Light Rail Transit, Boston (August 29-31 1977).

Kuyt, W.C. and J.D. Hemstock (City of Calgary Transportation Department). "Selection of LRT for Calgary's South Corridor." A Paper prepared for presentation at the American Public Transit Association Western Conference, Calgary (April 15-19, 1978).

Martin, J. Edward. *On A Streak of Lightning, Electric Railways in Canada.* British Columbia: Studio E, 1994.

McCauley, Thomas H. (Calgary Street Railway). "One-Man Operation in Calgary Alberta." *Electric Railway Journal* 50, No. 12 as found in "Selections from 1917 Electric Railway Journal." *Traction Heritage* 14, No. 82.

Meikle, John M. "Saskatoon Municipal Railway." *Canadian Rail,* No. 163 (February 1965).

Meikle, John M. "Calgary Municipal Railway." *Canadian Rail,* No. 166 (May 1965).

Meikle, John M. "Calgary Municipal (Streetcar Roster)." *Canadian Rail,* No. 171 (November 1965).

Newinger, Scott. "The Street Cars of Calgary." *Alberta Historical Review* 22, No. 3, (Summer 1974).

North American Trolley Association (NATTA). "Trolleybus Data Book." *Trolley Bus Bulletin,* No. 105 (April 1973).

North American Trolley Association (NATTA). "Trolleybus Data Book II." *Trolley Bus Bulletin,* No. 109 (1979).

North American Trolley Association (NATTA). *Trolley Coach News* 11 (September - December 1970).

North American Trolley Association (NATTA). *Trolley Coach News* 12 (January - April 1971).

Above: Single truck streetcar 26 operated as an auxiliary car from 1924 until the mid-1940s. Its rear platform was used in the construction of one of the four double truck cars built from single truck trams in 1924. (Percy W. Browning)

North American Trolley Association (NATTA). *Trolley Coach News* 15 (February - June 1972).

North American Trolley Association (NATTA). *Trolley Coach News* 19 (October - December 1972).

North American Trolley Association (NATTA). *Trolley Coach News* 24 (Winter 1973).

North American Trolley Association (NATTA). *Trolley Coach News* 28 (Fall 1974).

North American Trolley Association (NATTA). *Trolley Coach News* 30 (1975).

North American Trolley Association (NATTA). *Trolley Coach News* 32 (1975).

North American Trolley Association (NATTA). *Trolley Coach News* 33 (Summer 1975).

Ohio Brass Company. *Traction News* (March - April 1959).

Passenger Services Division of Calgary Transit. *History of Calgary Transit*. Calgary: 1977.

Railway and Marine World. Toronto: Acton Burrows, Ltd. (January 1908 - July 1912).

Roberts, Earl W. and David P. Stremes. *Canadian Trackside Guide*. Ottawa: Bytown Railway Society Inc., 2009.

Ruse, Joseph and C.A. Owens. *Calgary That Was and Is & Will Be, The Story of Calgary 1911 & Tuxedo Park*. Calgary and Toronto: The Land & General Investment Company, Limited, 1911.

Seebree, M. and P. Ward. "The Trolley Coach in North America." *Interurbans Special* 59 (Summer 1974).

Ward, Tom. *Cowtown, An Album of Early Calgary*. Calgary: McClelland and Stewart West Limited, 1975.

Wayman, Easten. *Saskatoon's Electric Transit*. Toronto: Railfare Enterprises Limited, 1988.

Wickson, Ted. *A Century of Moving Canada, Public Transit 1904 – 2004*. Toronto: Canadian Urban Transit Association, 2004.

INDEX AVAILABLE

A comprehensive Index for *Calgary's Electric Transit* is available from the publisher. (The lengthy Index was removed from this book's contents to provide space for inclusion of important historical information and last-minute photos that were discovered and deemed essential.)

To secure the free Index, go to: *www.railfare.net* – then select "Titles" ... select "Calgary's Electric Transit" ... select "Index" ... save and print on your computer's printer ... or mail cheque or money order for $4 (to cover shipping, handling, costs) to:

Railfare*DC Books,
Box 666,
St. Laurent Station,
Montreal, Quebec,
Canada H4L 4V9

APPENDIX 2: NOTES AND REFERENCES

Chapter 1

1   Chapter 1 is based on information found in W.B. Fraser, *Calgary* (Toronto: Holt, Rinehart and Wilson of Canada Limited, 1967).

Chapter 2

1   City of Calgary (City Clerk's Office), *City Council Minutes,* 6 May 1907.
2   City of Calgary (City Clerk's Office), "Proposed Car Line for Electric Street Railway," 13 September 1907.
3   City of Calgary (City Clerk's Office), *City Council Minutes,* 6 May 1907.
4   *Railway and Marine World: December 1907* (Toronto: Acton Burrows, Ltd.), p. 927.
5   City of Calgary (City Clerk's Office), H.E. Gillis, "Call for Tenders for Street Railway Franchise," 13 March 1908.
6   City of Calgary (City Clerk's Office), Correspondence to H.E. Gillis from J.T.D. Aitken, undated.
7   *Railway and Marine World: August 1908,* p. 583.
8   *Railway and Marine World: November 1908,* p. 816.
9   *The Morning Albertan,* 26 December 1908, p. 1.
10 *Railway and Marine World: November 1908,* p. 816.
11 City of Calgary (City Clerk's Office), "Commissioners' Report to Mayor and Council," 15 January 1909 as found in *City Council Minutes,* 18 January 1909.
12 City of Calgary (City Clerk's Office), "Supplement to Commissioners' Railway Report to Council," 18 January 1909.
13 "Commissioners' Report to Mayor and Council," 15 January 1909.
14 City of Calgary (City Clerk's Office), "Returning Officer's Statement," as found in *City Council Minutes,* 2 April 1909.
15 City of Calgary (City Clerk's Office), *City Council Minutes,* 13 April 1909.
16 City of Calgary (City Clerk's Office), "Commissioners' Report to Mayor and Aldermen," 26 February 1909.
17 *Ibid.*
18 City of Calgary (City Clerk's Office), "Commissioners' Report to Mayor and Council," 23 March 1909.
19 City of Calgary (City Clerk's Office), *City Council Minutes,* 28 August 1909.
20 H.W. McCauley, private correspondence with the author, 27 October 1974.
21 City of Calgary (City Clerk's Office), "Commissioners' Report to Council," 20 April 1909.
22 City of Calgary (City Clerk's Office), "Commissioners' Report to Council," 8 May 1909.
23 City of Calgary (City Clerk's Office), "Commissioners' Report to Mayor and Council," 31 July 1909.
24 City of Calgary, Correspondence from Board of Commissioners, R.R. Jamieson, Chairman, to Ottawa Car Company Limited, 3 July 1909.

Chapter 3

1   *The Morning Albertan,* 5 July 1909, p. 1.
2   Calgary *Herald,* 5 July 1909, p. 1.
3   *Ibid.*
4   *Railway and Marine World: August 1909,* p. 608.
5   *Railway and Marine World: May 1909,* p. 369.
6   *Railway and Marine World: April 1909,* p. 286.
7   Calgary *Herald,* 9 July 1909, p.1.
8   *The Morning Albertan,* 14 July 1909, p. 1.
9   *The Morning Albertan,* 20 July 1909, p. 5.
10 *The Morning Albertan,* 5 July 1909, p. 1.
11 *Ibid.,* p. 3.
12 Calgary *Herald,* 26 July 1909, p. 4.
13 Calgary *Herald,* 3 August 1909, p. 1.
14 City of Calgary (City Clerk's Office), "Street Railway Correspondence and Report File," 1909.
15 Calgary *Herald,* 6 August 1909, p. 1.
16 Calgary *Herald,* 14 August 1909, p. 1.
17 Calgary *Herald,* 25 August 1909, p. 10.
18 Calgary *Herald,* 26 August 1909, p. 1.
19 Calgary *Herald,* 15 September 1909, p. 1.
20 City of Calgary (City Clerk's Office), "Commissioners' Report to Council," 28 August 1909.
21 City of Calgary (City Clerk's Office), "Returning Officer's Summary of Bylaw #998," 26 October 1909.
22 Calgary *Herald,* 3 September 1909, p. 1.
23 *Ibid.*
24 Calgary *Herald,* 28 October 1909, p. 1.
25 City of Calgary (City Clerk's Office), "Commissioners' Report to Council," 8 December 1909.
26 City of Calgary (City Clerk's Office), "Commissioners' Report to Council," 28 December 1909.
27 City of Calgary (City Clerk's Office), Correspondence from R.R. Jamieson, Chairman, Preston Car & Coach Co., 31 December 1909.
28 City of Calgary (City Clerk's Office), "Commissioners' Report to Council," 8 December 1909.
29 City of Calgary (City Clerk's Office), "Calgary Electric Railway Superintendent's Report to Commissioners Year Ending 1909", 14 January 1910.
30 *Ibid.*
31 City of Calgary (City Clerk's Office), "Commissioners' Report to Mayor and Council," 4 June 1910.

32 Calgary *Herald*, 7 July 1910, p. 1.

33 *The Morning Albertan*, 28 February 1911, p. 22.

34 Calgary *Herald*, 8 April 1910, p.1.

35 Calgary *Herald*, 7 July 1910, p.1.

36 *The Morning Albertan*, 28 February 1911, p. 22.

37 *Ibid.*

38 *Ibid.*

Chapter 4

1 City of Calgary (City Clerk's Office), *Bylaw #1095,* 15 September 1910.

2 City of Calgary (City Clerk's Office), "Returning Officer's Election Statement," 15 September 1910.

3 City of Calgary (City Clerk's Office), T.H. McCauley, "Calgary Municipal Railway's Yearend Report 1910," 17 January 1911.

4 City of Calgary (City Clerk's Office), Correspondence: File 25, "Street Railway," 17 May 1911.

5 City of Calgary (City Clerk's Office), "Specifications," 30 November 1910.

6 *The Morning Albertan*, 23 June 1911, p. 1.

7 *The Morning Albertan*, 30 June 1911, p. 1.

8 Calgary *Herald*, 3 July 1911, p. 14.

9 Calgary *Herald*, 11 August 1911, p. 1.

10 Calgary *Herald*, 24 August 1911, p. 24.

11 Calgary *Herald*, 18 September 1911, p. 14.

12 Calgary *Herald*, 18 October 1911, p. 1.

13 Calgary *Herald*, 16 November 1911, p. 4

14 Calgary *Herald*, 13 November 1911, p. 1

15 City of Calgary (City Clerk's Office), Correspondence: File 26, "Street Railway," 13 November 1911.

16 City of Calgary (City Clerk's Office), "Commissioners' Report to Council," 1 February 1911.

17 *The Morning Albertan*, 25 July 1911, p. 1.

18 City of Calgary (City Clerk's Office), "Commissioners' Report to Council," 31 March 1911.

19 Calgary *Herald*, 3 August 1911, p. 1.

20 Calgary *Herald*, 14 October 1911, p. 32.

21 Calgary *Herald*, 2 January 1912, p. 1.

22 *Ibid.,* p. 16.

23 Calgary *Herald*, 3 January 1913, p. 20.

24 Calgary *Herald*, 2 January 1913, p. 1.

25 Calgary *Herald*, 17 December 1913, p. 1.

26 Calgary *Herald*, 26 September 1912, p. 20.

27 City of Calgary (City Clerk's Office), "Plan of South East Calgary Corporation," 16 July 1912.

28 City of Calgary (City Clerk's Office), "Commissioners' Report to Council," 23 February 1924.

29 Robert Dorman, *A Statutory History of Steam and Electric Railways of Canada 1836-1936* (Ottawa: The Queen's Printer, 1938).

30 Calgary *Herald*, 10 May 1912, p. 17.

31 Calgary *Herald*, 27 September 1912, p. 17.

32 Calgary *Herald*, 5 December 1912, p. 5.

33 Calgary *Herald*, 21 December 1912, p. 40.

34 Calgary *Herald*, 18 December 1913, p. 1.

35 Calgary *Herald*, 12 September 1911, p. 4.

36 City of Calgary (City Clerk's Office), "Commissioners' Report to Council," 11 October 1911.

37 City of Calgary (City Clerk's Office), "Commissioners' Report to Council," 9 December 1911.

38 Calgary *Herald*, 17 October 1911, p. 20.

39 City of Calgary (City Clerk's Office), "Commissioners' Report to Council," 21 November 1911.

40 Calgary *Herald*, 15 December 1911, p. 28.

41 Calgary *Herald*, 13 May 1912, p. 1.

42 Calgary *Herald*, 27 May 1912, p. 1.

43 City of Calgary (City Clerk's Office), Correspondence from T.H. McCauley to the Commissioners, 1 June 1912.

44 Calgary *Herald*, 3 July 1912, p. 1.

45 Calgary *Herald*, 6 July 1912, p. 6.

46 Calgary *Herald*, 15 July 1912, p. 16.

47 Calgary *Herald*, 5 July 1912, p. 1.

48 Calgary *Herald*, 6 July 1912, p. 6.

49 Calgary *Herald*, 15 July 1912, p. 1.

50 Calgary *Herald*, 5 November 1912, p. 1.

51 City of Calgary (City Clerk's Office), "Commissioners' Report to Council," 5 December 1912.

52 Calgary *Herald*, 21 May 1913, p. 1.

53 Calgary *Herald*, 3 January 1913, p. 20.

54 Calgary *Herald*, 7 January 1913, p. 1.

55 Calgary *Herald*, 17 March 1913, p. 1.

56 Calgary *Herald*, 19 March 1913, p. 1.

57 Calgary *Herald*, 23 February 1913, p. 1.

58 Calgary *Herald*, 14 October 1913, p. 32.

59 Calgary *Herald*, 29 July 1913, p. 1.

60 Calgary *Herald*, 2 December 1913, p. 18.

61 Calgary *Herald*, 27 November 1913, p. 9.

62 Calgary *Herald*, 17 September 1913, p. 13.

63 City of Calgary (City Clerk's Office), Correspondence from T.H. McCauley to the Commissioners, 10 October 1913.

64 City of Calgary (City Clerk's Office), "Commissioners' Report to Mayor," 13 October 1913.

65 Calgary *Herald*, 13 October 1913, p. 1.

66 Calgary *Herald*, 2 December 1913, p. 18.

67 City of Calgary (City Clerk's Office), Correspondence from T.H. McCauley to the Commissioners, 26 September 1913.

68 Calgary *Herald*, 16 September 1913, p. 1.

69 Calgary *Herald*, 5 August 1913, p. 15.

70 Calgary *Herald*, 31 October 1913, p. 13.

Chapter 5

1 Calgary *Herald*, 18 December 1913, p. 1.

2 Calgary *Herald*, 4 February 1914, p. 1.

3 Calgary *Herald*, 2 June 1914, p. 1.

4 T.C. Scatcherd (Retired Calgary Municipal Railway motor-conductor), private interview with the author, 16 December 1974.

5 City of Calgary (City Clerk's Office), *Bylaw #1535,* 7 May 1913.

6 City of Calgary (City Clerk's Office), *Bylaw #1704,* 26 June 1914.

7 Calgary *Herald,* 19 September 1914, p. 18.

8 Calgary *Herald,* 19 November 1914, p. 11.

9 Calgary *Herald,* 4 February 1915, p. 1.

10 Calgary *Herald,* 5 February 1915, p. 1.

11 Calgary *Herald,* 16 February 1915, p. 12.

12 Calgary *Herald,* 25 January 1915, p. 1.

13 Calgary *Herald,* 12 February 1915, p. 4.

14 Calgary *Herald,* 16 April 1915, p. 11.

15 Calgary *Herald,* 15 January 1915, p. 13.

16 City of Calgary (City Clerk's Office), Correspondence from T.H. McCauley to the Commissioners, 7 April 1915.

17 Calgary *Herald,* 10 April 1915, p. 1.

18 Calgary *Herald,* 21 August 1915, p. 12.

19 Calgary *Herald,* 20 August 1915, p. 7.

20 Calgary *Herald,* 25 September 1915, p. 7.

21 Calgary *Herald,* 30 September 1915, p. 10.

22 Calgary *Herald,* 5 October 1915, p. 3.

23 Calgary *Herald,* 6 October 1915, p. 12.

24 Calgary *Herald,* 12 October 1915, p. 10.

25 Calgary *Herald,* 13 November 1915, p. 11.

26 Calgary *Herald,* 27 November 1915, p. 9.

27 Calgary *Herald,* 4 December 1915, p. 1.

28 City of Calgary (City Clerk's Office), Correspondence from T.H. McCauley to the Commissioners, 2 March 1914.

29 Calgary *Herald,* 23 June 1915, p. 10.

30 Calgary *Herald,* 3 April 1916, p. 4.

31 Calgary *Herald,* 15 April 1916, p. 16.

32 Calgary *Herald,* 1 June 1915, p. 1.

33 City of Calgary (City Clerk's Office), Correspondence from City Solicitor Clinton J. Ford to the Mayor and Commissioners, 18 June 1915.

34 Calgary *Herald,* 20 May 1916, p. 9.

35 Calgary *Herald,* 15 April 1916, p. 16.

36 Calgary *Herald,* 16 May 1916, p. 5.

37 Calgary *Herald,* 19 July 1916, p. 14.

38 *Ibid.*

39 Calgary *Herald,* 15 July 1916, p. 14.

40 Calgary *Herald,* 10 August 1916, p. 5.

41 Calgary *Herald,* 16 September 1916, p. 20.

42 Calgary *Herald,* 22 February 1917, p. 14.

43 Calgary *Herald,* 12 May 1917, p. 14.

44 Calgary *Herald,* 24 July 1917, p. 11.

45 Calgary *Herald,* 18 July 1917, p. 5.

46 Calgary *Herald,* 24 July 1917, p. 11.

47 Calgary *Herald,* 6 May 1918, p. 5.

48 Calgary *Herald,* 4 September 1918, p. 10.

49 Calgary *Herald,* 16 September 1918, p. 9.

50 Calgary *Herald,* 24 January 1919, p. 3.

51 John Meikle, private interview with the author, 10 December 1974.

52 City of Calgary (City Clerk's Office), "Commissioners' Report to the Mayor and Council," 15 August 1919.

53 City of Calgary (City Clerk's Office), *City Council Minutes,* 18 August 1919.

54 Calgary *Herald,* 11 June 1917, p. 5.

55 Calgary *Herald,* 21 July 1917, p. 5.

56 Calgary *Herald,* 16 May 1918, p. 9.

57 Calgary *Herald,* 4 July 1916, p. 5.

58 Calgary *Herald,* 18 May 1917, p. 9.

59 City of Calgary (City Clerk's Office), *City Council Minutes,* 22 January 1916.

60 Calgary *Herald,* 13 January 1916, p. 15.

61 Calgary *Herald,* 9 March 1917, p. 9.

62 Calgary *Herald,* 12 April 1917, p. 9.

63 Calgary *Herald,* 25 April 1917, p. 9.

64 Calgary *Herald,* 27 May 1917, p. 9.

65 Calgary *Herald,* 4 May 1917, p. 10.

66 Calgary *Herald,* 7 May 1917, p. 1.

67 Calgary *Herald,* 10 May 1917, p. 9.

68 Calgary *Herald,* 20 August 1917, p. 5.

69 Calgary *Herald,* 16 October 1917, p. 14.

70 Calgary *Herald,* 22 October 1917, p. 4.

71 F.F. Angus, "The Class 80 Cars of St. John, NB," *Canadian Rail* 202 (1968), 193.

Chapter 6

1 City of Calgary (City Clerk's Office), "Map: Car Line Routes to Ogden," 2 February 1918.

2 City of Calgary (City Clerk's Office), "Plan: Proposed Improvement of Route of Ogden Car Line," 12 July 1918.

3 City of Calgary (City Clerk's Office), *City Council Minutes,* 14 September 1918.

4 Calgary *Herald,* 27 June 1918, p. 5.

5 Calgary *Herald,* 23 July 1918, p. 10.

6 *Ibid.*

7 Calgary *Herald,* 20 July 1918, p. 10.

8 Calgary *Herald,* 19 October 1918, p. 1

9 Amalgamated Transit Union (Division 583), "50th Anniversary Booklet," (1965), p. 4.

10 Calgary *Herald,* 29 May 1917, p. 1.

11 Calgary *Herald,* 23 October 1918, p. 4.

12 Calgary *Herald,* 25 October 1918, p. 9.

13 *The Morning Albertan,* 4 January 1919, p. 4.

14 *The Morning Albertan,* 17 February 1919, p. 3.

15 City of Calgary (City Clerk's Office), "Commissioners' Report to the Mayor and Council," 27 September 1919.

16 Calgary *Herald,* 23 July 1917, p. 5.

17 Calgary *Herald,* 17 August 1917, p. 1.

18 City of Calgary (City Clerk's Office), "Commissioners' Report to the Mayor and Council," 27 September 1919.

19 *The Morning Albertan,* 20 November 1919, p. 2.

20 *The Morning Albertan,* 24 September 1919, p. 7.

21 City of Calgary (City Clerk's Office), "Commissioners' Report to the Mayor and Council," 20 December 1919.

22 *The Morning Albertan,* 10 November 1919, p. 5.

23. City of Calgary (City Clerk's Office), "Commissioners' Report to the Mayor and Council," 27 September 1919.

24. *The Morning Albertan,* 5 November 1919, p. 3.

25. City of Calgary (City Clerk's Office), "Commissioners' Report to the Council," 10 November 1919.

26. City of Calgary (City Clerk's Office), "Commissioners' Report to the Council," 6 December 1919.

27. Calgary *Herald,* 5 December 1917, p. 5.

28. City of Calgary (City Clerk's Office), "Commissioners' Report to the Council," 6 December 1919.

29. J.A. Beatty (Former CMR motor-conductor), Correspondence to author, 8 November 1974.

30. Calgary *Herald,* 2 May 1918.

31. *The Morning Albertan,* 16 December 1919, pp. 1 & 5.

32. City of Calgary (City Clerk's Office), "Commissioners' Report to the Council," 20 December 1919.

33. Calgary *Herald,* 30 March 1920, p. 13.

34. Calgary *Herald,* 5 February 1920, p. 9.

35. *The Morning Albertan,* 2 July 1920, p. 3.

36. *Railway and Marine World: August 1920,* p. 449.

37. *The Morning Albertan,* 17 July 1920, p. 1.

38. *The Morning Albertan,* 18 August 1920, p. 1.

39. *The Morning Albertan,* 17 September 1920, p. 3.

40. C. Dwight Powell and John C. Ewing, Correspondence, 30 September 1974 and personal interviews, 31 October 1974 and 10 December 1974.

41. City of Calgary (City Clerk's Office), *City Council Minutes,* 15 April 1924.

42. *Railway and Marine World: July 1928,* p. 425.

43. City of Calgary (City Clerk's Office), "Commissioners' Report to the Council," 12 September 1925.

44. City of Calgary (City Clerk's Office), *City Council Minutes,* 1 March 1924.

45. *Ibid.*

46. City of Calgary (City Clerk's Office), *City Council Minutes,* 18 August 1924.

47. City of Calgary (City Clerk's Office), "Commissioners' Report to the Council," 3 September 1927.

48. City of Calgary (City Clerk's Office), *City Council Minutes,* 22 May 1927.

49. *The Morning Albertan,* 21 March 1924, pp. 5 & 9.

50. City of Calgary (City Clerk's Office), *City Council Minutes,* 9 June 1928.

51. *The Morning Albertan,* 14 November 1924, p. 2.

52. T.C. Scatcherd, 16 December 1974.

53. City of Calgary (City Clerk's Office), "Bulletin re: Calgary Municipal Railway cars 84 to 86," Canadian Car & Foundry Co. Ltd., Montreal.

54. City of Calgary (City Clerk's Office), *City Council Minutes,* 25 May 1929.

Chapter 7

1. City of Calgary (City Clerk's Office), "Commissioners' Report to the Council," 28 April 1930.

2. City of Calgary (City Clerk's Office), "Mayor's Report to the Council," 2 March 1931.

3. *Ibid.*

4. City of Calgary (City Clerk's Office), "Text of Agreement Between City and Brewster," 20 February 1931.

5. City of Calgary (City Clerk's Office), *City Council Minutes,* 13 February 1932.

6. Amalgamated Transit Union (Division 583), "50th Anniversary Booklet."

7. City of Calgary (City Clerk's Office), Correspondence from Chas. Corba to J.M. Miller (City Clerk) in response to Alderman Mahaffy, 21 June 1938.

8. City of Calgary (City Clerk's Office), "Mayor's Report to the Council," 2 March 1931.

9. *The Morning Albertan,* 9 June 1930.

10. J.K. Gush, "Recollections From Calgary Street Car Days," Presentation to Calgary and South Western Branch, Canadian Railroad Historical Association, 24 October 1974.

11. City of Calgary (City Clerk's Office), "Report of City Engineer to Commissioner Graves," 7 May 1931.

12. Calgary *Albertan,* 21 June 1944, p. 7.

13. Calgary *Albertan,* 27 June 1944, p. 9.

14. City of Calgary (City Clerk's Office), "Report of R.A. Brown to Commissioners," 26 June 1934.

15. City of Calgary (City Clerk's Office), "Report of R.A. Brown to Mayor Davison and Commissioner Riley," 22 January 1934.

16. *Ibid.*

17. City of Calgary (City Clerk's Office), "Recommendation of Special Street Railway Investigation Committee to Mayor and Council," 5 March 1934.

18. City of Calgary (City Clerk's Office), "Report of R.A. Brown to Mayor, Commissioners, and Council re: Fares," Letter #32, index 58, 17 January 1934 *(sic):* should read 1935.

19. J.K. Gush, "Recollections From Calgary Street Car Days."

20. *Ibid.*

21. Amalgamated Transit Union (Division 583), "50th Anniversary Booklet."

22. James Hughes (Retired CMR motor-conductor), private interview with the author, 16 December 1974.

23. Calgary *Herald,* 1 April 1933.

24. City of Calgary (City Clerk's Office), "Special Street Railway Investigation Committee's Report to the Mayor and Council," 28 March 1934.

25. Calgary *Albertan,* 4 July 1934, p. 3.

26. City of Calgary (City Clerk's Office), *City Council Minutes,* 29 August & 28 September 1934.

27. City of Calgary (City Clerk's Office), "Special Street Railway Investigation Committee's Report to the Mayor and Council."

28 City of Calgary (City Clerk's Office), Correspondence from T.S. Glover and A.I. Hibbard to City Council, 3 January 1935.

29 City of Calgary (City Clerk's Office), *City Council Minutes,* 21 January 1935.

30 City of Calgary (City Clerk's Office), "Commissioners' Report to the Council," 18 June 1937.

Chapter 8

1 J.A. Beatty (ex-CMR motor-conductor), Correspondence, 8 November 1974.

2 City of Calgary (City Clerk's Office), "Superintendent C. Comba's Report to Council," 29 March 1943.

3 City of Calgary (City Clerk's Office), "Superintendent C. Comba's Report to Council," 5 April 1943.

4 City of Calgary (City Clerk's Office), "Superintendent C. Comba's Report to Council," 25 November 1943.

5 City of Calgary (City Clerk's Office), "Calgary Transit, Schedule and Routes," 22 January 1945.

6 James Hughes, private interview with the author.

7 Calgary *Albertan,* 30 January 1946, p. 1.

8 City of Calgary (City Clerk's Office), Correspondence from C. Comba to the Commissioners, 1 August 1946.

9 City of Calgary (City Clerk's Office), Correspondence from C. Comba to the Commissioners, 18 March 1946.

10 City of Calgary (City Clerk's Office), "Commissioners' Report to the Council," 14 February 1946.

11 City of Calgary (City Clerk's Office), "Commissioners' Report to the Council," 19 July 1946.

12 Calgary *Herald,* 31 May 1947.

13 James Hughes, private interview with the author.

14 Calgary *Herald,* 30 July 1947.

15 City of Calgary (City Clerk's Office), *City Council Minutes,* 27 September 1948.

15a Calgary *Albertan,* 28 October 1948, p. 2.

15b Calgary *Albertan,* 16 November 1948, p. 9.

15c Calgary *Albertan,* 29 November 1948.

16 Calgary *Albertan,* 6 December 1949.

17 Calgary *Albertan,* 7 November 1949.

18 Anonymous, undated newspaper clipping.

19 Calgary *Herald,* Library photograph files.

20 Les Longpre (Retired Officer Calgary Transit), private interview with the author, 15 November 1974.

21 J.K. Gush, "Recollections From Calgary Street Car Days."

22 L.A. Armour (Superintendent Passenger Services Division: Calgary Transit), private interview with the author.

23 Calgary *Herald,* 30 December 1950.

Chapter 9

1 Calgary *Herald,* 5 June 1941.

2 Calgary *Herald,* 17 December 1943.

3 Calgary *Herald,* 11 August 1944.

4 *Ibid.*

5 Calgary *Herald,* 16 February 1945.

6 Calgary *Herald,* 6 June 1945.

7 Calgary *Herald,* 8 June 1945.

8 Calgary *Herald,* 27 June 1945.

9 *Ibid.*

10 Calgary *Herald,* 10 May 1946.

11 Calgary *Herald,* 28 May 1946.

12 Calgary *Herald,* 8 August 1946.

13 Calgary *Herald,* 15 October 1946.

14 Calgary *Herald,* 17 October 1946.

15 *Ibid.*

16 *Ibid.*

17 Calgary *Herald,* 31 May and 2 June 1947.

18 Calgary *Herald,* 30 July 1947.

19 *Ibid.*

20 Calgary *Herald,* 27 November 1947, p. 1 sect. 2 and 19 December 1947, p. 16.

21 Calgary *Herald,* 19 December 1947, p. 16.

22 Calgary *Herald,* 31 December 1947.

23 Calgary *Herald,* 19 June 1948.

24 Calgary *Herald,* 12 July 1948.

25 *Ibid.*

26 Calgary *Herald,* 8 October and 27 November 1947.

27 Calgary *Herald,* 31 August 1948.

28 Calgary *Herald,* 21 October 1949.

29 Calgary *Herald,* 25 October 1949.

30 Calgary *Herald,* 30 November 1949.

31 Calgary *Herald,* 6 December 1949.

32 Calgary *Herald,* 30 November 1949.

33 Glenbow Archives, Calgary Transit records: File 537, Note H-1 by RHW (Wray), "Conversion to Trolley Coach and Extensions," second page (not numbered), 29 April 1966.

34 *Ibid.*

35 Glenbow Archives, Calgary Transit records: File 22, 16 July 1953.

36 Calgary *Herald,* 20 July 1949, p. 16 and 26 July 1949, p. 4.

37 Glenbow Archives, Calgary Transit records: Box 1, File 66.

38 Glenbow Archives, Calgary Transit records: File 22.

39 *Ibid.*

40 Calgary *Herald,* 2 January 1954.

41 Glenbow Archives, Calgary Transit records: File 22, 16 July 1953.

42 Glenbow Archives, Calgary Transit records: Correspondence: File 44, from R.S. Trusslec (Electrical Engineer and Technical Assistant CTA) to R.R. Mills (District Manager: Ohio Brass), 25 May 1953.

43 *Ibid.*

44 Calgary *Herald,* 21 May 1954.

45 Calgary *Herald,* 21 April 1956.

46 Calgary *Herald,* 31 August 1957.

47 Glenbow Archives, Calgary Transit records: File 174.

48 Calgary *Herald,* 12 February 1957.

49 Calgary *Herald,* 10 March 1958.

50 *Ibid.*
51 Calgary *Herald*, 18 August 1958.
52 Glenbow Archives, Calgary Transit records: File 78.
53 Glenbow Archives, Calgary Transit records: File 685.

Chapter 10

1 Glenbow Archives, Calgary Transit records: Correspondence: File 106, to Patton, 30 March 1960 and to British United, 6 January 1960.
2 Anonymous, "Annual Review: Trolley Coach Operations," *Canadian Transportation,* (June 1959): 58.
3 Glenbow Archives, Calgary Transit records: Correspondence: File 127, R.H. Wray to F. McHenry (City Engineering Department), 27 April 1960.
4 Glenbow Archives, Calgary Transit records: File 139, 2 August 1960.
5 Glenbow Archives, Calgary Transit records: File 127, 30 November 1960.
6 Glenbow Archives, Calgary Transit records: File 127, 23 June 1960.
7 Glenbow Archives, Calgary Transit records: File 143.
8 Glenbow Archives, Calgary Transit records: File 144.
9 Glenbow Archives, Calgary Transit records: File 174.
10 *Ibid.*
11 Calgary *Herald*, 27 August 1961.
12 Glenbow Archives, Calgary Transit records: File 198.
13 Glenbow Archives, Calgary Transit records: "Calgary Transit System Comparison of Operation and Costs of Motor Buses and Trolley Coaches," January 1961.
14 *Ibid.*
15 Glenbow Archives, Calgary Transit records: File 279.
16 Glenbow Archives, Calgary Transit records: File 283.
17 Glenbow Archives, Calgary Transit records: File 279.
18 Glenbow Archives, Calgary Transit records: File 246.
19 Glenbow Archives, Calgary Transit records: File 279, "Route Data (as of Dec. 31, 1961),"15 May 15 1962.
20 *Ibid.*
21 Glenbow Archives, Calgary Transit records: Correspondence: File 269, R.H. Wray to W. Hawkins (Manager Electric System, Manchester), 24 January 1962.
22 Glenbow Archives, Calgary Transit records: File 269.
23 Glenbow Archives, Calgary Transit records: File 267.
24 Glenbow Archives, Calgary Transit records: File 334.
25 Glenbow Archives, Calgary Transit records: File 382.
26 Glenbow Archives, Calgary Transit records: File 382, "Questionnaire of Trolley Bus Operation on the Calgary Transit System," RHW (Wray), 11 October 1963.
27 Glenbow Archives, Calgary Transit records: File 404.
28 Glenbow Archives, Calgary Transit records: File 382, 15 August 1964.
29 Glenbow Archives, Calgary Transit records: File 476, *North Hill News,* 20 May 1965.

30 Glenbow Archives, Calgary Transit records: File 476 + 505.
31 Glenbow Archives, Calgary Transit records: File 505.
32 Glenbow Archives, Calgary Transit records: File 476 + 382, 15 August 1964.
33 Glenbow Archives, Calgary Transit records: File 505, "Route Revisions and Extensions Approved for 1965 (In Progress)," p. 7 + 9.
34 Glenbow Archives, Calgary Transit records: File 505.
35 Glenbow Archives, Calgary Transit records: File 493.
36 Glenbow Archives, Calgary Transit records: File 537, reply to letter, 25 October 1966.
37 Glenbow Archives, Calgary Transit records: Correspondence: File 550, R.H. Wray to R.F. Triffo, 29 December 1966.
38 Glenbow Archives, Calgary Transit records: File 550.
39 *Ibid.*
40 Glenbow Archives, Calgary Transit records: File 537, Anonymous ("LA"), "A Calgary Transit System Report on the Condensed History of the Trolley Coach," 25 October 1966.
41 Glenbow Archives, Calgary Transit records: File 537.
42 Seebree, M. and P. Ward, "The Trolley Coach in North America," *Interurbans Special* 59 (Summer 1974),p. 293.
43 North American Trolley Association (NATTA), *Trolley Coach News* No. 11, (September - December 1970).
44 Correspondence, R.H. Wray to Harry Porter, editor *Trolley Coach News,* 23 April 1976.
45 North American Trolley Association (NATTA), *Trolley Coach News* No. 12, (January - April 1971).
46 *Ibid.*
47 North American Trolley Association (NATTA), *Trolley Coach News* No. 15, (February - June 1972).
48 North American Trolley Association (NATTA), *Trolley Coach News* No. 24, (Winter 1973).
49 *Ibid.*
50 North American Trolley Association (NATTA), *Trolley Coach News* No. 28, (Fall 1974).
51 North American Trolley Association (NATTA), *Trolley Coach News* No. 30, (1975) and *UCRS Newsletter* (March - April 1974), p. 56.
52 North American Trolley Association (NATTA), *Trolley Coach News* No. 33, (Summer 1975).
53 North American Trolley Association (NATTA), *Trolley Coach News* No. 32, (1975).
54 North American Trolley Association (NATTA), *Trolley Coach News* No. 33, (Summer 1975). See Chris Radkey's report and updates from Don C. McDermid (Calgary Transit Passenger Services Division).
55 North American Trolley Association (NATTA), *Trolley Coach News* No. 34, (Fall - Winter 1975).

Chapter 11

1   W.C. Kuyt and J.D. Hemstock (City of Calgary Transportation Department), "Calgary's Light Rail Transit System," a Paper prepared for presentation at the Second National Conference on Light Rail Transit, Boston (August 29-31 1977), p. 2.

2   *Ibid.,* pp. 2-3.

3   *Ibid.,* p. 3.

4   *Ibid.,* pp. 3-4.

5   *Ibid.,* pp. 8-9.

6   W.C. Kuyt and J.D. Hemstock (City of Calgary Transportation Department), "Selection of LRT for Calgary's South Corridor," a Paper prepared for presentation at the American Public Transit Association Western Conference, Calgary (April 15-19, 1978), p. 4.

7   J.D Hemstock, (City of Calgary Transportation Department), "Siemens-DuWag Light Rail Vehicle for Calgary," a Paper prepared for the 1979 APTA Rapid Transit Conference, Montreal (June 1979), unpaginated.

8   "Selection of LRT for Calgary's South Corridor," p. 18.

9   Anonymous, "C-Train Facts," typescript paper (*circa* 1979), unpaginated.

10   Hemstock, p. 5.

11   *Ibid.,* pp. 5-6.

12   Siemens Specification Sheet, "Light Rail Vehicle RTC 1 of the City of Calgary," Ref. E1, E6: 80/47.

13   *Ibid.*

14   *Ibid.*

15   *Ibid.*

16   *Ibid.*

17   Physical site visit, 24 April 1981.

18   *Ibid.*

19   *Ibid.*

20   "C-Train Facts."

21   *Ibid.*

22   *Ibid.*

23   City of Calgary (Transportation Department), "Light Rail Transit – C-Train," brochure, undated (*circa* 1980).

24   "C-Train Facts."

25   City of Calgary (Transportation Department), "On Track: LRT Update," July 1980.

26   "C-Train Facts."

27   *Ibid.*

28   "Light Rail Transit – C-Train."

29   Calgary *Herald,* 1 June 1981, p. B1.

Chapter 12

1   Calgary *Herald,* 27 April 1985, p. G15.

2   *Ibid.*

3   Physical site visit & interview, 9 February 1987.

4   *Ibid.*

5   Calgary *Herald,* 27 April 1985, p. G15.

6   City of Calgary (Transportation Department), "Airport 57," route brochure, 4 April 1986.

Chapter 13

1   Anonymous, Title Unknown, *Branchline* 27, No. 7 (July-August 1988), p. 21.

2   Donald M. Bain, "Western Canada's Newest Rail Commuter Service," *Branchline* 35, No. 6 (June 1996), pp. 8-9.

3   Calgary *Herald,* 12 April 1996, p. 7.

4   Calgary *Herald,* 6 September 2001, p. B3.

5   Anonymous, "Calgary Transit and The Environment Ride the Wind," http://www.calgarytransit.com/environment/ride_d_wind.html, (accessed 14 December 2008).

6   Canada Post, *Canada's Stamp Details* XIII, No. 1 (January - March 2004), p. 28.

7   Calgary *Herald,* 4 October 2001, p. B1 and 6 October 2001, p. B5.

8   Calgary *Herald,* 12 December 2003.

9   Calgary *Herald,* 16 December 2007, p. B5.

10   Donald M. Bain, "Calgary Transit's CTrain and the Dalhousie Extension," *The Trip Sheet* 14, No. 2 (April 2004), p. 3.

11   Siemens Data Sheet, "Siemens SD 160 Light Rail Vehicle," http://www.usa.siemens.com/transportation, (accessed 6 August 2009).

12   "Calgary Transit's CTrain and the Dalhousie Extension," p. 3.

13   Anonymous, "Calgary Celebrates Arrival of New CTrain Cars Funded Through Municipal-Provincial-Federal Partnership," http://www.infc.gc.ca/media/news.nouvelles/gtf.fte/2007/20070718/calgary-eng.html, (accessed 15 December 2008).

14   Anonymous, "Calgary Transit Schedule Lookup," http://tripplanning2.calgarytransit.com route 201 and 202, (accessed June 2009).

15   Anonymous, "Calgary Opens Crowfoot Station," http://www.buildingcanada-chantierscanada.gc.ca/media/news-nouvelles/2009/20090613, (accessed 28 June 2009).

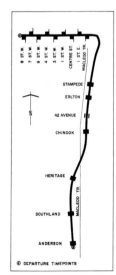
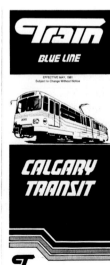

APPENDIX 3: CALGARY MUNICIPAL RAILWAY ROSTER PASSENGER STREETCARS

Unit No.	Builder/Year	Roof	Brakes	Windows Style Number	Trucks Builder Type
1 – 8	Ottawa 1909	M	H	Arch 5 X 2	Brill 27-G-1
9 – 12	Preston 1909	M	H	Arch 5 X 2	Bemis 45
13 – 15	Ottawa 1910	M	A	Arch 6 X 2	Brill 27-G-1
16 – 18	Preston 1910	M	A	Arch 6 X 2	Brill 27-G-1
19 – 30	Preston 1911 S.O. 158	D	H	Square 8 X 1	Taylor
31 – 36	Preston 1912	D	H	Square 8 X 1	Taylor
37 – 42	Preston 1912	M	A	Arch 5 X 2	Brill 27-G-1
43 – 48	Ottawa 1911	M	A	Arch 6 X 2	Brill 27-G-1
49, 51 - 55	Preston 1912	M	A	Arch 6 X 2	Brill 27-G-1
50 Scenic Car	Preston 1912 S.O. 177	C	A	–	Brill 27-G-1
50 (2nd) 56 – 66	Ottawa 1913	M	A	Arch 6 X 2	Brill 27-G-1
67 – 78	Ottawa 1913	M	A	Arch 5 X 2	Brill 27-G-1
79	Preston 1914	M	A	Arch 5X2	Brill 27-G-1
78 – 79 (2nd)	Wason	M	A	Square 10 X 1	Standard 0-50
80 - 81	Wason	M	A	Square 10 X 1	Standard 0-50
82 – 83	Newburyport	M	A	Square 3-6-3	Standard 0-50
84 – 86	CC&F 1928 Lot No. 768	A	A	Square 12 X 1	CC&F F-790
87 – 92	CC&F 1929 Lot No. 847	A	A	Square 12 X 1	CC&F F-790
201-206	Ottawa 1913	A	A	Square	Brill 27-G-1
300ex 1st 8	Ottawa 1909 Rebuilt Calgary 1918	A	A	Square 4 X 1	Brill27-G-1
8 (2nd)ex 1st 78	Ottawa 1913	M	A	Arch 5 X 2	Brill 27-G-1
19 – 21, 24, 28, 33 (2nd) ex Saskt'n 21 – 26	Preston 1913	M	A	Arch 6 X 2	Standard 0-50
27 (2nd) ex 57	Ottawa 1913	M	A	Arch 6 X 2	Brill 27-G-1
25, 29, 30, 32 (2nd)	Preston 1911 Rebuilt Calgary 1924	D	A	Square 12 X 1	Standard 0-50
31 (2nd) ex 1st 79	Preston 1914	M	A	Arch 5X2	Brill 27-G-1
36 (2nd) ex 8 (1st) ex 300	Ottawa 1909 Rebuilt Calgary 1918, 1932	A	A	Square 10 X 1	Brill 27-G-1

Trucks Single/Double Wheelbase	Control/Traction Motors	Length Overall Body	Width / Height	Seats	Weight
Double 4'6"	K 6 WH 101 BE	41'6" 28'6"	8'6" 8'9"	38 44	20,000 lbs 44,000 lbs
Double 4'6"	K 6 WH 101 BE	41'6" 28'6"	8'6" 8'9"	38 42	20,000 lbs 44,250 lbs
Double 4'6"	K 6 WH 101 BE	46'6" 33'6"	8'6" 8'9"	44 54	46,000 lbs
Double 4'6"	K 6 WH 101 BE	46'6" 33'6"	8'6" 8'9"	44 52	46,000 lbs
Single 8'0"	K 10 GE 80 A	32'0" 21'0"	8'2" 8'4"	28 32	15,000 lbs 27,000 lbs
Single 8'0"	K 10 GE 80 A	32'0" 21'0"	8'2" 8'4"	28 36	15,000 lbs 27,000 lbs
Double 4'6"	K 6 WH 101 B2	41'6" 28'6"	8'6" 8'9"	38 46	20,000 lbs 44,000 lbs
Double 4'6"	K 6 WH 101 B2	46'6" 33'6"	8'6" 8'9"	44 56	46,000 lbs
Double 4'6"	K 6 WH 101 B2	46'6" 33'6"	8'6" 8'9"	44 54	46,000 lbs
Double 4'6"	K 6 WH 101 B2	45' 33'	8'4¾"	50	16,000 lbs 40,500 lbs
Double 4'6"	K 6 WH 101 B2	46'6" 33'6"	8'6" 8'9"	44 52	??
Double 4'6"	K 6 WH 101 B2	41'6" 28'6"	8'6" 8'9"	38 48	20,000 lbs 44,000 lbs
Double 4'6"	K 6 WH 101 B2	41'6" 28'6"	8'6" 8'9"	38 48	20,000 lbs 44,000 lbs
Double 4'6"	K 6 GE 67	39'6" 28'6"	?	45 48	42,500 lbs
Double 4'6"	K 6 GE 67	39'6" 28'6"	??	45 48	42,500 lbs
Double 4'6"	K 6 GE 67	44'6" 33'6"	??	53 58	44,500 lbs
Double	K 35 XB WH 510 A2	46' 2" –	8'3" 10'10½"	53 53	37,800 lbs
Double	K 35 XB WH 510 A2	46' 2" –	8'3" 10'10½"	53 53	37,800 lbs
Double 4'6"	–	44'	??	60 68	?
Double 4'6"	K 6 WH 101 BE	41'6" 28'6"	8'6"	16	??
Double 4'6"	K 6 WH 101 B2	41'6" 28'6"	8'6" 8'9"	38 48	20,000 lbs 44,000 lbs
Double 4'6"	K 6 WH 101 B2	45' 32'	8'6" 8'9"	44 54	47,000 lbs
Double 4'6"	K 6 WH 101 B2	46'6" 33'6"	8'6" 8'9"	44 52	??
Double 4'6"	K 6 GE 80 A	43'0" 30'0"	8'2" 8'4"	46	?
Double 4'6"	K 6 WH 101 B2	41'6" 28'6"	8'6" 8'9"	38 48	20,000 lbs 44,000 lbs
Double 4'6"	K 6 WH 101 BE	41'6" 28'6"	8'6" 8'9"	-	??

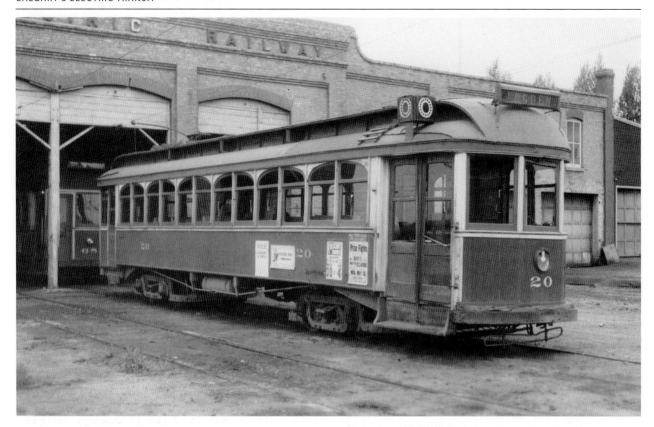

Above: Former Saskatoon car 20 outside the CMR barns. This was the second Calgary tram to carry the number 20 – the first being one of the small single truck units traded to Saskatoon for the larger, heavier, double truck cars.
(CRHA – Fonds R.F. Corley)

Below: The motorman patiently waits with the entrance door open to allow the photographer to capture this image of car 12 operating on Route 5, the Belt Line. The car is standing on 17th Avenue SE facing east and about to turn north into 2nd Street SE. This is one of the four original 1909 Preston-built cars. Note its Bemis trucks.
(Percy W. Browning photograph)

ROSTER NOTES – PASSENGER CARS

A-1 Car Builders

Calgary: Calgary Municipal Railway, Calgary, AB

CC&F: Canadian Car & Foundry Company, Limited, Montreal, QC

Newburyport: Newburyport Car Manufacturing Company, Newburyport, MA

Ottawa: Ottawa Car Company, Ottawa, ON (1893 – 1913)

Ottawa: Ottawa Car Manufacturing Co., Ottawa, ON (1913 – 1939)

Peteler: Peteler Car Co., Minneapolis, MN

Preston: Preston Car & Coach Company, Preston, ON

Wason: Wason Manufacturing Company, Springfield, MA

A-2 Dates

Date shown is the year built and in most cases year delivered compiled from contracts, dates in newspapers and industry related publications such as *Railway and Marine World*, *Canadian Railway and Marine World*, *Electric Railway Journal*. In some instances cars were ordered one or two years earlier, and details can be found in the text. "S.O." depicts "Shop Order Number" where known.

A-3 Construction

a) All bodies were of wooden construction with composite wood and steel underframes except car 50 (1st), the scenic car, which had a metal chariot-style front dash and sides finished in plate beveled glass mirrors, and cars 84 to 92 which were all steel.

b) Roof design: A = arched roof.
                       D = deck roof.
                       M = monitor roof or "railroad" roof.
                       C = canvas canopy (Scenic Car).

c) Brakes: H = hand brakes.
                   A = air brakes.

A-4 Doors

All of the cars numbered 1 through 79 (original numbers) were delivered as pay-as-you-enter two-man cars with a single-width front door and a double-width rear door. All passengers boarded at the rear of the car and paid their fare to the conductor stationed on the rear vestibule. Passengers could leave via the front motorman's vestibule or via the longer rear vestibule where the wider doorway could accommodate exiting and entering passengers simultaneously.

In 1916 the process of converting all of the cars for one-man operation commenced. Superintendent Thomas H. McCauley invented an entry system which could be applied to all cars on the system at the time. It involved the removal of the right front dash panel and the window above it and the installation of a door in that space. That door became the entrance for boarding passengers. All passengers could now board at the front of the car and place their fare in the fare box located beside the motor-conductor. Disembarking passengers left simultaneously via the original front vestibule doorway. The rear doors were closed off and became emergency exits only. With the exception of some unspecified single-truck cars in the 19 to 36 series, all cars were so converted.

Entry and exit doorways differed with the acquisition of additional cars and the rebuilding of some of the existing cars. Cars 19 to 21, 24, 28, and 33 (2nd) received from Saskatoon had long front vestibules so that boarding and disembarking could take place simultaneously via the double-width front doors. The rear doors were closed off and became emergency exits only. Similarly cars 25, 29, 30 and 32 (2nd) received long front vestibules in their rebuilding. Car 16 was rebuilt with its long rear platform forward so it too had double-width front doors. Of course, steel cars 84 to 92 were built and delivered with double-width front doors. Second hand cars 78 and 79 (2nd) and cars 80, 81, 82 and 83 retained their original single-width doors and the McCauley Patent door was never installed. Since these six cars generally operated exclusively in Ogden service, they only picked up passengers along the way, then all disembarked at once upon arrival at Ogden. The process was reversed on the return trip at the end of the day.

Trailers 201 to 206 were delivered with triple-width centre doorways providing space for two exits and one entry. These doorways were later reduced to single-width centre entry/exit doorways.

Treadle rear exits were applied to cars 1, 2, 16, 29 (2nd), 36 (2nd) and 67 to 72. Cars 84 to 92 delivered with treadle rear exits.

A-5 Trucks

All cars had 33" wheels, except cars 84 to 92 which had 26" wheels.

A-6 Control

All cars had single-end (SE) control except car 22 converted to double-end (DE) in 1918, and cars 78 to 83 (q.v.).

A-7 Motors

All cars had all axles motored except for two experimental periods. For a brief period in 1910-11 cars 1 to 18 operated with only two of their axles powered. In 1911 CGE four-motor sets were installed on cars 13 to 18 and all WH 101 BE motors were returned to cars 1 to 12. According to an article in *Electric Railway Journal* of November 4 1916 in an effort to economize during WW I, most cars operated with two motors during the summer season and four motors during the winter season.

Three of the cars traded from Saskatoon had two controllers and four motors. The remaining three had one controller and two motors. All were standardized with one controller and four motors for service in Calgary.

Motor ratings were as follows:

GE 67, GE 80, WH 101	40 HP
WH 510 A2	42 HP
GE 247	42 HP
DK 20	40 HP

A-8 Gearing

All cars had 59:17 spur gearing except 15, 18, 50 (1st), 53, 70 which had 63:15 helical gearing and 84 – 92 not known.

A-9 Seating

Two figures are shown. The first figure shows seating capacity of cars as they were delivered. The next figure represents seating capacities after alterations following the introduction of one-man operation, other car rebuilds and other changes in seating configurations. On conversion to one-man operation in the 1916-1919 period, most cars appeared to lose space for two passengers at the front, but gained about ten spaces in the smoking compartment set on the rear platform. Cars 61 and 78 to 83 had longitudinal seating which provided greater standee capacity.

A-10 Weights

The first weight listed in the column for each car group is that of the car body without running gear as described in the builders' contracts with the CMRy. The second weight in the column represents the total weight of the car in running order and comes from data provided by the late R.F. Corley. The running order weight listed for cars 19 to 36 (1st) is estimated based on the body weight noted in the contracts, plus half the weight of the running gear for short (41'6") double-truck cars. The running order weight for cars 84 to 92 is that given in the CC&F descriptive bulletin. No. P. 30 issued in December, 1928.

A-11 Modernization

A modernization program commenced in 1927 was intended to cover all cars on the system, but only a few selected cars were so modified.

Modernization included:

    Lifeguard (safety cradle).

    Improved headlight.

    Folding front steps.

    Interior dome lighting.

    Pneumatically operated treadle exit.

Many cars received the lifeguard, fewer cars received the folding front step.

Cars completely modernized were: 1, 2, 16, 29 (2nd), 36 (2nd) and 67 to 72.

A-12 Couplers

Cars 13 to 16 and 63 to 66 were equipped with Ohio Brass couplers and triple valve air brakes to haul trailers 201 to 206.

A-13 Brakes

Cars 1 to 12 delivered with hand brakes only (H) as were single-truck cars 19 to 36. Straight air brakes installed on cars 1 to 12 in 1912. All other double truck cars delivered with straight air brakes whereby the motorman's brake valve applied air to stop the car. Cars assigned to haul trailers noted in A-11 were equipped with triple valve brakes and the motorman's brake valve released air to stop the car or the two-car train.

A-14 Dimensions

Height data noted for all cars except cars 84 to 92 is from the bottom of the frame to the top of the roof.

A-15 Car Notes

Cars 1 to 12

These cars equipped with air brakes in 1912. Cars 1 and 2 modernized in 1927. (Note A-10). Car 7 body sold for use as cottage at Ghost Dam and salvaged in 1974 for parts to build a new car operating as number 14 in Calgary's Heritage Park. Car 8 burned June 10th 1917 and rebuilt as car 300 in 1918. Car 10 burned in April 1930 and scrapped.

Cars 13 to 18

These cars delivered with no motors. Two motors were removed from each of cars 1 to 12 and two of these surplus motors installed on each of cars 13 to 18. All subsequently equipped with four CGE motors in 1911. (Note A-6). Cars 13 to 16 equipped with couplers and triple valve brakes to haul trailers 201 to 206. By the 1940s only car 13 from this group retained capability to haul trailers, usually trailer 201. Cars 15 and 18 equipped with GE 247 motors and 63:15 gearing (Note A-7) for use on Ogden line. Motors and gearing transferred from Scenic Car following its withdrawal from service to car 15 in 1932. Similar equipment installed on car 18 about 1918. Car 16 burned April 1930, rebuilt in 1937 with K-35G control, arch roof, square windows, turned end-for-end, eliminating the need for McCauley front door in favour of standard double width doors on the front platform and modernized. (Note A-10). Car 14 was last car to operate on the system. It was stored as a relic but deteriorated. Its frame was used to build replica at Heritage Park in 1974.

Cars 19 to 36

In 1914 selected cars from this series were, with minor modifications, placed in operation as one-man cars on three stub lines. Another six cars followed in June 1916 when all cars on the Belt Line service were equipped for one-man operation. By that time modifications included closing in the rear platform as an observation and smoking area, providing seating for 10 passengers thereby increasing the total seating capacity of the car to 38. The original single-width door on the front vestibule continued to be used for both entry and exit. In January 1917 the McCauley patent front door with its associated safety features was applied to the single-truck cars providing an entry through the removal of the right front platform or vestibule panel. Exiting passengers used the original front vestibule door. These were therefore the prototype cars

Above: "Dinky" 35 parked off-track at the carbarns. During its latter days, the body was used as an employees' lunchroom. (J.A. Beatty)

for the McCauley patent appliances. Once this one-man concept proved to be workable on the 32-foot single-truck cars, it was gradually applied to all of the 41'6" and 46'6" double-truck cars.

Cars 19 to 21, 24, 28, 31 and 33 sent to Saskatoon Municipal Railway in 1919 in exchange for six SMR double truck cars which became Calgary Municipal Railway 19 to 21, 24, 28 and 33 (q.v.). Car 22 converted for double-end operation in 1918 and retired in 1944. Car 26 converted to work auxiliary car 26 (q.v.) in 1924 when its rear platform was removed and used in the rebuilding program for cars 25, 29, 30 and 32 (all 2nd numbers) (q.v.). Cars 25, 29, 30 and 32 combined with cars 34 and 36 and the rear platform of car 26 to build double-truck cars 25, 29, 30 and 32 (all 2nd numbers) in 1924 (q.v.). Cars 23, 27, 35 were retired in the mid-1930s. Car 35 used as a lunchroom at the carbarns. Most of the K-10 controllers on these cars replaced with K-6 controllers.

Cars 37 to 42

Cars 41 and 42 had 44 (revised) seats. The route box indicators on most cars were fixed, displaying the route number to the front and side only at the right front of the car and to the rear and left side only at the left rear of the car. In order to change the route number display someone had to climb up on the roof, remove the currently displayed route number in the forward and right side facing positions and insert the desired route number displays in their places. The same procedure had to be employed to change the numbers in the rear display box. The route number boxes on cars 38, 39 and 40 had the capacity to carry a second set of route numbers on the

otherwise blank two sides of the display boxes and both front and rear boxes could be rotated from inside the car by the motor-conductor by means of a crank allowing the motor-conductor the flexibility to display one of two pre-selected route numbers without having to climb up on the roof to change the display. Cars with this adjustable route display capacity could be identified by an interested observer as they were equipped with a shield at the rear of the front roof-mounted route number box and at the front of the rear roof-mounted route number box. The purpose of the shield was to cover the display of the alternate route number, leaving only the two sides of the box displaying the intended route number. Cars with this feature were available for assignment to route 4 Crescent Heights and route 5 the Belt Line where some runs were required to alternate from one route to the other.

Cars 49, 51 to 55

Car 49 had 56 (revised) seats. Car 53 equipped with GE 247 motors and 63:15 gearing (Note A-7) c1918.

Car 50 Scenic Car

No road number applied after 1913. Equipped with GE 247 motors and 63:15 helical gearing (Note A-7) c1918. Withdrawn from service in 1932 and motors and gears transferred to car 15. (Note A-7). In the 1940s placed on Standard 0-50 trucks and used to advertise Victory Bond sales. Dismantled or scrapped September 1946.

Cars 50 (2nd), 56 to 66

Car 50 had 56 (revised) seats. Car 57 renumbered 27 in 1944. Car 59 rebuilt with square windows in the 1940s. Car 60 burned at East Calgary loop on May 1st 1918 and rebuilt with square windows, arch roof and 66 seats. Car 61 equipped with Brill 27 G trucks date unknown. Car 62 rebuilt with square windows. Cars 63 to 66 equipped in late 1913 with Ohio Brass couplers (Note A-11), additional sanders ahead of the rear trucks and triple valve brakes to haul trailers 201 to 206. Cars 64 and 65 did not initially carry a Hunter roof-mounted destination sign but by 1949 car 64 did carry such a sign.

Cars 67 to 78

Car 67 and 68 converted to K-35 control. Cars 67 to 72 were modernized in 1927. (Note A-10) Car 68 involved in accident December 15th 1919 and rebuilt in 1920 with arch roof. Car 70 equipped with GE 247 motors and 63:15 gearing c1918. Car 72 equipped with square windows in 1940 and 41 (revised) seats. Car 78 renumbered car 8 (2nd) in 1920. Cars 67 to 69 had 39 (revised) seats. Cars 73 to 77 equipped with adjustable route number boxes and associated shields making it possible for the motor-conductor to change the display of the route number to the second of two pre-selected route numbers by the simple turn of a crank inside the car which rotated the box to the desired display position.

Car 79

This was one of an order of six cars. The balance of the order was cancelled due to declining traffic. The car was renumbered 31 (2nd) in 1920.

Cars 78 to 79 (2nd) and 80 to 83

Received in 1920 either from Springfield MA or the New York & Stamford Railway as second hand cars. Jack Beatty who was a motor-conductor in Calgary in the 1930s notes in a letter to the author dated March 26th 1976 from Montreal that he recalled seeing Wason decals on the bulkheads of cars 78 and 79 (2nd). They were received as double-end cars but rebuilt for single-end operation on arrival in Calgary. Cars 79 and 81 were converted back to double-end operation in 1934 and then to single-end operation again about 1940. Car 80 converted to work auxiliary c1940. (q.v.) Car 78 received WH 101B2 motors c1940. Although operated as one-man cars, no physical modifications for one-man operation were ever carried out on cars 78 to 83 except for closing off rear doors and placing the fare box at the front. None of these cars carried the Hunter roof-mounted destination signs. All of these cars had longitudinal seating.

Cars 84 to 92

All of these cars equipped with roller bearings, air-operated front doors, rear treadle exit and safety control. Height noted is full height from top of rail to top of roof. They were delivered with "Montreal"-type route number indicators but these were replaced with the Calgary-type roof-mounted indicators in 1936. No colour route indicators ever applied. Cars 84, 88, 90 and 92 had roof-mounted headlight brackets for use on night Bowness assignments. Car 89 withdrawn from service January 29th 1946 on account of an accident and scrapped. Car 91 burned at the carbarn yard and re-entered service in April 1930.

Cars 201 – 206

These were all non-powered trailer cars. Ohio Brass couplers provided air braking capabilities from the lead powered car. Window arrangement on door side as follows: 6-door-6 and on blind side 6-2-6. Conductor's pull-cord single stroke bell mounted on outside front signalled motorman to stop or proceed. Converted to single centre door in 1917.

Car 300

Car 300 was a combination freight/passenger car built for milk pick-up on Ogden, Sarcee and Bowness lines. Rebuilt by CMR in 1918 from car 8 (1st) after a 1917 fire. Withdrawn in 1936 and rebuilt again to car 36 (2nd).

Car 8 (2nd)

Renumbered from 78 (1st) in 1920 to fill gap left by rebuilding of number 8 (1st) to car 300.

Cars 19 to 21, 24, 29, 33 (2nd)

Delivered new to Saskatoon Municipal Railway as cars 21 to 26. Exchanged for seven single Calgary Municipal Railway truck cars 19 to 21, 24, 28, 31 and 33 in 1919 (q.v.). Three cars were received from Saskatoon in December 1919 and three in December 1920. All converted to single-end four motor cars. (Note A-6).

Car 27 (2nd)

Renumbered from car 57 as a result of accident on May 31st 1944.

Cars 25, 29, 30, 32 (2nd)

These cars rebuilt by the Calgary Municipal Railway from single-truck cars 25, 29, 30, 32, 34, 36 and the rear platform of car 26. Bodies of cars 34 and 36 cut in half. These with the rebuilding and fabrication of additional structures provided four double-truck cars with long platforms at both ends. The "operative remainder" of car 26 converted to auxiliary 26.

Car 31 (2nd)

Renumbered from car 79 (1st) in 1920 to fill gap left by the seventh car traded to Saskatoon.

Car 36 (2nd)

Rebuilt from car 300 in 1932 with McCauley patent front door and modernized (Note A-10).

Above: Portable substation 2 was one of two such units used on the Calgary Municipal Railway. They were placed toward the outer ends of the Bowness and Ogden lines to ensure an even distribution of power to these outer extremeties of the system. Convoys of streetcars operated to Bowness in summer and year-round to Odgen, drawing heavily on electric current. The substations provided the extra energy. (W.C. Whittaker)

Below: Calgary's original single truck single-broom sweeper A was an Ottawa Car Company product of 1912. (Glenbow Archives NA-2935-16)

APPENDIX 4: CALGARY MUNICIPAL RAILWAY ROSTER WORK AND FREIGHT EQUIPMENT

Unit No.	Builder / Year	Description	Brakes	Trucks Builder Type	Trucks Single or Double/ Wheelbase	Control Traction Motors	Length	Width	Other Equipment
A	Ottawa 1913	Sweeper, double broom	H	Pedestal	Single ?	K 10 WH 101 B2			Side plow wings
B	Calgary 1913	Motor flat car, centre cab	A	Brill 27-G-1	Double 4'6"	Dick, Kerr Dick, Kerr 20	?	?	
C	Preston 1909	Sprinkler	?	Bemis 45	Double 4'6"	K 6 WH 101 B2	30'0"	? 10'6"	5000 gallon tank, Allis-Chalmers centrifugal type pumps and McGuire-Cummings sprinkler heads, steel frame.
D	Calgary 1911	Motor flat car	H	?	Single ?	K 6 WH 101 B2	?	? ?	
D (2nd)	Ottawa 1920	Sweeper, single broom	H	Pedestal	Single ?	K 6 WH 101 B2	?	? ?	Side plow wings
E	Preston 1912	Sprinkler	?	Brill 27-GE-1	Double 4'6"	K 6 WH 101 B2	30'0"	? 10'6"	5000 gallon tank
F	Preston 1914	Sprinkler	?	Brill 27-G-1	Double 4'6"	K 6 WH 101 B2	30'0"	? 10'6"	5000 gallon tank
G	Calgary c1916	Motor flat car, end cab	A	Brill 27-G-1	Double 4'6"	K 6 WH 101 B2	42'0"	? ?	
H Mary Ann	Ottawa 1928	Sweeper, double broom, centre cab	A	Brill 27-G-1	Double 4'6"	GE Type M GE (65 HP)	39'6"	9'5" 12'1 ½"	WH 101 B2 sweeper motors. Side plow wings. All steel construction.
26 (2nd)	Preston 1911 Rebuilt Calgary 1924	Auxiliary	H	Taylor	Single 8'0"	K 10 GE 80 A	c-25'	8'2" 8'4"	
Auxiliary	Wason ?	Auxiliary	A	Stan'd 0-50	Double 4'6"	K 6 GE 67	39'6"	? ?	
1, 2	Calgary 1924	Portable electrical sub stations	?	-	Double ?	-	?	? ?	One unit known to contain mercury arc rectifier.
A-1?	Dominion Bridge Co. Calgary1920s	Depressed-centre flat car	?	Brill 27-G-1	Double 4'6"	-	?	?	Used to convey Insley gas-powered shovel to Bowness.
	Calgary 1911	Flat cars (4)	?	2-axle home-made	Single ?	-	?	? ?	
	Peteler 1913	Gravel dump cars (4)	?	?	Single ?	-	?	? ?	8 yard capacity, wooden bodies
100-103	Calgary 1916	Box cars	?	2-axle home-made	Single ?	-	?	? ?	Four box car trailers mounted on dump car trucks for Sarcee line.
109	Calgary 1916	Single-truck box locomotive	?	2-axle home-made	Single ?	K 6 WH 101 B2	?	? ?	Used to haul box car trailers on Sarcee line.
	Calgary 1916	Motor flat-car, end cab.	?	?	Double ?	K 6 WH 101 B2	?	? ?	Used to carry cordwood to Sarcee and haul a trailer flat.
	Calgary 1916	Trailer flat-car	?	2-axle home-made	Single ?	-	?	? ?	Used to carry bales of hay behind motor flat on Sarcee line.

ROSTER NOTES – WORK AND FREIGHT EQUIPMENT

Identification

Considerable confusion exists regarding identity, dates built, and rebuildings of work equipment, particularly in early years. While it is certain that each of these pieces of equipment existed the assignment of unit letters to C, D (1st), E and F is uncertain.

Some but not all of the equipment built as temporary units for the Sarcee service carried identifying numbers. See article about Calgary Municipal Railway by John Meikle in *Canadian Rail* No. 166, May 1965, pp.77 - 83. Specific identifying numbers were found along with a written description in an article headed Extemporizing Equipment to Camp Sarcee which appeared in *Electric Railway Journal*, Vol. 52, No. 13, September 28th 1918, pp. 544 and 546.

"Not listed in either Mr. J. Meikle's roster (*Canadian Rail* No. 171, November 1965) or the one in [your book, *Stampede City Streetcars* / Railfare / 1973] is the track rebuilding train which I remember seeing in action in the general rebuilding of the 12th Avenue East line from 2nd Street East to the Elbow River Bridge. I was attending Victoria Public School at the time and our home was on 11th Avenue in the six hundred block, going home via 12th Avenue was an unauthorized detour but I couldn't resist dawdling to watch the operation. This must have been sometime between 1928 and 1932.

The train consisted of several four wheel cars – perhaps originally the Sarcee cars or the sprinklers – with very high bearing pedestals resembling those of the four wheel sweepers. One of the cars had a box body containing a motor, which through a belt drove a rock crusher on another car. I had a photo of these two which meant that they still existed at the back of the barns around 1937-38. I believe the other cars were tool storage cars. A picture of the car is in *"Cowtown"* [a local publication -- *ed*] page 239.

The crusher was supplied by those dump cars which were also still around in 1937-38."

– *From a letter dated July 30 1984 addressed to the author from Percy W. Browning of Stoney Creek, Ontario and formerly of Calgary, Alberta.*

It is possible that the cars described by Mr. Browning were the unnumbered gravel dump cars which were built by Peteler in 1913.

Control

All motor cars had single-end control except sweeper A (which was later converted from double-end to single-end control) and sweeper H.

Motors

For ratings see passenger car Note A-6.

Car Notes

Sweeper A converted to single broom, single-end operation at unknown date. It had a wood underframe and wood box body.

Motor flat D featured a rudimentary cab. It became a shop crane without a cab and fitted with a boom. Its unit identity was removed in 1920 and transferred to a new sweeper.

Sprinklers C, E and F were out of service by 1920.

Sweeper D (2nd assignment of unit number) was built on a steel underframe with a wood box body.

Sweeper H was of all steel construction and had a centre cab locomotive style carbody. It weighed 72,000 lbs.

Auxiliary car 26 was converted from passenger car 26 in 1924. The rear platform was removed and used in passenger car rebuild program. Retired about 1944.

Auxiliary was converted from passenger car 80 about 1940 to replace 26. It was painted silver, and was not assigned a letter or number.

Portable sub-stations 1 and 2 were used on the Ogden and Bowness lines to help maintain an even distribution of direct current electricity on these system extremities.

A-1 depressed centre flat car trucks were supplied by the Calgary Municipal Railway. "The shovel was used mainly for deepening, widening and dredging the channel from the Bow River to the lagoon system at the west end of Bowness Park. The shovel would be unloaded from the low-boy on the trackage at the entrance to the park and driven under its own power to the dredging site. The gravel dredged from the channel was crushed and used as ballast on various lines of the system." The information came from Tommy Ridley who retired in 1963 as garage superintendent after fifty years of service with the city. Letter addressed to the author dated January 21st 1975 from L.A. Armour, Superintendent, Passenger Services Division, The City of Calgary Transportation Department.

Below: Single truck sweeper D, a 1920 product of the Ottawa Car Manufacturing Company, stands stored in the summer sun at the carbarns. (Glenbow Archives NA-2935-17)

The Cars Retired

1930: car 10.

1946: car 89, observation car.

1947: cars 4, 5, 7, 9, 11, 12, 37, 40, 70, 72, 74, 76, 81, 203, 204. Total 13 cars and 2 trailers.

1948: cars 1, 2, 3, 6, 8, 15, 24, 30, 31, 36, 49, 51, 61, 65, 79, 201, 202, 205, 206. Total 15 cars, 4 trailers.

1949: cars 17, 18, 21, 25, 27, 33, 39, 41, 44, 52, 54, 56, 63, 66, 69, 71, 73, 84, 86, 87, 91, 92. Total 25 cars. *

1950: cars 13, 14, 16, 19, 20, 28, 29, 32, (38), 42, 43, 45, 46, 47, 48, 50, (53), 55, 58, 59, 60, 62, 64, (67), (68), 75, 77, (78), 82, 83, (85), 88, (90). Total 30 cars. *

* City of Calgary Annual Reports for 1949 and 1950 list thirty passenger cars on the roster at the end of each successive year. The above cars listed for 1949 were taken off the roster during that year presumably leaving thirty cars available for service at the end of that year. Twenty cars from the 1950 list above appear in dated photos in the author's collection. *The Calgary Herald* reported that two steel cars were destroyed in the December 27th 1950 carbarn fire. Cars listed ( ) are thought to have been available for service early in 1950 but off trucks and still on the property later in 1950. Three cars noted in the 1950 list were off the roster before 1950 but which specific three is not known. Those three would therefore be listed with the 1949 retirements.

Above: At the south end of the abandoned plant, freight motor B rests some time after concluding its part in dismantling the railway. Officials and staff of the Calgary Transit System make a final inspection of the equipment. The gentleman without a hat is Ken Gush who was a motor-conductor and inspector with the Calgary Municipal Railway. He remained with Calgary Transit in an official capacity until his retirement some years after the abandonment of the streetcar system. (Glenbow Archives PA-1689-16)

Below: Motor flatcar B and the single truck derrick car remain at the spur track at the derelict standby power plant along the banks of the Elbow River some time after the abandonment of the streetcar system in Calgary. Both pieces of equipment were involved in the dismantling of the Calgary Municipal Railway. Note the scrap track materials in the foreground. (Glenbow Archives PA-1689-17)

APPENDIX 5: CPR FREIGHT SPUR TO VICTORIA PARK STORE YARDS

A Canadian Pacific Railway spur line into the steam-driven power-generating plant along the Elbow River located south of 17th Avenue SE provided the Calgary Municipal Railway with an opportunity to expedite the handling of incoming freight for the City. The spur handled coal cars destined for the plant. With the rapid growth of the city and the street railway system, the City expected very considerable and continuous shipments of streetcars, rail, track special work, ties, power poles, water and sewer pipe and other supplies over an extended period of time. In a letter dated January 17th 1911, addressed to the City Commissioners, Mr. McCauley, Superintendent of the Calgary Municipal Railway, proposed a connection of the street railway tracks with the CPR spur to the Victoria Park store yards. He also proposed a spur from the street railway at 9th Avenue SE and 6th Street SE to be placed on the south side of 9th Avenue SE so that material could be loaded after CPR freight cars had completed their delivery. Mr. McCauley pointed out that this 9th Avenue SE track would not be on any CPR property; thus, no permission from the railway would be required from them in this regard.

In a letter addressed to Mr. Maharg, Superintendent of the Canadian Pacific Railway at Calgary and dated January 30th 1911, Mr. McCauley outlined his plan. He proposed to erect the trolley wires the standard height of 22' 6" above, and clear of, the CPR rails. The span poles would be placed any safe distance from the track that the CPR specified. A cut-off switch at either 12th Avenue

SE or 17th Avenue SE would be installed, to disconnect this line from the rest of the trolley system during times that CPR crews are shunting, or when the street railway was not using it. He noted that the spur would not be used at any time by the street railway system when it would interfere with CPR service. Mr. McCauley stated that the City would no doubt agree to assume any liability. Mr. McCauley's desired choice for the spur connection was at 12th Avenue SE. He proposed running over the CPR tracks as it would be easier to offload freight from CPR cars onto the ground, remove the CPR cars and then run the Calgary work cars in to load the material for delivery to desired points in the city. An application with the Dominion Railway Board would be submitted by the City with all of the necessary supporting plans and specifications.

The outcome of the 9th Avenue SE unloading spur is uncertain, but the 12th Avenue SE connection was built and remained active until after the 1950 close of streetcar service in Calgary. In fact, some of the work equipment used to dismantle the street railway system languished on this trackage for some time after their task was completed.

In a letter to the author dated July 30th 1984, the late Percy W. Browning describes the spur as follows: "Another interesting piece of trackage … is that leading off the Twelfth Avenue eastbound track southbound onto Sixth Street East. A couple of hundred feet further this track joined the CPR siding leading into the Exhibition grounds along the bank of the Elbow River. The CPR had one track leading to the east side of the standby power city powerhouse, and before natural gas for boilers was installed the occasional hopper car of coal was delivered there. Another track went around the west side of the plant and broke into several curved sidings south of the powerhouse. This was the storage yard for large right of way items such as rails, ties, poles and timbers. This was a convenient arrangement since the CPR could deliver cars with these supplies right to the storage area for unloading. When required the motor flats used the same siding to pick up these items directly from storage, since all sidings had trolley wire.

Once I saw this track used in an even handier way. The CPR parked a gondola load of new wheels just south of Twelfth (Avenue SW – ed.) where the wheels were transferred directly to motor flats parked alongside for delivery to the carbarns (sic). I don't remember the lifting device – it may have been the shop crane or the machine shovel. Getting onto this track was easy, getting out was a little more involved. The workcar motorman had a choice of running west on Twelfth (Avenue SE – ed.) on the wrong side to Second Street East (SE – ed.), or running east to the Elbow River Bridge single track switch and then west from there. – Incidentally maintenance jobs would have to be carefully planned because Royal American Shows during Stampede week and circuises (sic) at other times stored their dormitory and stock cars on these tracks, completely blocking them. During racing weeks when horses went by rail, the horse cars were stored there."

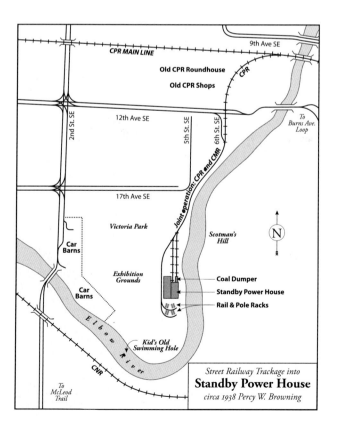

Street Railway Trackage into
Standby Power House
circa 1938 Percy W. Browning

Above: Trolley coach 409 on 7th Avenue SE eastbound near 3rd Street SE. The pedestrians are more interested in the photographer with his 4x5 camera than the new form of transportation being photographed. June 1947 soon after the start of service.
(Ohio Brass photo, Tom Schwarzkopf collection)

Below: LRV 2025 leads a C-Train out of the Cemetery Hill tunnel. It is about to cross 25th Avenue SE and pull into Erlton/Stampede station. In the background is the Macleod Trail. (Ted Wickson)

APPENDIX 6: TROLLEY BUS ROSTER

Bus Type	Wheel Base	Length	Width	Height	H.P.	Circle Radius	Weight - Ratio		Weight Lbs.	Passengers
							Front Axle	Rear Axle		
Canadian Car Brill T-44[1]	198½"	36'1"	8'6"	10'4½"	140	43'0"	6435	12,075	18,510	44
Canadian Car Brill T-48A[1]	247"	38'9½"	8'6"	10'6¼"	140	39'4"	7300	12,220	19,170	48
ACF Brill TC44[2]	20'4"	37'0"	8'6"	10'5"	140	43'0"			20,760	44

1. Data for Canadian Car Brill bus types supplied by Don Mann, Edmonton Transit, from 1972 ETS bus records

2. ACF Brill data from Electric Railway Historical Association of Southern California <www.erha.org/latltc44diagram.html>

Fleet Nos.	Builder	Year	Model	Serial Nos.	Qty	Seats	Notes
400 – 429	CCF-Brill	1947	T44	5138-167	30	44	GE motors for all
430 – 459	CCF-Brill	1948	T44	5211-240	30	44	
460 – 470	CCF-Brill	1949	T44	5682-692	11	44	
471 – 476	CCF-Brill	1950	T44	5693-698	6	44	
477 – 480	CCF-Brill	1950	T48A	8161-164	4	48	
481 – 484	CCF-Brill	1953	T48A	8320-323	4	48	
485 – 504	ACF-Brill	1948	TC44	vary	20	44	See note 3

3. ex-Baltimore units purchased 1957
(Calgary #/Baltimore #/serial #)*
485/2172/581 • 489/2177/587 • 493/2187/601 • 496/2189/600
499/2176/593 • 502/2181/591 • 486/2173/583 • 490/2179/588
494/2180/592 • 497/2175/590 • 500/2188/599 • 503/2186/596
487/2171/585 • 491/2178/589 • 495/2182/598 • 498/2190/602
501/2184/595 • 504/2183/597 • 488/2174/586 • 492/2185/594

4. Removed from service Oct/64:
485-489 and 495-499 inclusive

5. In May 1973 stored as serviceable:
400-419, 491-493, 502 + 504†.
Subsequently, nos. 400-419 were disposed of as in notes 4, 5
+ 10. Disposition of ACF coaches 491-3, 502 + 504 unknown,
but assumed to have been scrapped.

6. Surplus coaches sold to Edmonton July 1974:
401, 403, 404, 405, 412, 413, 415, 416, 428, 429, 435, 453, 454,
466, 469, 477, 479, 480, 481, 482*

7. Surplus coaches sold to Vancouver July 1974:
402, 407, 408, 409, 410, 411, 414, 424, 438, 478*

8. Scrapped per CTS records:
485-490 and 496-501 inclusive

9. Used as portable passenger shelters: 494 and 503 (CTS)

10. As of February 1975 acquired by T.S. Holdings:
402, 407-411, 414, 424, 438, 478**

11. After close of system, last run coach 422 preserved by
Reynolds - Alberta Museum in Wetaskiwin, AB. (Walton).
Coach 432 sold to M. Vondrau, Preston ON in September
1974; then donated to Halton County Radial Railway
museum, Rockwood, ON. Subsequently sold to Vintage
Electric Streetcar Co., Windber, PA in July 1993. (Young/
Sandusky). Coaches 446 and 459 preserved at Sandon, BC
(via the Vancouver acquisitions).***

12. All remaining coaches not previously sold or scrapped at
close of system sold to Vancouver in August 1975, namely:
28 non operational coaches @ $500 each -
  400, 406, 417-421, 423, 425-427, 430, 431, 433, 434, 436,
  437, 439-449.
25 operational coaches @ $1,000 each -
  450-452, 455-465, 467, 468, 470-476, 483, 484 *

*   Information from NATTA – Trolley Bus Data Book II,
     Trolley Bus Bulletin 109 with corrections by T.S.
**   Transit Canada Jan/Feb/75 p.32
*** Historic Sandon web site: Canadian Car & Foundry
     Brill Trolleys, July 2006 <http://www.sandonbc.com/
     brilltrolleys.html> visited February 2008
†   Information from NATTA – Trolley Bus Data Book,
     Trolley Bus Bulletin 105 May 1973

Sandusky = Robert J. Sandusky, transit historian
Walton = Mark W. Walton, transit historian
Young = Wally Young, transit historian

APPENDIX 7: LIGHT RAIL VEHICLES ROSTER

Unit No.	Builder	Date	Type	Motors	Length	Width	Height	Weight	Passenger Capacity
2001 to 2027	Siements Duewag Dusseldorf, W. Germany + CTS Anderson	1980-1981	U2	Two DC	23.150 m^A 24.170 m^B	2650 mm	978 mm^C 3320 mm^D	32,600 kg	64 seated 97 standing 161 total
2028 to 2030	Siements Duewag Dusseldorf, W. Germany + CTS Anderson	1982	U2	Two DC	23.150 m 24.170 m	2650 mm	978 mm^C 3320 mm^D	32,600 kg	64 seated 97 standing 161 total
2031 to 2065	Siements Duewag Dusseldorf, W. Germany + CTS Anderson	1983	U2	Two DC	23.150 m 24.170 m	2650 mm	978 mm^C 3320 mm^D	32,600 kg	64 seated 97 standing 161 total
2066 to 2083	Siements Duewag Dusseldorf, W. Germany + CTS Anderson	1984	U2	Two DC	23.150 m 24.170 m	2650 mm	978 mm^C 3320 mm^D	32,600 kg	64 seated 97 standing 161 total
2101 to 2102	Siemens Duewag, Dusseldorf, West Germany.	1988*	U2	Four AC	23.150 m 24.386 m	2650 mm	978 mm^C -	36,000 kg	64 seated 97 standing 161 total
2201 to 2215	Siemens Transportation Systems Inc., Sacramento, CA	2000-2001	SD160	Four AC	- 24.820 m^B	2654 mm	985 mm^C 3840 mm^E	40,624 kg	60 seated 113 standing 173 total
2216 to 2232	Siemens Transportation Systems Inc., Sacramento, CA	2003	SD160	Four AC	- 24.820 m^B	2654 mm	985 mm^C 3840 mm^E	40,624 kg	60 seated 113 standing 173 total
2233 to 2265	Siemens Transportation Systems Inc., Sacramento, CA	2007	SD160	Four AC	- 24.820 m^B	2654 mm	985 mm^C 3840 mm^E	40,624 kg	60 seated 113 standing 173 total
2266 to 2272	Siemens Transportation Systems Inc., Sacramento, CA	2008	SD160	Four AC	- 24.820 m^B	2654 mm	985 mm^C 3840 mm^E	40,624 kg	60 seated 113 standing 173 total

Notes:

+ CTS Anderson = Assembly completed by Calgary Transit's Anderson Shops, Calgary, Alberta
A: Over buffers
B: Over couplers
C: Top of rail to floor
D: Top of rail to top of roof
E: Top of rail to top of roof with pantograph locked down

Upper figures in each height cell represent height from top of rail to floor. The lower figues for the U2-type cars denote car height from top of rail to top of roof. The lower figues in the SD160-type height cells denote top of rail to top of vehicle with pantographs locked down. All LRVs are articulated, bi-directional, mounted on three bogies (six axles). Wheelbase on each bogie is 1800 mm.
All are configured for high platform operation.

Unit Numbers 2101 to 2102 built 1988* by Siemens Duewag of Dusseldorf, West Germany. They were purchased by the Government of Alberta to be used as alternating current demonstrators in Edmonton and Calgary and assigned numbers 3001 and 3002. They arrived in Calgary in 1990. Calgary Transit purchased the units in 1992 and assigned them numbers 2101 and 2102.

Credits: Bain, D.M., *Calgary Transit Then & Now*;
Bain, Donald M., Calgary Transit's *CTrain and the Dalhousie Extension*;
Canadian Trackside Guide 2007, 2009;
Cooper, Ron via Robert J. Sandusky and the Light Rail Transit Association Reports;
Siemens *Specifications for Light Rail Vehicle RTC 1 of the City of Calgary*; Siemens *Specifications Light Rail Vehicle U2-AC City of Calgary – City of Edmonton Province of Alberta/Canada*;
Siemens Transportation Systems Inc., *Specifications for SD160 Light Rail Vehicle*.